Colorado
Ice
Climber's
Guide

Colorado
Ice
Climber's
Guide

Cameron M. Burns

Chockstone Press, Inc.
Evergreen, Colorado

ISBN: 1-57540-086-3

PUBLISHED AND DISTRIBUTED BY
Chockstone Press
Post Office Box 3505
Evergreen, Colorado 80437

Cover photo: Robert Cordery-Cotter on The Fang (WI6), Vail

All photos by Cameron M. Burns unless otherwise labeled.

Dedication

This book is dedicated to my wonderful wife and most regular ice climbing partner, Ann Robertson, for the hundreds of frozen, soggy, wildly sadistic belays and routes she has endured over the years. Folks, when you find a real ice climbing partner, cherish it.

WARNING: CLIMBING IS A SPORT WHERE YOU MAY BE SERIOUSLY INJURED OR DIE.
READ THIS BEFORE YOU USE THIS BOOK.

This guidebook is a compilation of unverified information gathered from many different climbers. The author cannot assure the accuracy of any of the information in this book, including the topos and route descriptions, the difficulty ratings, and the protection ratings. These may be incorrect or misleading and it is impossible for any one author to climb all the routes to confirm the information about each route. Also, ratings of climbing difficulty and danger are always subjective and depend on the physical characteristics (for example, height), experience, technical ability, confidence and physical fitness of the climber who supplied the rating. Additionally, climbers who achieve first ascents sometimes underrate the difficulty or danger of the climbing route out of fear of being ridiculed if a climb is later down-rated by subsequent ascents. Therefore, be warned that you must exercise your own judgment on where a climbing route goes, its difficulty and your ability to safely protect yourself from the risks of ice and rock climbing. Examples of some of these risks are: falling due to technical difficulty or due to natural hazards such as holds breaking, falling rock or ice, climbing equipment dropped by other climbers, hazards of weather and lightning, your own equipment failure, and failure or absence of fixed protection.

You should not depend on any information gleaned from this book for your personal safety; your safety depends on your own good judgment, based on experience and a realistic assessment of your climbing ability. If you have any doubt as to your ability to safely climb a route described in this book, do not attempt it.

The following are some ways to make your use of this book safer:

1. **Consultation:** You should consult with other climbers about the difficulty and danger of a particular climb prior to attempting it. Most local climbers are glad to give advice on routes in their area and we suggest that you contact locals to confirm ratings and safety of particular routes and to obtain first-hand information about a route chosen from this book.

2. **Instruction:** Most climbing areas have local climbing instructors and guides available. We recommend that you engage an instructor or guide to learn safety techniques and to become familiar with the routes and hazards of the areas described in this book. Even after you are proficient in climbing safely, occasional use of a guide is a safe way to raise your climbing standard and learn advanced techniques.

3. **Fixed Protection:** Many of the routes in this book use bolts and pitons which are permanently placed in the rock. Because of variances in the manner of placement, weathering, metal fatigue, the quality of the metal used, and many other factors, these fixed protection pieces should always be considered suspect and should always be backed up by equipment that you place yourself. Never depend for your safety on a single piece of fixed protection because you never can tell whether it will hold weight, and in some cases, fixed protection may have been removed or is now absent.

Be aware of the following specific potential hazards which could arise in using this book:

1. **Misdescriptions of Routes:** If you climb a route and you have a doubt as to where the route may go, you should not go on unless you are sure that you can go that way safely. Route descriptions and topos in this book may be inaccurate or misleading.

2. **Incorrect Difficulty Rating:** A route may, in fact, be more difficult than the rating indicates. Do not be lulled into a false sense of security by the difficulty rating.

3. **Incorrect Protection Rating:** If you climb a route and you are unable to arrange adequate protection from the risk of falling through the use of fixed pitons or bolts and by placing your own protection devices, do not assume that there is adequate protection available higher just because the route protection rating indicates the route is not an "X" or an "R" rating. Every route is potentially an "X" (a fall may be deadly), due to the inherent hazards of climbing – including, for example, failure or absence of fixed protection, your own equipment's failure, or improper use of climbing equipment.

THERE ARE NO WARRANTIES, WHETHER EXPRESS OR IMPLIED, THAT THIS GUIDEBOOK IS ACCURATE OR THAT THE INFORMATION CONTAINED IN IT IS RELIABLE. THERE ARE NO WARRANTIES OF FITNESS FOR A PARTICULAR PURPOSE OR THAT THIS GUIDE IS MERCHANTABLE. YOUR USE OF THIS BOOK INDICATES YOUR ASSUMPTION OF THE RISK

Acknowledgments

This guide wouldn't have been possible without a lot of help and encouragement from a whole bunch of people. My sincerest thanks goes out to all them.

Benny Bach, for his highly knowledgeable tours of Rocky Mountain National Park; Jeff Singer at Backcountry Experience in Durango, and Bill Gamble for their help in the Durango area; Bill Whitt of the Victorian Inn in Ouray, who along with Gary Wild has boosted ice climbing's place in Ouray; Mike Gruber for his help on Summit County ice routes; Jon Butler for his help in Grand Junction; and, Doug and Daiva Berry, for their excellent help in Telluride.

I'd like to mention David and Nancy Nystrom, and John and Christy Plymell of East Vail. Every year, David, patriarch of the family, plows an access trail for ice climbers through the side of his yard and across Gore Creek. Although he is not an ice climber himself, David is thoroughly supportive of our sport and is a guy to bow down and worship.

Thanks to the folks at B.J. Adams & Co. in Snowmass Village for the use of the xerox machine. Without it, there'd be no maps in here!

Charlie Fowler and Richard DuMais' previous work documenting the ice routes in Colorado should not be ignored. Both men did an excellent job, and set the stage for this publication.

Thanks also to all the folks I've ever climbed ice or hung out in the mountains with, including: Luke Laeser, Rob Hering, Jeff Widen, Tony Asnicar, Mike and Claire Schillaci, Kent Robinson, Brian Takei, Mike Lyons, Paul Fehlau, Mike Walker, Charlie French, Julian Fisher, Chris Lomax, Mike Baker, Micah McKee, Jeff and Erica, Hall, Carlo Torres, Ethan, Iris and Walden Putterman, Steve, Sandy, Tori and Angelo Porcella, Bob and Sylvia Robertson, Brian Gonzales, Kerry and Mary Burns, Mary Gardner, Margaret Montgomery, Barbara New, Karen Gilbert, Candace Welch, Mary Hayes, John and Jennifer Catto, Jeffrey and Celina Hancox, Arlan and Wendy Hemphill, Mike Gross, Paul Lambdin, Karen and Dale Wooldridge, John Middendorf, Eric Bjørnstad, Robin Bartlett, The Walton Clan, Leslie Henderson, Dave and Christie Sessions, Elizabeth Ward, Cliff, Audrey, and Maria Ahumada, Chris Pomeroy, Jon Krzak, Mike, Penny, Jessica, Natalie, and Katie Sandy, Jenn Kleiser, Dottie Wolcott, Laurie Vagneur, Margot, Ruth and Peter Frey, Chris and Stan Cheo, Gillian Burns, Andy Stone, John Colson, Jon Klusmire, Dale Strode, Sara Garton, Gayle Johnson, David Bentley, Jim and Terry, Becca Magill, Scott Condon, Devon Meyers, Roy Willey, Tom and Scott Holt, Loren Jenkins, Stewart Oksenhorn, Melissa Schmitt, and old Bobbie Ward.

Cam Burns, 7/96

Contents

Boulder Canyon Ice   Photo: Bill Pelander

Introduction

"Am I a victim of my own madness."
— Warren J. Harding, Downward Bound

In January, 1986, I swung an ice tool for the first time. Benny Bach and I were in Boulder Canyon for the afternoon, skipping our classes at the University of Colorado and thwacking our way into the world of alpinism.

We knew little about using tools, and absolutely zero about placing ice screws, (we weren't even sure what the term "alpinism" meant), so we soloed up and down the flows, wondering if our feeble pecking would hold us.

It took only a few trips up and down the ice before I was hooked, so to speak, and ice climbing became as much a pastime as rock climbing. All my friends seemed to have taken it up, and I became a tool-bashing, Molson guzzling, gimpy-walking, metal-plate-in-the-head, kitchen-magnet-wearing ice climber.

Eight years later, after compiling a feature on Colorado ice climbing for the now-defunct British publication Mountain Review, I felt I knew most areas in the state fairly well. The magazine folded — many blamed my involvement with the magazine — and I tossed my piles of notes.

Then, in March, 1996, my wife Ann and a devious publisher named George Meyers suggested I rewrite all my notes and put together a guidebook. It was a silly idea, as I knew of several chaps who were already working on such a guidebook. But, the quarter-inch plate warped my thinking, and thus I began to re-write all that I knew. The joy, the tears, the laughter, the sorrow. What a drag. My wife simply plucked the magnets off my forehead and went about her business.

Of course, several references already existed, namely Charlie Fowler's exceptional "San Juan Ice Climbs" and Richard DuMais' 1987 book, "The High Peaks," which proved invaluable.

Anyway, this guide is the result of my labors. It's not got every route in Colorado in it. In fact, it doesn't include a lot of the newer, super hard, mixed routes that are going up in many places. It even misses a few areas I just couldn't get to before publication, or decided were better left undiscovered. Each area has to have its stash.

But this guide does get you to most of the classic ice climbs in the state, and will keep you busy for at least a winter. I hope you enjoy it. More importantly, I hope you enjoy some of these routes as much as I did.

About This Guide

The guide is divided into sections encompassing generally large areas. And, like my plate-crushed brain, it sort of wanders all over the place. It might seem random to you, but it made sense to me, sort of. It starts in the north, with Rocky Mountain National Park, and then moves south to the Boulder/Golden area, then west, into the mountains. Around Grand Junction, it heads south, into the San Juans (Blue Mesa Reservoir, Telluride, etc.), then swings east across the bottom of the state finishing with Colorado Springs.

Like my friends in Cañon City, each route has its own personalized number. You'll see the numbers on maps, as well as in many photos.

The maps are drawn to scale, however, the maps aren't necessarily of the same scale. Something to remember when you're trying to figure out why the masochistic, posthole approach to Deep Creek is taking longer than the walk to Cascade Creek.

There are a lot of photos in this guide too, which I should mention. In summer, a cliff's a cliff, right? In winter, however, a dry, sunny cliff with a blue runnel down it one day can be under 25 feet of snow the next. In short, routes can look like anything. Be prepared for that. Use the images in this book to study the rock buttresses and mountains behind the routes you're planning to climb. Combined with the maps and written material, the photos should help you get where you want to be. And if there is no photo, sorry. That'll be corrected in the next edition.

There are approach time estimates and a note on where you can see the climbs from the comfort of your clunker. With any luck, you might not have to get out of your car.

First ascent information is so lacking in many areas that I chose to leave it out altogether. Perhaps in a future edition I will include it.

Anyway, I hope all this information is helpful. I also hope I got it all down correctly. (I know something's bound to be wrong, but that's how guides go.) If you have any corrections, additions, comments, gripes or spare beer money, you can send them to me at P.O. Box 1925 Basalt, CO, 81621.

Ratings

For the most part, this guide uses the "WI" (the initials for "Water Ice") system for rating climbs. In it, WI 1 is the easiest climb, and, generally, WI 6 is at the top end of the scale. A lot of climbers simply call routes "Grade something or other," with Grade replacing WI. In other words, a WI 5 climb is often called a Grade 5.

This system is different to rock climbing's Yosemite decimal system, in that the overall difficulty of a pitch is generally considered, not one single move. For example, both a pitch of WI 4 ice and a pitch of WI 5 ice might include some vertical ice on it. If they were rock climbs, they'd get the same grade. But the WI system takes into account the rest of the route.

Just quickly, a run down of what you might expect:

WI 1. A walk, basically. You only need crampons.

WI 2. A steep walk, where a tool can be useful.

WI 3. Sections of steep ice are encountered. Vertical ice can occur, but it is generally in short steps of a few feet with plenty of rests between. Crampons and two hand tools are needed.

WI 4. More continuous sections of steep ice are encountered, with rests being only stances between vertical sections of ice. You'll want a rope.

WI 5. Vertical ice. Rest stances might occur, but are few and far between. Placing protection generally means hanging off tools or the rope.

WI 6. Overhanging ice. Can also include vertical ice that is very rotten and cauliflowered ice, where protection is sparse.

Beyond WI 6, most modern ice climbers switch to the MI (the initials for "Mixed Ice") system. There are only a few of these routes mentioned, and they involve

Rifle Ice Cave

exceptionally hard rock climbing (usually with tools) with sporadic sections of ice. M5 is pretty straightforward and generally well-protected mixed rock and ice, while M8 is wildly gymnastic climbing (usually out the roof of something) that is sometimes poorly protected.

There are a few routes in this guide that are given the AI or "Alpine Ice" rating. Alpine Ice ratings, in my experience, tend to be fairly close to WI ratings, but are slightly easier by about half a grade. For instance, AI 3 feels like WI 2+. The designation AI is often used to warn climbers that pure ice climbing isn't all they're likely to encounter. To tell the truth, 95 percent of every route I've ever done with an Alpine Ice rating has been a steep snow climb.

The thing to remember about ice climbing is that, as Charlie Fowler once wrote, "Ratings Don't Mean Shit." Ice changes, gear evolves, climbers are hung over, anything can happen. When you get to the route, you're the one who's got to decide if you can climb it, not the guy who wrote the guidebook.

Equipment

Your choice of equipment is entirely up to you. However, we're talking about ice here, and the stuff changes in shape, size and strength every second of the day. The bulk of the routes in this guide require only ice screws (the short ones are always best), but, whenever I go out, I grab a handful of wired stoppers, a few pitons (two knifeblades, two Lost Arrows and two small angles) a set of small camming units and a whole bunch of slings, just in case. Most of the time I don't need all this extra stuff, but it's nice to know I've got it in case spring comes early.

I also carry a few old screws and slings for descents, in case I can't find an anchor.

Descents

Descents are the crux of any route, rock, ice or otherwise. The descents off routes are described with each route. This information — while based on a pretty good memory, notes, and conversations with other climbers — is not infallible. A three inch snowfall can easily cover up a rappel anchor. The ice itself can form differently and leave you high and dry thirty feet below an anchor. Pretty much, anything can happen. As I mentioned above, that's why it's always smart to carry a few old screws and a pile of rap slings, at the very least. (Rock gear's always a darn good idea.)

When it comes to getting down safely, you're in charge!

Avalanches

Avalanches are another key consideration for ice climbers. They can occur anywhere and they do. You are absolutely in charge when it comes to deciding whether or not to climb a particular route.

A friend and I were doing Horsetail Falls near Ouray about five years ago, when, on the last easy pitch, he knocked off a slab of snow 20 feet by 20 feet, and about a foot thick. The thing landed near me on a ledge and the force of the wind knocked me over. That was a small slab, in conditions we felt were very safe for climbing! I don't remember how many times I've driven to Silverton only to decide against climbing that day.

And don't think that after an avalanche, everything's okay. A couple of climbers I know who started up The Ribbon were hit by one small spindrift avalanche and figured it was okay to go on. They were hit by a second, and decided maybe climbing on wasn't such a good idea. They rapped to the bottom, and stepped out of the way just as the Mother avalanche came ripping down the gully. The bottom line? Once an avalanche — or two or three or four — has taken place, it doesn't mean that area is safe.

Again, use your brain. If it doesn't smell right, stay away!

Seasons

Generally, ice in Colorado is good in the Dec.-March period. In a lot of the high mountain areas in the southwest part of the state, routes can stay in shape until mid-May!! Of course, it all depends on the weather. And, of course, a lot of the routes in Rocky Mountain National Park are intended to be done in summer and/or fall.

Access Issues

Ah, the finicky subject of access. Unfortunately, I don't have much to add other than what I've told you for descents and avalanches — use your head.

In most cases, these routes have no access problems. Some of them do, and generally those problems are noted with the individual route. But, access is always changing, so keep your eyes open and don't push it when crossing private land. Remember, there are tons of excellent routes on public land.

Also, please write me at the above address if you have any info/concerns/whatever about access issues in a specific area.

Barrows Worm on Jaws, Rocky Mountain National Park

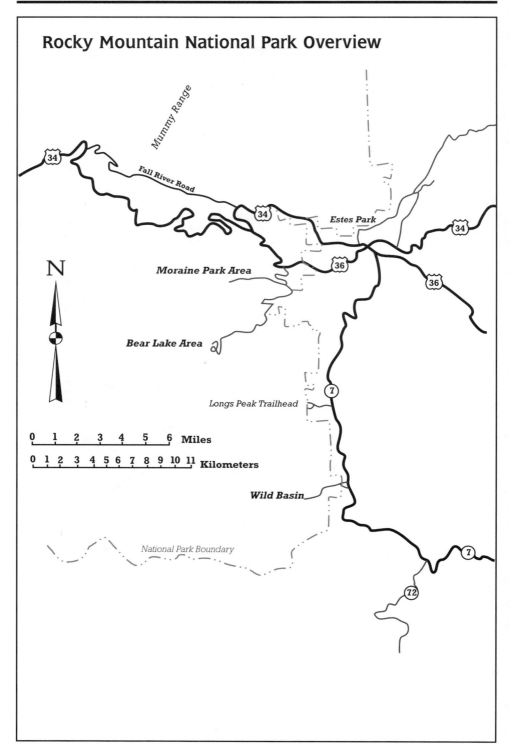

Rocky Mountain National Park Overview

NORTHEAST MOUNTAINS

Rocky Mountain National Park

(Routes 1-68)

"...an area of high mountains rising above wooded valleys and open meadows, offering a wide spectrum of recreational opportunities to the outdoor enthusiast."
— Richard DuMais, "The High Peaks," 1987

Besides the San Juan Mountains in the southwestern part of the state, and a few unique areas like Vail and Rifle, Rocky Mountain National Park offers the highest concentration of climbable ice in Colorado.

The approaches are generally much longer than anywhere else in the state, however, the serene beauty of the park in winter make the ski in and ski out trips an integral part of a day's ice climbing.

Ice routes in the park range from forearm popping vertical waterfalls to long snow slogs on remote peaks. In short, there's something for every level of ice climber here.

Because of the large number of Front Range climbers compared with other areas in the state, this section includes a lot of moderate alpine routes (basically snow cruises up steep couloirs). Certainly these types of routes exist all over the state, but being so close to Denver, they're in greater demand in the Park.

Park Geography

Rocky Mountain National Park, at first look, appears to be a jumbled mess of mountains and canyons, high cirques and low valleys.

In reality, it's not. The east side of the Continental Divide, the area of most interest to Front Range climbers, is really a series of east-west, or nearly east-west canyons, leading into the mountains.

To make things easy to comprehend, this guide is primarily divided up into a number of valleys from north to the south. For example, it starts with climbs in the Mummy Range, at the north side of the park, then moves south, ending with routes in Wild Basin. Within each valley, however, routes are laid out depending on how they are approached by the climber. In other words, within a specific valley or cirque, the routes might not be arranged from north to south. Anyway, you're a big kid. You'll figure it out.

U.S. Park Service Requirements/Permits

While most ice/alpine routes in Rocky Mountain Nation Park can be done in a long, tendon-grinding day from a car parked at the trailhead, it's often a much more enjoyable trip if it includes a remote bivouac.

To spend a night out, a permit is required. (A permit is not required for day trips.) Fortunately, Rocky Mountain National Park is extremely accommodating of climbers, and offers climbers a "bivouac permit."

The permits restrict climbers to camping in certain "zones" around the base of climbing objectives, or on a face during a "climb" (see definition below.) There are a few other restrictions, including:

- the climbing party must be limited to 4 people, all of whom must climb;
- the bivouac site must be 3.5 miles or more from a trailhead;
- a "climb" must be four or more pitches, of roped, technical climbing;
- the bivouac site must be off all vegetation. You must sleep on rock or snow;
- no tents are allowed. A ground cloth or tarp is okay. Bivouac bags ("bivie sacks") and sleeping bags are allowed.
- the camp must be established after sundown and removed before sunup. In short, between dusk and dawn;
- it has to be at least 100 feet from a body of water.

The Park has a reservation system whereby bivouac permits can be reserved for specific dates. Reservations are not required, but they are recommended during the busy summer months. Reservations for the summer months of a particular calendar year cannot be made until March 1 or after. They can be made by mail, in person, or by phone (until May 20).

For more information on obtaining a bivouac permit, call (970) 586-1242, or write:

Backcountry Permits
Rocky Mountain National Park
Estes Park, CO 80517

Unfortunately, there's a $10 administration fee that you must pay when you pick up your permit, whether its a reserved permit or not.

And, you need a "Vehicle/Parking Permit" to park at the trailhead parking lots overnight. These can be picked up when you get your bivouac permit. (Bring your license plate number.) The parking permit must go on your dashboard while you're in the mountains.

Mummy Range
(Routes 1–5)

"The Mummies" are an intriguing and often overlooked section of Rocky Mountain National Park. While they are generally ignored, for the most part by serious climbers, they offer several long, high-quality alpine routes, most notably the Y Couloirs on Ypsilon Mountain and several routes on the massive east face of Fairchild Mountain.

Getting there To get to the Mummy Range from Estes Park, drive west through town to the Fall River Entrance Station to the park, the northernmost of the entrances on the east side.

For those unfamiliar with the Estes Park/Rocky Mountain National Park, which is an ungodly jumble of tourons and cars during the summer, the Park lies just west of the city, and can be accessed via two entrance stations. The most popular is the Beaver Meadow Entrance Station, as it is the most direct route to the more popular areas of the park (Bear Lake, Glacier Gorge, etc.) The Fall River Entrance Station lies along U.S. 34 (the main highway between Loveland and Granby), which skirts the northern side of Estes Park. Anyway, get on U.S. 34 in Estes Park, and head west.

From the Fall River Entrance Station, drive 2.1 miles into the park and turn right, onto Fall River Road, which leads to the Endovalley Picnic area. Drive 0.1 miles on Fall River Road, to the Lawn Lakes trailhead and Parking area, on your right. Park here.

The trail to Ypsilon and Fairchild Mountains leaves the northern side of the parking lot and switchbacks up the big hill. About 200 feet into the hike, there's a branch in the trail. The right branch leads to "Deer Mountain Trails;" the left leads to "Lawn Lake, 6.2 miles." Go left and follow the beautiful Roaring River up into the mountains.

After about a mile and a half, the trail forks. The left branch goes to "Ypsilon Lake" while the right branch goes to "Lawn Lake."

If you're heading to the Y Couloirs on Ypsilon Mountain, go left. If you're heading for routes on Fairchild Mountain, go right.

The trail to Ypsilon Lake crosses the Roaring River, then heads southwest, almost the direction you came from, before circling around to the West and heading up towards Ypsilon Lake and Ypsilon Mountain. After reaching Ypsilon Lake, skirt the lake and hike up the valley past the two Spectacle Lakes, below the East Face. From this point, the Y Couloirs cannot be missed.

If you headed to Fairchild Mountain, continue past the branch in the trail, past the Ypsilon Creek, Cutbank and Golden Banner campgrounds, to the junction with the Black Canyon Trail (which will come in from the right). The impressive walls of Mummy Mountain's southwest face will be above you, and Lawn Lake will be off to the left (northwest). Continue up the trail to Lawn Lake.

On the right, about three quarters of a mile past Lawn Lake, and left (west) of the main rock walls of Mummy Mountain, is Mummy Falls. This waterfall spills down a cleft in the rock that faces left (west), so it is impossible to see until you've passed Mummy's southwest face altogether. The trail continues up to Crystal Lake, under the east cirque of Fairchild Mountain, and the routes Winterlong and Abadoo Scronch. Although this approach is long (7.5 miles in all) it gets flatter the higher one gets in the valley.

1. Winterlong, Fairchild Mountain
(III, AI 2-3, 5.8 rock, 900 feet) ★★

This route follows a series of ramps on the left-hand (south) side of the northeast face. Start by climbing an obvious, very easy, left-angling snow ramp on the left end of the main face, that leads to a long, low-angled, ramp that traverses back right, into the center of the northeast face where it meets a small snowfield. There are several sections of tricky rock climbing along the second, right-angling ramp. Getting across this traverse is often considered the logistical crux of the route. From the top

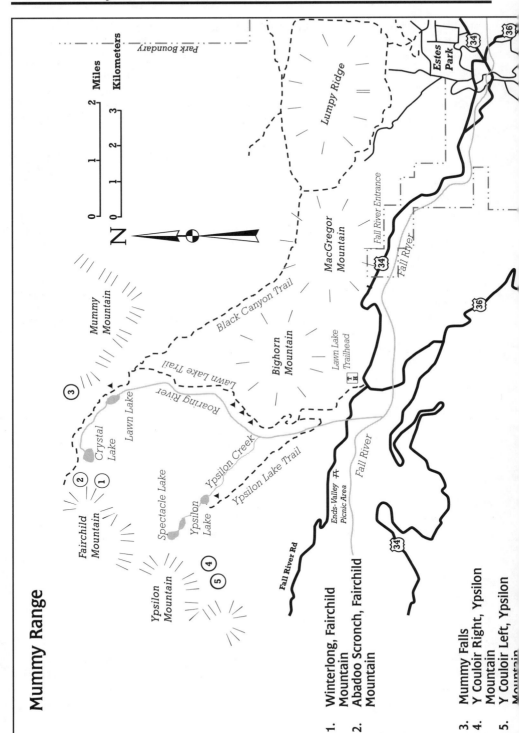

Mummy Range

1. Winterlong, Fairchild Mountain
2. Abadoo Scronch, Fairchild Mountain

3. Mummy Falls
4. Y Couloir Right, Ypsilon Mountain
5. Y Couloir Left, Ypsilon Mountain

Fairchild Mountain.
Left to right: Winterlong, Abadoo Scronch

of the small snowfield, the route climbs straight up, on a buttress right of a prominent chimney. Depending on the exact route chosen, one may encounter rock to 5.8.
Several pitches above the buttress, the large hanging snowfield in the top center of
the face is reached, and skirted to its left. The top of the northeast face is just a
short scramble from the snowfield. A great early winter outing.

Approach time: Although a fast party can do it in 2, allow 3-4 hours for the hike
from the Lawn Lakes Trailhead.

Descent: Hike off the summit to the north, to the saddle between Fairchild
Mountain and Hague Peak (the next mountain to the northeast). From this
wide saddle, a trail leads down the easy slopes to Crystal Lake and Lawn
Lake.

Season: Spring/Fall. It melts out entirely in mid-summer

Road/Highway the climb is visible from: None.

2.   Abadoo Scronch, Fairchild Mountain
(III, AI 4-5, 5.7 rock, 900 feet) ★

This route lies right of Winterlong, in almost the center of the northeast face. It
follows a massive and steep, right-angling cleft that cuts the face in two, and skirts
the hanging snowfield in the top center of the face on the snowfield's right side.
Several steep, often difficult sections of ice are encountered in this long gully
climb before it eases near the top.

Approach time: Allow 3-4 hours.

Descent: Same as for the previous route, Winterlong.

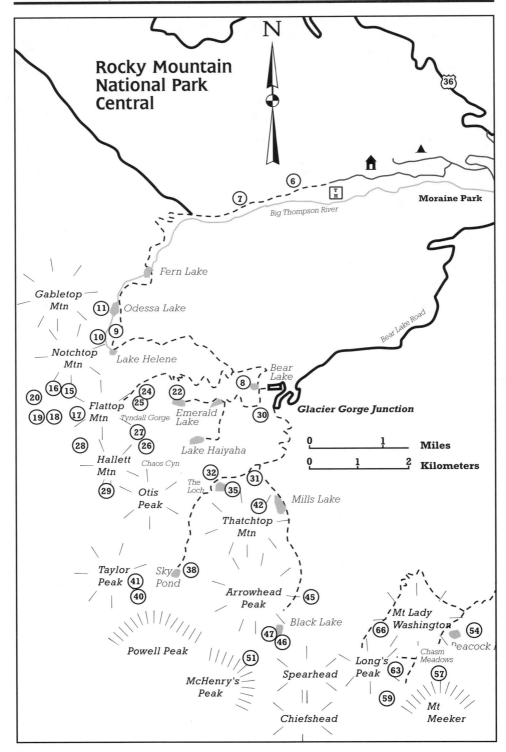

Rocky Mountain National Park Central

N

Moraine Park

Big Thompson River

Bear Lake Road

Fern Lake

Gabletop Mtn

Odessa Lake

Notchtop Mtn

Lake Helene

Bear Lake

Glacier Gorge Junction

Flattop Mtn

Tyndall Gorge

Emerald Lake

Lake Haiyaha

Hallett Mtn

Chaos Cyn

Otis Peak

The Loch

Mills Lake

Thatchtop Mtn

Taylor Peak

Sky Pond

Arrowhead Peak

Mt Lady Washington

Powell Peak

Black Lake

Peacock

Chasm Meadows

Long's Peak

McHenry's Peak

Spearhead

Mt Meeker

Chiefshead

0   1   Miles

0   1   2   Kilometers

Rocky Mountain National Park Central

6. Windy Gulch Cascades
7. Jaws Falls
8. Bear Lake Ice Fall
9. Grace Falls
10. Odessa Wall
11. Guide's Wall
15. Southeast Couloir Right, Notchtop Mountain
16. Southeast Couloir Left, Notchtop Mountain
17. East Couloir, Northwest Face Flattop Mountain
18. Central Couloir, Northwest Face Flattop Mountain
19. West Couloir, Northwest Face Flattop Mountain
20. Ptarmigan Point Glacier
22. The Squid
24. Dragon's Tail Gully, Flattop Mountain
25. Tower Gully, Flattop Mountain
26. East Couloir, Hallett Peak
27. Hallett Chimney
28. Tyndall Glacier
29. Chaos Canyon Icefield
30. Parking Lot Wall
31. Loch Vale Gorge
32. The Crypt
35. Necrophilia
38. Thatchtop-Powell Icefield
40. Taylor Glacier
41. Taylor Glacier Buttress
42. All Mixed Up
45. Reflections
46. Black Lake Slabs
47. West Gully
51. Big Mac Couloir, McHenry's Peak
54. Columbine Falls
57. Dream Weaver
59. The Loft
63. Notch Couloir
66. North Face

Ypsilon Mountain. Left to right: Y Couloir Left, Y Couloir Right

Season: Spring/Fall. It melts out entirely in mid-summer.
Road/Highway the climb is visible from: None.

3. Mummy Falls (WI 4, 200 feet) ★
A classic cascading waterfall climb, lying on the absolute western end of
Mummy's southwest face. Can be snow-choked or thin.
Approach time: Allow 3-4 hours.
Descent: Scramble down left.
Season: Spring/Fall. A snowfield above supplies the water, so cautious eyes
   should examine it thoroughly.
Road/Highway the climb is visible from: None.

4. Y Couloir Right, Ypsilon Mountain
(AI 2, Class 4 rock, 1500 feet) ★★★
The dramatic bowl shaped southeast face of Ypsilon Mountain, and the Y-shaped
gully that bisects it, gave this beautiful peak its name. They really are two separate
climbs and are described separately.
   The right couloir is the classic route here. Although it is easier than classic
alpine cruises of similar lengths (i.e. Dream Weaver, The Notch Couloir), a massive cornice of snow tends to hang around most of the spring and early summer,
making climbing it a rather daunting undertaking. Stonefall is also sometimes
high in the gully, so late summer/early fall ascents are generally preferred.
   The description is easy: Climb the gully. A regularly occurring break in the
snow/ice halfway up is negotiated by climbing left, on rock, around the break.
The summit cornice is passed by going left also.
Approach time: 3-4 hours.

Descent: The best way down is via the Donner Ridge, a ridge that runs from the summit south, to the amphitheater between Ypsilon and Mt. Chiquita, the next mountain to the southwest. Take care to stay well right (south) of the steep cliffs on the southeast face of Ypsilon Mountain.

Season: Late summer/early fall are the safest times. However, the later in the summer, the less snow/ice there is.

Road/Highway the climb is visible from: Many parts of Rocky Mountain National Park. It's best viewed from Highway 34, a few miles west of the Fall River Entrance to the Park.

5.   Y Couloir Left, Ypsilon Mountain
(AI 2, Class 3 rock, 1500 feet) ★

This branch of the couloir is a little easier, lacks the massive cornice found on the Right Couloir, and generally holds snow all summer long.

Approach time: 3-4 hours.

Descent: Same as for the previous route, the Y Couloir Right.

Season: Summer/fall.

Road/Highway the climb is visible from: Many parts of Rocky Mountain National Park. It's best viewed from Highway 34, a few miles west of the Fall River Entrance to the Park

Moraine Park
(Routes 6–7)

Moraine Park is a big, open, marshy area, on the banks of Big Thompson River, between the Park's Beaver Meadows Entrance Station and the Bear Lake area. There's not much of interest to the serious climber here, except for two nearby ice routes that form along the northern side of the Big Thompson Valley—Jaws and the Windy Gulch Cascades.

Getting there Jaws Falls and the Windy Gulch Cascades lie west of the Moraine Park area. They are accessed by hiking up the Fern Lake trail.

To get to the parking area for these climbs, drive 0.2 miles west of the Beaver Meadows Entrance Station to the Park and turn south, onto the Moraine Park/Bear Lake Road. (The Beaver Meadows Entrance Station is the regular east entrance to the park, and lies just outside of Estes Park, west of town.)

Follow the Moraine Park/Bear Lake Road for 1.3 miles. Turn right (west) and drive towards the Moraine Park Campground and the Fern Lake Trailhead.

After 0.55 miles, and before the campground is reached, turn left. Follow this road for 1.5 miles, past a livery, and to the end of the road. The Fern Lake trailhead and parking lot will be obvious, on the right side. The road up the valley is closed in winter and a gate bars vehicular access.

Park here and ski directly west, into the mountains. The Windy Gulch Cascades, a series of low-angled ice flows, lie about 1/2 a mile up the valley on the right (north) side.

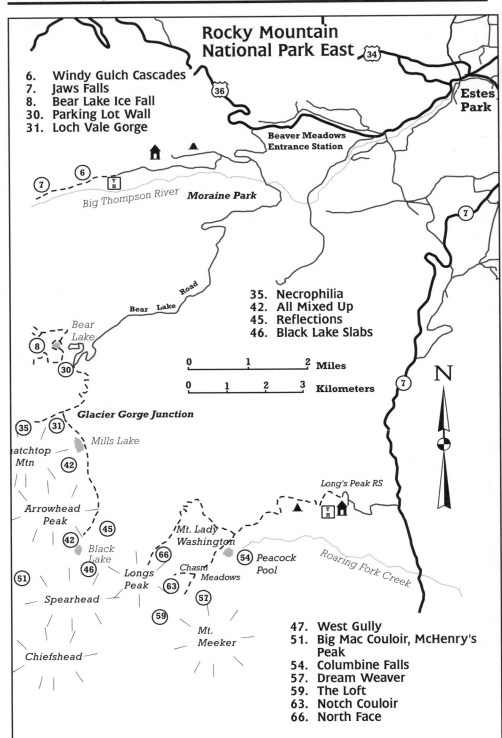

Rocky Mountain National Park East

6. Windy Gulch Cascades
7. Jaws Falls
8. Bear Lake Ice Fall
30. Parking Lot Wall
31. Loch Vale Gorge

Beaver Meadows
Entrance Station

Big Thompson River **Moraine Park**

Bear Lake Road

Bear
Lake

35. Necrophilia
42. All Mixed Up
45. Reflections
46. Black Lake Slabs

0   1   2 **Miles**

0   1   2   3 **Kilometers**

Glacier Gorge Junction

Mills Lake

atchtop
Mtn

Arrowhead
Peak

Mt. Lady
Washington

Long's Peak RS

Black
Lake

Longs
Peak

Chasm
Meadows

Peacock
Pool

Roaring Fork Creek

Spearhead

Mt.
Meeker

Chiefshead

N

47. West Gully
51. Big Mac Couloir, McHenry's
    Peak
54. Columbine Falls
57. Dream Weaver
59. The Loft
63. Notch Couloir
66. North Face

Jaws Falls is about a mile up the valley, also on the right side. Skis are a must!

6. Windy Gulch Cascades (WI 2, 200 feet)

This name was one of the names originally used for Jaws Falls, however, it has subsequently been used for this small stream that boasts some short pillars and steps. The route faces south into the sun, so catch it in midwinter.

Approach time: 30 minutes

Descent: To descend, rappel off trees or scramble down.

Season: Midwinter. It faces south and gets the sun, so start early.

Road/Highway the climb is visible from: None.

7. Jaws Falls (WI 4, 170 feet) ★★★

Jaws, as it's known, is one of the finest routes in the state. A thick wide waterfall that cascades over a cave, the route gets its name from the icicles that dangle from the roof of the cave and help give the appearance of an open mouth.

Jaws Falls

Thin, brittle ice leads up 50 feet to the cave, then climb up and out the roof (the crux) to easier ground above. The route faces south into the sun, so catch it in midwinter (and, early in the morning).

Approach time: 45 minutes

Descent: To descend, rappel off a big tree at the top, on the left.

Season: Midwinter.

Road/Highway the climb is visible from: None.

Bear Lake Area
(Routes 8-29)

The Bear Lake area of Rocky Mountain National Park is easily the most popular among tourists, and on a summer day, it's nearly impossible to not find yourself smashed in a crowd as you wander around the Lake.

However, the area also boasts a number of excellent easy-moderate alpine routes, along with a handful of hard ice routes, and as soon as you break away from the Bear Lake Nature Trail, you're likely to find yourself almost alone.

This chapter includes routes in the three drainages west of Bear Lake simply because the starting point for climbers headed into these areas is the Bear Lake parking lot and trailhead. The drainages, from north to south, are the Fern Creek Valley, Tyndall Gorge and Chaos Canyon.

In the Fern Creek Valley are Grace Falls, Guide's Wall, Odessa Wall, the Northeast Face of Notchtop Mountain, the Southeast Face of Notchtop, the Ptarmigan Point Glacier, and the three couloirs on the Northwest Face of Flattop Mountain.

In Tyndall Gorge, the beautiful valley below Hallett Peak's dramatic North Face, are the Tyndall Glacier, Tentacles, the Squid, Calamari, Tower Gully, Dragon Tail's Gully, the East Couloir of Hallett Peak and the Hallett Chimney.

The Chaos Canyon Icefield is found at the head of Chaos Canyon.

Getting there To get to the Bear Lake trailhead and parking lot, drive 0.2 miles west of the Beaver Meadows Entrance Station to the Park and turn south, onto the Moraine Park/Bear Lake Road, as you would to get to Moraine Park.

Follow the Moraine Park/Bear Lake Road for about 9.5 miles. The parking lot will be obvious, as it happens to also be the end of the road. A note of warning for alpine climbers seeking to do summer routes: the Bear Lake area is so popular in summer that it is generally impossible to get a parking space anytime after 8 a.m. So, the park service has instituted a free shuttle system whereby you can park several miles back down the road and ride to the Bear Lake parking lot.

Once at the Bear Lake trailhead and parking lot, you can choose your destination: the Fern Creek Valley, Tyndall Gorge, or Chaos Canyon.

Fern Creek Valley Area

From the Bear Lake trailhead and parking lot, wander past the west end of the parking lot, between a restroom and a Park Service information booth. After you cross a large bridge, the trail will split. A brown sign points the way to various destinations and their mileages.

Go right, and within a few hundred feet you'll reach the Bear Lake Nature Trail, which circumnavigates the lake. Here, you have the option to go left or right, around the lake.

The Bear Lake Ice Fall, which rarely has good climbing, forms up at the western side of the lake, several hundred feet above the trail. It should be obvious. You can reach it by either going left or right around Bear Lake, though going left (along the south side of the lake) is fastest.

To reach the Fern Creek Valley, go right, and skirt Bear Lake on its right hand (east) side for several hundred feet, until a sign points out the trail to "Flattop Mountain, 4.4 miles, Odessa Lake, 4.0, Fern Lake, 4.7 miles," and Bierstadt Lake, 2.7 miles" which branches off up the hill to the right (northeast). Follow this right branch. It winds up around the eastern spur of Flattop Mountain for 0.4 miles, before splitting again. At this intersection, the right branch goes to Odessa Lake and Fern Lake," while the left branch goes to "Flattop Mountain." Go left.

After several miles of hiking, the trail enters a small, hanging east-west valley that, to the west, intersects with the Fern Creek Valley proper. You'll pass a lake, Two Rivers Lake, and the massive northeast face of Notchtop will be in plain view before you. After Two Rivers Lake, the trail cuts back right and drops down the hill towards Odessa Lake. Leave the trail before it begins its descent to Odessa Lake, and walk west, to Lake Helene. Grace Falls, the Odessa Wall, and Guide's Wall are all easily

**Benny Bach Soloing
The Black Lake Slabs**

seen from this area, as are the routes on Notchtop's northeast face.

Routes on the northeast face of Notchtop should be obvious. Grace Falls is the big thick waterfall that spills out of the upper Fern Creek Valley toward Odessa Lake. For greater reference, it lies just north of Lake Helene.

Right of Grace Falls is the Odessa Wall, essentially a cliff band at the base of Notchtop's northeast face. Guide's Wall is the low-angled slab above Odessa Lake and north across the valley from Lake Helene.

To reach these routes, cut across the hillside toward them. This is mostly a matter of picking and choosing the best way, as no regular route exists.

For routes on Notchtop's southeast face, and Flattop's northwest face, continue west, up the upper Fern Creek Valley, into the basin between Flattop and Notchtop. (There are two small tarns up in this basin and it's easily recognized in summer because it's the snowiest place around.)

The couloirs on the southeast face of Notchtop will become visible up to the right (northwest), behind the magnificent ridge on the south face of Notchtop. Over to the left (south) will be the couloirs on the northwest face of Flattop, and finally, at the head of the valley, at the furthest point to the west, is the Ptarmigan Point Glacier.

Guide's Wall. Guide Wall Route

8.   Bear Lake Ice Fall (WI 2-3, 100 feet)

This climb is not really in the Fern Creek Valley, it's sort of on the approach to Fern Creek. Anyway, for simplicity's sake, it's included here. It faces east, so get there early.

Approach time: 10 minutes from the Bear Lake parking lot.
Descent: Scramble off left, or rappel.
Season: Midwinter.
Road/Highway the climb is visible from: None.

9.   Grace Falls (WI 4, 120 feet) ★★★

A classic waterfall climb with many variations. The best climb is the main falls itself, a WI 4 pillar of thick blue ice. To the left of the main falls, a thin route with several mixed variations often forms. To the right of the main falls is a shorter, easier (WI 3) route.

Approach time: Allow 2 hours, from the Bear Lake parking lot.
Descent: Scramble off either right or left of the falls.
Season: Midwinter
Road/Highway the climb is visible from: None.

10. Odessa Wall (WI 5, various lengths) ★

Right of Grace Falls, and below the bowl of Notchtop's northeast face, this wide cliff band often produces thin, yet climbable ice. There are many individual routes

Fern Creek Valley Area. Left to right: Ptarmigan Point Glacier, Northeast Face Route, Notchtop, Grace Falls, Northeast Face Left, Notchtop, Direct Northeast Face, Notchtop, Odessa Wall

with varying lengths.

Approach time: Allow 2-3 hours, from the Bear Lake parking lot.
Descent: Scramble off either right or left of the cliff.
Season: Midwinter
Road/Highway the climb is visible from: None.

11. Guide's Wall (WI 2, 100 feet) ★★★

Right of Odessa Wall and the bowl of Notchtop's northeast face, this low-angled granite cliff regularly sports a number of high quality ice slabs. The main flow lies on the left-hand edge of the slabs.

Approach time: Allow 2-3 hours, from the Bear Lake parking lot.
Descent: Walk off left.
Season: Midwinter.
Road/Highway the climb is visible from: None.

12. Northeast Face Left, Notchtop
(IV, AI 4, 5.7, 1,000 feet)

This route is reportedly not very good. The route starts by climbing a left slanting ramp on the left side of the face. Climb the ramp for three leads to a big ledge system leading back to the right. The ledge system terminates at the base of a snow

Fern Creek Valley Area, Notchtop Mountain. Left to right: Southeast Couloir Left, Southeast Couloir Right

gully near the center of the face. The gully is climbed to the top, near the notch. Bring much rock gear.

Approach time: Allow 2-3 hours, from the Bear Lake parking lot.

Descent: The standard descent off Notchtop is via the West Gully-North Ridge of the mountain. In short, this descent route heads west from the summit, and follows the north ridge down to the huge hanging valley on the northwest side of the mountain.

Season: Midwinter.

Road/Highway the climb is visible from: The face can be seen from various points throughout the park, but its condition is difficult to estimate from such long distances.

13. Direct Northeast Face, Notchtop
(III, AI 4, 5.8, 1,000 feet)

Start at the foot of the slabby wall on the left side of the face (a few hundred feet right of the previous route). Several leads of mixed rock and ice put one on the big ledge system that bisects the face horizontally. From this ledge, the route joins the Northeast Face Left route. Belay ledges are reportedly scarce on the lower part of the route. Bring rock gear.

Approach time: Allow 2-3 hours, from the Bear Lake parking lot.

Descent: Same as for the previous route.

Season: Midwinter

Road/Highway the climb is visible from: The face can be seen from various points throughout the park, but its condition is difficult to estimate from such long distances.

14. Northeast Face Route, Notchtop
(III, AI 4, 1,000 feet) ★★

This is the classic outing on Notchtop's northeast face. Start at the back of the bowl that forms the northeast face, a climb a snow cone to the foot of the first rock band on the face. A steep ice pitch climbs the rock band. Easy snow slopes are followed by another steep pitch of ice up the second rock band, and leads to more snow slopes. These are followed by snow and ice climbing to the notch.

Southeast Couloir, Left

This route can be hazardous, as it is prone to rock and ice fall. Bring rock gear.

Approach time: Allow 2-3 hours, from the Bear Lake parking lot.

Descent: Same as for the previous route.

Season: Midwinter.

Road/Highway the climb is visible from: The face can be seen from various points throughout the park, but its condition is difficult to estimate from such long distances.

15. Southeast Couloir Right, Notchtop Mountain
(II, AI 2-3, 1000 feet) ★

On the Southeast face of Notchtop, just left of the prominent South Ridge, are two long couloirs which offer easy-moderate cruising material for alpinists. The right-hand (east) of the two has many possible variations at the top, as the couloirs breaks up into fingers. Do it in early summer, as it tends to melt out later in the year.

Approach time: Allow 2-3 hours, from the Bear Lake parking lot.

Descent: Same as for the previous route.

Season: Early summer.

Road/Highway the climb is visible from: None.

Flattop Mountain. Left to right: East Couloir, Northwest Face, Central Couloir, Northwest Face, West Couloir, Northwest Face, Ptarmigan Point Glacier

16. Southeast Couloir Left, Notchtop Mountain
(II, AI 2-3, 1000 feet) ★★★

Left of the previous route is another long couloir. However, this couloir is just one line, and tends to retain its snow and ice throughout the summer. The interesting jogs to the right make this a stimulating climb, and perhaps a little safer than similar types of couloirs..

Approach time: Allow 2-3 hours, from the Bear Lake parking lot.

Descent: Same as for the previous route.

Season: Summer.

Road/Highway the climb is visible from: None.

17. East Couloir, Northwest Face Flattop Mountain
(II, AI 2-3, 1000 feet) ★★★

On the broad northwest face of Flattop are a series of snow gullies that last well through the summer, and offer superb but easy alpine climbs in the middle of summer. The East Couloir is the leftmost (easternmost) and longest of the three.

Approach time: Allow 2-3 hours, from the Bear Lake parking lot.

Descent: Walk off the summit of Flattop via the Flattop Trail. This trail follows along the top of Flattop and descends to Bear Lake. Or, it's possible to descend the Ptarmigan Point Glacier, or the route itself.

Season: Summer.

Road/Highway the climb is visible from: The face can be seen from various points throughout the park.

Tony Asnicar on Ptarmigan Point Glacier

18. Central Couloir, Northwest Face Flattop Mountain (II, AI 3, 900 feet) ★★★

This route lies just right (west) of the previous route. It's very similar to the east gully, just a little steeper and shorter.

Approach time: Allow 2-3 hours, from the Bear Lake parking lot.
Descent: Same as for the previous route.
Season: Summer.
Road/Highway the climb is visible from: The face can be seen from various points throughout the park.

19. West Couloir, Northwest Face Flattop Mountain (II, AI 2-3, 800 feet) ★★★

This route is the right-hand of the three couloirs, and the top of it is broken up by a rock band that pokes through the snow. It's slightly easier than the Central Couloir.

Approach time: Allow 2-3 hours, from the Bear Lake parking lot.
Descent: Same as for the previous route.
Season: Summer.
Road/Highway the climb is visible from: The face can be seen from various points throughout the park.

20. Ptarmigan Point Glacier (I, AI 1, 700 feet) ★★★

This is the big, wide snowfield at the head of the Fern Creek Valley. It can be ascended in any number of locations, and the big bergschrund that traverses its top edge can offer some interesting ice bouldering.

Approach time: Allow 2-3 hours, from the Bear Lake parking lot.

Descent: Same as for the previous route.

Season: Summer.

Road/Highway the climb is visible from: The face can be seen from various points throughout the park.

Rocky Mountain National Park. Hallett Peak Storm

Tyndall Gorge Area

Getting there: From the Bear Lake trailhead and parking lot, wander past the west end of the parking lot, between a restroom and a Park Service information booth. After you cross a large bridge, the trail will split. A sign points the way to various destinations and their mileages.

Instead of going right, as you would for the Fern Creek Valley, go left, onto the Emerald Lake Trail. This highway-like trail cruises up to Dream Lake and Emerald Lake into the heart of the Tyndall Gorge. Watch out for tourists with Camcorders glued to their heads!

After passing the elongated Dream Lake, the trail wanders through the forest to Emerald Lake. Up on the hillside to the right (north) — just before Emerald Lake — is a short cliff band that is home to Calamari, The Squid, and Tentacles, three short hard ice routes.

Beyond the lake, on the same (north) side of the valley, are the spectacular rock towers of the Dragon's Tail and Tyndall Spire. (These two formations are really neighboring fins of rock on the south edge of Flattop Mountain.) The most prominent fin, in the center of the area, is the Dragon's Tail. The Dragon's Tail Gully goes up the wide chute right of this fin. Tower Gully goes up the left side of the Dragon's Tail.

From Emerald Lake, the north face of Hallett Peak will also be obvious, up the valley on the left (south) side. The obvious wet cleft in the face is the Hallett

Tyndall Gorge, Flattop Mountain. Left to right: Tower Gully, Dragon's Tail Gully

Chimney. To the left of this route, and skirting the steep rock walls of the north face, is an easy couloir that leads to Hallett's East Ridge. This is the East Couloir of Hallett Peak.

If you continue hiking up the gorge, past Hallett's north face, you'll reach the Tyndall Glacier at the head of the valley. Above Emerald Lake, however, there is not much of a trail and it gets pretty rough.

21. Calamari (WI 4-5, 180 feet) ★

In a good year, three separate flows of ice form up on the north side of the Emerald Lake Trail, just east of (before you get to) Emerald Lake, about 400 feet up the hillside. Calamari, which lies 150 feet right of the Squid, is the route lying furthest right. It can range from being thick, easy to climb ice, to desperate and runout 5.9 rock with a few icicles on it.

Approach time: 45 minutes from the Bear Lake parking lot.
Descent: Rappel off a tree or scramble down.
Season: Midwinter
Road/Highway the climb is visible from: None.

22. The Squid
(WI 5, 150 feet) ★★★

This is the most regularly forming of the three routes on the north side of the Emerald Lake trail. It follows a right facing dihedral, then thin slabs above. Often thin or mixed. Bring rock gear.

Approach time: 45 minutes from the Bear Lake parking lot.

Descent: Rappel off a tree or scramble down.

Season: Midwinter

Road/Highway the climb is visible from: None.

23. Tentacles
(WI 5, 120 feet) ★

A series of thin ice sheets 100 feet left of the Squid, Tentacles is the leftmost of the three, and rarely forms well. Bring rock gear.

Approach time: 45 minutes from the Bear Lake parking lot.

Descent: Rappel off a tree or scramble down.

Season: Midwinter

Road/Highway the climb is visible from: None.

The Squid   Bill Pelander photo

24. Dragon's Tail Gully, Flattop Mountain (II, AI 2-3, 600 feet) ★★

A straightforward gully that follows the right side of the Dragon's Tail. There are several short but steep sections, before it tops out on Flattop. Can be prone to avalanche.

Approach time: 1 hour from Bear Lake parking lot.

Descent: Wander east, down the Flattop Mountain Trail back to Bear Lake., or downclimb the route

Season: Late summer/early fall.

Road/Highway the climb is visible from: None.

25. Tower Gully, Flattop Mountain (II, AI 1-2, 500 feet) ★

Another straightforward gully, this one follows the left side of the Dragon's Tail. It terminates on the summit plateau, and can be prone to avalanche danger. Remember, it faces south.

Approach time: 1 hour from Bear Lake parking lot.

Descent: Wander east, down the Flattop Mountain Trail back to Bear Lake or downclimb the route.

Season: Late summer/early fall.

Road/Highway the climb is visible from: None.

Hallett Peak. Hallett Chimney Route

26. East Couloir, Hallett Peak (AI 1-2, 500 feet)

A very direct couloir that leads to the East Ridge on Hallett Peak. Often holds snow through the summer, but the snow stays only in the couloir and melts off the East Ridge proper. You can continue up the East Ridge all the way to the summit.

Approach time: 1 hour from Bear Lake parking lot.

Descent: Downclimbing the route is the most straightforward.

Season: Summer.

Road/Highway the climb is visible from: None. It's hidden by rock buttresses left (east) of the route.

27. Hallett Chimney (III, AI 5, 5.6, 900 feet) ★★

The big cleft left of the first buttress on Hallett Peak makes a better ice climb than rock route (it's always dripping). The route gets harder as you get higher, and can be prone to avalanche in the winter. Bring a full rack of rock gear.

Approach time: 1 hour from Bear Lake parking lot.

Descent: Downclimbing the East Couloir is the easiest. Or, the standard descent from Hallett Peak Routes lies just right (west) of the steep part of the face and follows a steep snow-filled gully down to the foot of the north face.

Season: Spring/fall.

Road/Highway the climb is visible from: None. While the Chimney is visible from many places in the park, the back of this cleft (i.e. the place where the ice is) is only visible from below the route.

Hallett Peak Summit, Tyndall Glacier Route

28. Tyndall Glacier (AI 1-2, 500 feet) ★★

This is the huge, wide glacier at the head of the valley. It can be climbed via numerous routes.

Approach time: 2 hours from Bear Lake parking lot.

Descent: Downclimbing the route is the most straightforward, or you can walk off to the right, over the top of Flattop Mountain, then down the Flattop Mountain trail to Bear Lake.

Season: Summer.

Road/Highway the climb is visible from: The glacier can be seen from various points throughout the park.

Chaos Canyon Area

Getting There

From the Bear Lake trailhead and parking lot, wander past the west end of the parking lot, between a restroom and a Park Service information booth. After you cross a large bridge, the trail will split. A sign points the way to various destinations and their mileages.

Go left, as you would for the Emerald Lake Trail. About a mile up this trail, just before the Emerald Lake Trail reaches Dream Lake, it splits. As the sign states, the left trail goes to "Lake Haiyaha, 1.1 miles" and Chaos Canyon, while the right trail leads to "Dream Lake, 0.1 miles" and Emerald Lake, 0.7 miles." Go left, towards Lake Haiyaha.

Unfortunately, the trail ends at Lake Haiyaha, and reaching the Chaos Canyon Icefield is a matter of stumbling up the valley floor for another mile and a half. The benefit is you'll have the place all to yourself.

29. Chaos Canyon Icefield (II, AI 2, 700 feet) ★
The big wide snowfield at the head of the valley. The sides are harder.
Approach time: 2 hours from Bear Lake parking lot.
Descent: Downclimbing the route is the most straightforward, or you can walk off to the right, over the top of Hallett Peak and down the Tyndall Glacier, or continue north (right), past Hallett Peak, and down the Flattop Mountain trail to Bear Lake.
Season: Summer.
Road/Highway the climb is visible from: The glacier can be seen from various points throughout the park.

Chaos Canyon Icefield

Glacier Gorge, Loch Vale
(Routes 30–52)

Glacier Gorge and Loch Vale are essentially two side-by-side valleys in the center of the park containing a variety of ice climbs.

The valleys are not quite parallel. It's easiest to think of them as spokes on a wheel, radiating out from the Glacier Gorge Junction trailhead and parking lot.

From the center of the wheel, Glacier Gorge runs directly south, along the west side of Longs Peak, to Chiefshead and Pagoda Mountain. Meanwhile, Loch Vale runs southwest, to the Sharkstooth, Taylor Peak and the Cathedral Spires (Petit Grepon) area.

Ice climbs are found throughout the length of the two valleys, ranging in difficulty from the easy ice bouldering around Black Lake to the mind-melting Necrophilia. There are even a few mega-classics like the West Gully and All Mixed Up.

Getting There: The first mile or so of the trail into both valleys is the same, then the trail splits, with one branch heading south towards Glacier Gorge and Black Lake, and the other going southwest toward Loch Vale sand Sky Pond.

The starting point for both trails is at the Glacier Gorge Junction Trailhead parking lot.

To get to the parking lot, drive 0.2 miles west of the Beaver Meadows Entrance Station to the Park and turn south, onto the Moraine Park/Bear Lake Road, as you would to get to Bear Lake.

The approach to Glacier Gorge and Loch Vale

Follow the Moraine Park/Bear Lake Road for 8.5 miles. The parking lot will be obvious, on the right side of a sharp bend in the road.

Parking Lot Wall will be visible across the road to the southwest.

From the parking lot, cross the street to the southwest and gain the Glacier Gorge trail, which heads south, up into the trees. As you ascend into the trees, Parking Lot Wall will be on your right.

Just past Parking Lot Wall, about two minutes walk from the parking lot, the trail splits for the first time into two separate branches. The main trail cuts left, and circles around to Alberta Falls and up towards Glacier Gorge and Loch Vale.

The trail to the left is a shortcut to the right. This trail — present during most winters — skirts the south side of the bluff containing Parking Lot Wall and follows a small drainage southwest where it rejoins the main trail. There are some low angled slabs along this drainage that sometimes form up offering easy ice bouldering and easy mixed leads.)

Benny Bach Raps off Cold Storage

After about 45 minutes to an hour, the trail will reach a sign, and will split once again (the second split, for reference). As the sign notes, the right branch goes up to "Loch Vale (0.8 miles), Sky Pond (2.8 miles) and Andrews Glacier (2.8 miles)", while the left branch heads towards "Mills Lake (0.6 miles), and Black Lake (2.8 miles)."

Go left towards Black Lake for several hundred yards. As you ski or snowshoe, the massive hanging valley of Glacier Gorge will become somewhat obvious up to the left (south), through the trees. After a few hundred yards, there'll be a small bridge with a single handrail and a sign pointing to Glacier Gorge. In the winter, with deep snow present, the bridge looks like little more than a fallen tree and the sign is not visible at all. Keep your eye open for tracks leading off left, up the valley. If you miss this turn, the trail continues up and rejoins the Loch Vale trail.

Once you've found the Glacier Gorge trail and ascended up into the gorge, the valley opens up, and offers views of all the surrounding peaks. The first landmark reached is Mills Lake, which is generally frozen and offers a big flat open area to ski across. Above and west of Mills Lake is where All Mixed Up, the Pipe Organ, and the Middle Finger of Dr. Wazz are all located.

To reach the Black Lake area from Mills Lake, continue south up the valley towards the massive northeast face of Chiefshead Peak. It takes another 1-2 hours, depending on your fitness, to reach Black Lake.

Black Lake, located at the head of Glacier Gorge, is an ice climber's paradise. It offers many ice routes of all grades, and during a good ice year, the slabs surrounding the south side of the lake can freeze up offering countless routes.

Black Lake is also the jumping off point for several alpine routes —such as the Big Mac Couloir on McHenry's — and many parties chose the Black Lake area as a base camp for longer routes.

To get to Loch Vale, take the right fork of the trail when it splits a second time, as mentioned above, in the Glacier Gorge approach description.

Within a few hundred yards, the trail reaches the Loch Vale Gorge, a steep canyon with rocky walls that boast a number of 60-100-foot ice routes. Continue up the canyon to its head, and Loch Vale will open up before you. The obvious frozen lake just beyond the head of the gorge is The Loch.

The Crypt is the obvious blue curtain of ice immediately north of the Loch on the northwest (southeast facing) side of the valley. Numerous other flows of all grades and lengths form in this area, but the Crypt is the most reliable, as well as the most striking piece of ice.

About a quarter mile left (southwest) of The Crypt on the same side of the valley are two regularly forming flows of ice on a cliff band, Cold Storage, and Freezer Burn.

On the opposite side of the valley is Thatchtop Mountain, where Necrophilia, Deep Freeze, and the Northwest Face Route lie.

Beyond the Loch area, the valley climbs toward Sky Pond. The long, even ridge on the left side of the valley is the Thatchtop-Powell ridge, and there are several snow and ice gullies along its northwest side that offer excellent alpine cruising material in the summer. At the head of the valley is Taylor Peak, and the Taylor Glacier.

Loch Vale Routes

30. Parking Lot Wall (WI 5, 120 feet)

During a really good ice season, this wall can offer good climbable ice close to the road. The climbs are generally top-roped because of their thin nature.

Approach time: 5 minutes

Descent: To descend, either rappel off trees or walk down to the left (south).

Season: Mid-winter. Rarely forms well.

Road/Highway the climb is visible from: The Moraine Park/Bear Lake Road in the Park.

31. Loch Vale Gorge (WI 3-5, various lengths) ★★★

Just beyond the small bridge that marks the trail into Glacier Gorge is Loch Vale Gorge. A number of ice climbs form at the bottom end of this narrow gorge, and offer some of the best ice climbing in the Park. They tend to be vertical or almost vertical, long enough to be challenging and access to them is fairly straightforward, since they lie only 100 to 200 feet off the trail.

Approach time: Allow 45 minutes to an hour.
Descent: Rappel off trees or scramble down.
Season: All winter.
Road/Highway the climb is visible from: None.

32. The Crypt (WI 4, 100 feet) ★★★

The Crypt is the obvious blue curtain of ice immediately north of the Loch.
Pumper for its grade, but quality. Numerous other flows of all grades and lengths
form in this area, but the Crypt is the most reliable, as well as the most striking
piece of ice.
Approach time: Allow two hours.
Descent: Rappel off trees.
Season: All winter.
Road/Highway the climb is visible from: None.

33. Cold Storage and 34. Freezer Burn (WI 4, 60 and 80 feet) ★★

About a quarter mile left (southwest) of The Crypt are two regularly forming
flows of ice on a cliff band. The left, Cold Storage, is about 60 feet tall and offers
WI 4 climbing. The right, Freezer Burn, is about 80 feet tall and offers slightly
harder climbing. Both routes are harder than they appear from the Loch. There
are numerous other similar icefalls in this area.
Approach time: Allow two hours.
Descent: Rappel off trees or hike down to the left (southwest).
Season: All winter.
Road/Highway the climb is visible from: None.

The Loch Area, looking northwest
Left to right: Cold Storage and Freezer Burn, The Crypt

The Loch Area, looking south.
Left to right: Necrophilia, Deep Freeze, Northwest Face Route

35. Necrophilia (WI 5, 300 feet) ★★

The ultimate RMNP mixed hard route, Necrophilia lies south of the Loch, on the lowest cliffband on the northwest face of Thatchtop. Bring plenty of rock gear as often Necrophilia boasts more rock than ice. This climb can be linked up with Deep Freeze for a long hard day's outing.

Approach time: Allow two hours.
Descent: Scramble off easy ground to the right (west), or rappel the route.
Season: Mid-winter.
Road/Highway the climb is visible from: None.

36. Deep Freeze (WI 5+, 300 feet)

Deep Freeze lies in the steep gully capped by huge roofs left of Necrophilia. If climbed from its base, it is much longer than 300 feet, although the lower portions of the route are mostly easy snow. Bring rock gear and expect some very difficult climbing.

Approach time: Allow two hours.
Descent: Descend by hiking off to the left (east).
Season: Mid-winter.
Road/Highway the climb is visible from: None.

37. Northwest Face Route, Thatchtop
(WI 4-5, 1,000 feet) ★

This route follows a massive cleft in the left side of Thatchtop's north face that angles up left, then cuts back right at about the mid-point. The route contains only

Thatchtop-Powell Area from the Loch Area.
Left to right: Thatchtop-Powell Icefield, North Gully of Thatchtop

a few hundred feet of real ice climbing (which is hidden from most views), and consists mostly of hiking up snow. The ice climbing occurs at the point where the route changes direction. Bring rock gear.

Approach time: Allow two hours.
Descent: Descend by hiking off to the left (east).
Season: Mid-winter.
Road/Highway the climb is visible from: None.

38. Thatchtop-Powell Icefield (II-III, AI 2-2+, 1,000 feet) ★

This route is also known as the Two-Ten Gully, after its position in Richard DuMais book, "The High Peaks." It ascends the massive, permanent snowfield south of Sky Pond. Although during the winter and early spring it is not recommended — due to avalanche danger — it is a fine alpine route in the summer and fall.

Approach the route directly from Sky Pond. The first few leads are relatively easy. About half way up, the route steepens. The gully also branches into fingers, with the two left-hand (eastern) fingers being relatively easy. The right finger, which climbs the rock buttress right of the route, is much harder, and offers five pitches of difficult mixed ground (AI 4).

Approach time: Allow three-four hours.
Descent: Descend by either downclimbing the route (a rappel or two may be nec-
essary) or hiking off to the right (west) and down the Taylor Glacier.
Season: Summer/fall
Road/Highway the climb is visible from: This climb is visible from all over the
Estes Park area, and the Bear Lake parking lot.

Taylor Glacier from the Loch Area
Left to right: Taylor Glacier, Taylor Glacier Buttress

39. North Gully of Thatchtop (II-III, AI 3-4, 900 feet)

Like the Two-Ten Gully, this route is often called the Two-Eleven Gully, for its position in DuMais' book. This route lies right of the Thatchtop-Powell Icefield and climbs the right side of a large rock buttress. After several hundred feet of easy snow climbing, the gully steepens to the point of overhanging. At this point, climb up and right, out the top of the gully, then traverse back left, into the gully proper, and climb it to the top.

Approach time: Allow three-four hours.

Descent: Descend by either downclimbing the route (a rappel or two may be necessary) or hiking off to the right (west) and down the Taylor Glacier.

Season: Summer/fall.

Road/Highway the climb is visible from: This climb is visible from all over the Estes Park area, and the Bear Lake parking lot.

40. Taylor Glacier (II, AI 2, 600 feet)

The Taylor Glacier lies at the head of the valley, on the south side of Taylor Peak. The route is simple — climb the Glacier to the ridge lining the cirque. Numerous variations are possible.

Descent: Descend by downclimbing the route.

Season: Summer/fall.

Road/Highway the climb is visible from: This climb is visible from all over the Estes Park area, and the Bear Lake parking lot.

41. Taylor Glacier Buttress (II, 5.0-5.6, AI 2, 1,000 feet) ★★

This climb is a classic of the area. It ascends a huge snow ramp that lies right of the buttress right of the Taylor Glacier. In other words, it traverses the east face of

Taylor Peak (angling from the bottom right of the face to the top left). The climb is often just a snow climb, but when conditions are right, it might require some easy rock climbing near the middle point on the ramp. From the top of the buttress, hike up and right (north) to the summit of Taylor Peak.

Descent: Descend by downclimbing the Taylor Glacier.

Season: Summer/fall.

Road/Highway the climb is visible from: This climb is visible from all over the Estes Park area, and the Bear Lake parking lot.

Glacier Gorge Routes

42. All Mixed Up (WI 4, 500 feet) ★★★

From Mills Lake, the famous moderate classic route All Mixed Up will become obvious up in the huge bowl west of — and high above — the lake. It follows the center of the bowl for several easy, low-angled pitches to the obvious big ledge. From the ledge, it is possible to avoid the last pitch of the route by escaping off left. The last pitch is a steep pillar of ice and can range from sinker plastic blue ice to thin, ice-coated rock. This climb is also known as the White Spider due to its resemblance of the famous ice gully at the top of the Eiger's North Face.

Approach time: Allow 2 hours for the approach.

Descent: To descend, either rappel the route if you can find anchors, or walk far off to the right side and scramble down. Many descent routes are possible.

Season: Early/late winter. Stays in shape well into the spring.

Road/Highway the climb is visible from: None.

Glacier Gorge. All Mixed Up Route from Mills Lake

43. The Pipe Organ (WI 5, 100 feet)

This steep route sometimes forms up to the right of All Mixed Up.

Approach time: Allow 2 hours for the approach.

Descent: Walk far off right and scramble down.

Season: All winter.

Road/Highway the climb is visible from: None.

44. Middle Finger of Dr. Waz (WI 5, 100 feet)

This is the well-named, vertical curtain that forms up downhill and right of the Pipe Organ.

Approach time: Allow two hours for the approach.

Descent: Walk off right.

Season: All winter.

Road/Highway the climb is visible from: None.

45. Reflections (WI 3, 160 feet)

As one nears Black Lake, many iced up slabs present themselves on the left side of the valley. The most obvious is a thin sheet of ice, about 40-feet wide and about a ropelength in height. Bring a few pieces of rock gear, as well as tie offs for your ice screws.

Approach time: Allow two-three hours for the approach.

Descent: Descend by walking off to the left (east).

Season: All winter.

Road/Highway the climb is visible from: None.

Speerhead, Chiefshead. Reflections Route

46. Black Lake Slabs
(WI 1-3, many variations possible, 400 feet) ★

Around the southeastern edge of Black Lake are a series of slabs that regularly boast a thick coating of blue ice. For the most part, these slabs offer WI 1-2 climbing, but occasionally some steeper ground (up to WI 3) can be found.

Approach time: Allow 2-3 hours for the approach.

Descent: Descend by downclimbing snow between the various ice sections, or walk off to the left (east).

Season: All winter.

Road/Highway the climb is visible from: None.

47. West Gully (WI 4, 450 feet) ★★★

The finest offering in the Black Lake area, the West Gully sits on the western side of the lake, directly below the basin below McHenry's Peak. It usually offers a steep pillar followed by 220 feet of thin slabs of high quality ice. Often, the pillar doesn't form, but the route still boasts good climbing.

Approach time: Allow two-three hours for the approach.

Descent: Wallow through snow along the base of Arrowhead Peak, right of the climb, or rappel.

Season: All winter.

Road/Highway the climb is visible from: None.

48. Stone Man (WI 5, 80 feet)

There are two short pillars that regularly form right of the West Gully, just above the west end of the lake. Stone Man, named for the famed rock tower on the ridge between Chiefshead and McHenry's Peaks is the leftmost of the two.

Approach Time: Allow two-three hours for the approach.

Descent: Scramble off right.

Season: All winter.

Road/Highway the climb is visible from: None.

49. Yellow Tears (WI 5, 80 feet)

This is the right-hand of the two pillars.

Approach time: Allow two-three hours for the approach.

Descent: Scramble off right.

Season: All winter.

Road/Highway the climb is visible from: None.

50. The Snow Bench Route, McHenry's Peak
(III, AI 2, 5.5, 500 feet) ★★★

From the Black Lake area, McHenry's is the triangular shaped peak to the west. It offers an interesting, though easy, alpine route up its east face. From Black Lake, skirt the lower flanks of Arrowhead Peak (the broken up summit right of McHenry's) to gain the bowl below McHenry's east face.

At the base of the East Face, just right of center, is the start of the route. There is a break in the rock bands that allows access to the long, left-angling snow ramp, the namesake of the route. Follow the ramp to a notch in the ridge, then to the summit. There are many variations. Bring rock gear.

Black Lake Area. Left to right: The Snow Bench Route, McHenry's Peak, West Gully, Big Mac Couloir, McHenry's Peak, Right Gully, McHenry's Peak

Approach time: Allow three-four hours for the approach.

Descent: Walk off via the southeast ridge, towards Stoneman Pass and Chiefshead.

Season: All winter, though avalanche danger can be high.

Road/Highway the climb is visible from: None.

51. Big Mac Couloir, McHenry's Peak
(III, AI 3-4, 5.6, A1, 500 feet) ★★

This route lies right of the Snow Bench route, and ascends the left side of a prominent buttress in the middle of the east face. Begin by climbing the first pitch of the Snow Bench Route, through the rock band. Then, climb the obvious large couloir up the left side of the buttress. Expect difficulties of up 5.6 rock and steep ice/snow climbing. At the top of the buttress, climb up and right, onto a steep wall. Climb this to the top. Bring rock gear.

Approach time: Allow three-four hours for the approach.

Descent: Same as for the previous route.

Season: All winter, though avalanche danger can be high.

Road/Highway the climb is visible from: None.

52. Right Gully, McHenry's Peak
(III, AI 3-4, 5.8, A1, 500 feet)

This route lies right of the prominent buttress in the middle of the east face. As for the Big Mac Couloir, climb the first pitch of the Snow Bench Route, through the rock band. Then, cut far right, to the right side of the buttress. Follow the right side of the buttress straight up, to the steep wall below the summit. Climb the wall to the top. Bring rock gear.

Approach Time: Allow three-four hours for the approach.

Descent: Same as for the previous route.

Season: All winter, though avalanche danger can be high.

Road/Highway the climb is visible from: None.

Longs Peak, Mt. Meeker & Chasm Meadows
(Routes 53-66)

The Longs Peak/Mt. Meeker area is one of the finest alpine climbing arenas in Colorado. Long winding gullies up sweeping mountain faces are the norm, and generally, a spectacular summit is at the end of the climb.

While the routes on Longs Peak and Mt. Meeker tend to be long, easy cruises — not the short, vertical forearm-blasters found in the rest of the state — they stay in shape well into the summer and fall, offering Front Range climbers an alpine climbing experience on a year-round basis.

Getting there The best way to reach Longs Peak and Mt. Meeker is from the Longs Peak Ranger Station and trailhead, on Colo. 7, between Estes Park and the small town of Meeker Park, west of Lyons.

To reach the ranger station, drive 25.2 miles from the junction of U.S. 36 and Colo. 7 in downtown Lyons west along Colo. 7. You'll pass the towns of Allenspark, Meeker Park and the Wild Basin trailhead. The ranger station will be on the left.

From the major intersection of U.S. 34 and U.S. 36, on the east side of Estes Park, drive south on U.S. 36 for 0.4 miles to the intersection with Colo. 7. Turn right, onto Colo. 7. Drive 9.3 miles south on Colo. 7. The Longs Peak Ranger Station will be on your right. Drive up the mile-long driveway to the parking lot. Plan on getting there early because it fills up in early summer, when alpine routes are in prime condition.

Once you're at the Longs Peak Ranger Station, it's about a 3-4 hour hike (depending on your condition, of course) to climbs on Longs Peak and Mt. Meeker, along the Longs Peak Trail.

The trail departs the area from immediately left of the ranger station building and follows several long switchbacks through the pine forest. At 0.5 miles, the trail branches, with the right branch leading to Eugenia Mine and Storm Pass, and the left branch continuing on towards Longs Peak and Mt. Meeker.

The trail emerges onto a flat mesa-like area, known as the boulderfield. This is not a good place to linger on summer afternoons, as there is not shelter from the dangerous lightning storms that sweep across the area.

Just a short ways onto the boulderfield, (at the 2.5 mile mark) the trail branches. You'll know you're there when you see a sign pointing left to "Chasm Lake 1.7

miles, and Longs Peak 5.9," and right to: "Battle Mountain Group Campground 0.3." Although not mentioned, it's also about a mile and a half to the base of the north face of Mt. Meeker the East Face of Longs Peak. Take the left branch in the trail, towards Longs.

Within another 0.5 miles, you'll reach the Chasm, the east-west valley that drains the Longs Peak/Mt. Meeker basin, at a sort of notch on the left (south) side of Mt. Lady Washington. The trail descends into the Chasm, as it skirts the southeast side of Mt. Lady Washington.

From here, it's possible to scope out routes on Mt. Meeker, with the exception of the Right Gully, which is hidden by the famed Flying Buttress, a rock spur on the north face.

Indeed, the Flying Buttress is perhaps the best landmark for locating ice/alpine routes on Mt. Meeker because the climbs are named in reference to the buttress. Dream Weaver — long known as The Left Gully — lies to the left of the Flying Buttress, while the Right Chimney lies right of the Flying Buttress. The Loft lies right of Mt. Meeker altogether, and ascends the broad saddle between Meeker and Longs.

The trail continues into the valley, and where, after about 0.7 miles, the trail reaches Chasm Meadows, the Park Service's Shelter Hut, and the valleys that drain Meeker and Longs split. There are several worthwhile ice climbs in the area around the Shelter, which are described below.

To reach the north face of Mt. Meeker and the East Face of Longs will be obvious. Hike directly south, up the snow and boulderfields to reach the base of Mt. Meeker. To get to Longs Peak's East Face, continue up the drainage to the right, skirting Chasm Lake on the right side (if it's frozen you can walk across it, of course).

Chasm Meadows is an ill-defined geographic area, at the junction where the drainages below the north face of Mt. Meeker and the East Face of Longs Peak meet.

The most prominent feature of the area is probably the Ship's Prow, a long, sloping, east-west ridge that divides the two drainages and the Peacock Pool, a small lake which lies several hundred yards downstream from the Ship's Prow.

Most climbers first view this area as they enter the Chasm, on the Longs Peak Trail as it skirts the southeast flank of Mt. Lady Washington.

As you descend into the Chasm and head towards the Ship's Prow, a rock buttress will become visible on the right side of the trail. Indeed, the trail passes right under it. This is the South Buttress of Mt. Lady Washington. This about 400-foot buttress often holds a number of mixed routes.

To the Left, below the South Buttress of Mt. Lady Washington and directly below the trail is a small waterfall, Columbine Falls, a popular ice route. Left of Columbine Falls, a number of thin ice climbs form around the western edge of the Peacock Pool.

About a half mile beyond the North Buttress of Mt. Lady Washington and Columbine Falls is the Park Service's shelter cabin. Directly west of this cabin (above it, really) is the Ship's Prow. The northern, lower (right-hand) end of this rock spur often holds several hard ice climbs.

Mt. Meeker. The Flying Buttress (right) and start of Dream Weaver (left)

Chasm Meadows Area

53. South Buttress of Mt. Lady Washington (WI 3-5, 400 feet, various routes) ★

From the Longs Peak Trail, directly below the buttress, climb up to it. Rock gear is a must.

Approach time: From the Longs Peak Ranger Station, allow 3 hours.
Descent: Walk off to the right or rappel.
Season: Most of the winter.
Road/Highway the climb is visible from: None.

54. Columbine Falls (WI 3-4, 100 feet) ★★

From the Longs Peak Trail, directly above the waterfall, scramble down to its base.

Approach time: From the Longs Peak Ranger Station, allow 3 hours.
Descent: Walk off to the right.
Season: Most of the winter.
Road/Highway the climb is visible from: None.

55. Peacock Pool ice (WI 3-5, various lengths) ★★

Directly left of Columbine Falls a number of short, hard routes occasionally form.
Approach time: From the Longs Peak Ranger Station, allow 3 hours.
Descent: Walk off to the right.
Season: Cold winters only.
Road/Highway the climb is visible from: None.

56. Ship's Prow (WI 5-5+, 50-200 feet) ★★

The right-hand end of this ridge offers about a half dozen short hard ice routes. The longest is about 200 feet, while some of the shorter routes (toward the right-hand end) are merely 20-30 feet and can be easily top-roped. For leading any of these routes, rock gear is essential.

Approach Time: From the Longs Peak Ranger Station, allow 3 hours.
Descent: Walk off to the right.
Season: Mid-winter.
Road/Highway the climb is visible from: None.

Mt. Meeker

While Mt. Meeker is wildly overshadowed by Longs Peak in terms of rock climbing, Mt. Meeker offers some of the best — and most popular — ice climbs in the Longs Peak area.

Dream Weaver, a classic gully climb up the north face is perhaps the ultimate moderate climb in the Park, and is a must do for any aspiring alpinist. The Loft is an excellent steep snowfield for giving a lesser experienced climber a few pointers, or even practicing self-arrest.

One of the best aspects of climbs on Meeker is that all of the ice/alpine routes lie on the complex and extensive north face, and can be easily seen and discerned from below the face, as well as points along the trail leading to Meeker and Longs.

57. Dream Weaver (II, 5.4, AI 3, 1,500 feet) ★★★

Dream Weaver, considered one of the best routes in the park, lies immediately left of the Flying Buttress.

The climb starts up a wide snowfield, about 600 feet long (it looks shorter from the base of the mountain). The gully then pinches down and climbs through a short rock cliff (AI 2/3-). Above the constriction, the gully angles up right for a pitch. It then pinches down a second time (often considered the crux) into a four-foot wide chimney which is often mixed. (The ice climbing is no harder than AI 3, and the rock difficulties are about 5.4.) The gully the opens up near the top of the Flying Buttress before necking down again for another 400 feet of excellent ice climbing. Two more tight spots are encountered before the climb opens up again; this time, on the summit snow/boulderfield.

Approach time: From the Longs Peak Ranger Station, allow 3-4 hours.
Descent: From the top of the difficulties, traverse right across the boulderfield towards

Benny Bach at the crux of Dream Weaver

Mt. Meeker, Chasm Meadows Area. Left to right: Dream Weaver, Right Chimney, The Loft, Ship's Prow, Lamb's Slide Cut-Off

The Loft. After several hundred feet, the Right Gully will come into view below you and the traverse will consist of verglassed slabs and is quite dangerous. Some parties rope up to cross the slabs, a practice that is recommended. Continue west towards Longs, then descend The Loft. While it is possible to descend The Loft almost anywhere, there is a trail that avoids the steep middle section by traversing south (right, as you look at the Loft from above) around a rock buttress, before rejoining the snow lower down.

Season: There is a short window of about three weeks in late spring/early summer when the route is in prime condition, but the exact dates of that window fluctuate. The route can also be in good condition in the late fall, before heavy snows make it a death wish. If your timing's off, the route is merely a snow grovel.

Road/Highway the climb is visible from: This climb is visible from many places in the Estes Park area, as well as from many points along Colo. 7.

58. Right Chimney (II, AI 4, 1,500 feet) ★★

The right chimney is a much more serious undertaking than Dream Weaver, for the simple reason that its much harder for the second to dodge falling ice should the leader happen to knock it down. It is rarely done.

The climb lies immediately right of the Flying Buttress, and starts with about 900 feet of grueling snow groveling up the obvious gully. The gully metamorphoses near the top of the Flying Buttress into a narrow slot — the chimney itself, which is climbed in four-six pitches.

The right wall of the right chimney also sporadically offers a thin, mixed outing, which moves out right from near the top of the Flying Buttress. This route bisects the upper face neatly in two and is pretty hard. Expect rock up to 5.9 and ice climbing to AI 5. Rock gear is essential.

Approach Time: From the Longs Peak Ranger Station, allow 3-4 hours.

Descent: As with Dream Weaver, from the top of the difficulties, traverse right across the obvious slabs towards The Loft. Descend The Loft.

Season: Late spring/early summer is generally the best time to catch this route, but it can also be in good condition in the late fall.

Road/Highway the climb is visible from: Like Dream Weaver and The Loft, this climb is visible from many places in the Estes Park area and from many points along Colo. 7. However, only the bottom of the route can be seen. The Flying Buttress blocks the upper portion of the route from view.

59. The Loft (II, AI 2-, 800 feet) ★★

The Loft is the ultimate first time alpinist's route. It offers a beautiful setting, a short manageable crux, then rewards the adventurous beginner with fantastic views of the western part of the Park.

Begin by hiking up the long easy snowfield. The snowfield gets progressively steeper, until the gully pinches tight, and climbs through a rock band (the crux). This section can be climbed on either the wide left side, or the narrower right side, both sides being about the same (about 75 degrees). Above the rock band, several hundred feet of snow scrambling leads to the top of the route, the saddle between Longs and Meeker.

Chasm Meadows Area. Left to right: Right Chimney, The Loft, Columbine Falls, Ship's Prow, Lamb's Slide Cut-Off, Alexander's Chimney, Notch Couloir, Lamb's Slide, South Buttress of Mt. Lady Washington

Approach Time: From the Longs Peak Ranger Station, allow 3-4 hours.

Descent: Downclimb the top section of the route to the top of the rock band. There are three options for getting down this, the steepest part of the route. One is to downclimb. The second option is to rappel. Rappels can be made off slings tied around boulders on the north (left side, as viewed from above) of the route. The third option is to bypass the steep section. A small informal trail leads south (right side, as viewed from above), out of the gully, around an obvious rock buttress, before rejoining the snowfield lower down. This trail is not always obvious, and care should be taken. Roping up is recommended.

From below the rock band, the descent is obvious. However, due to the large quantity of snow that accumulates in The Loft, late spring avalanches are frequent. Descend the lower portion of the route by keeping off to either side in case the Loft decides to cut loose.

Season: Late spring/early summer is best, but the route can be done well into the summer. Early fall is also good. Stay off it in the winter, as the large amount of snow that accumulates in the gully makes it a death wish.

Road/Highway the climb is visible from: This climb is visible from many places in the Front Range, the Estes Park area, as well as from many points along Colo. 7.

Longs Peak

The history of Colorado alpinism could not have been written without Longs Peak. This high mountain, with its wild East Face, has played an important role in Colorado mountaineering for over a century.

Although there are no pure ice climbs on the east face, there are a number of excellent alpine (ice/rock/snow, or some combination thereof) routes located here.

They are described from left to right, across the east face.

60. Lamb's Slide Cut-Off (II, AI 2, 3rd Class, 800 feet) ★

This easy snow gully, very similar in nature to Lamb's Slide, lies left of Lamb's Slide, and in front of it (to the east.) Beginning just above Chasm Lake, it ascends Glacier Rib, the rock spire that bounds Lamb's Slide on the left. About three-quarters of the way up, it pinches through a rock band (the crux) and tops out near the top of Lamb's Slide.

Approach time: From the Longs Peak Ranger Station, allow 3.5 hours.

Descent: The quickest way down is to downclimb the route. However, descending Lamb's Slide is slightly easier.

Season: Late spring/early summer is best, after avalanches are no longer a threat. However, the route can be done well into the summer and early fall is also good. Not recommended as a winter climb.

Road/Highway the climb is visible from: This climb is visible from many places in the Estes Park area, as well as from many points along Colo. 7.

Looking up the Lamb's Slide, Longs Peak

61. Lamb's Slide (II, AI 2, 800 feet) ★★

Lamb's Slide is the broad, long, easy angled snow ramp that bounds the lower left side of the East Face of Longs Peak. Named after Elkanah Lamb, who slid down it during the first descent of the East Face in 1871, Lamb's Slide is generally climbed as the first half of a combination of routes (such as the Lamb's Slide-Notch Couloir combination). However, for neophyte alpinists, the wide ramp offers an excellent outing within itself.

Approach Time: From the Longs Peak Ranger Station, allow 4 hours.

Descent: The easiest descent is to downclimb the route. Bring plenty of rock anchors if you plan to rappel.

Season: Summer and fall are best, as the route regularly avalanches all winter, and well into May and June.

Road/Highway the climb is visible from: This climb is visible from many places in the Front Range, the Estes Park area, as well as from many points along Colo. 7.

62. Alexander's Chimney (II, WI 4, 5.5, 500 feet) ★★

A wet, rotten and generally unenjoyable grovel as a rock climb, Alexander's Chimney ices up during the fall months and is one of the more classic outings in the Park. Because it climbs only the Lower part of the East face, it is often combined with other routes, such as the Notch Couloir.

Alexander's Chimney is the prominent chimney system on the left side of the Lower East Face of Longs Peak. To reach it, climb several hundred feet up Lamb's Slide. The first big chimney system in the right wall is Alexander's Chimney.

Climb it to Broadway, the large horizontal ledge that divides the East Face. Rock gear is highly recommended.

Approach time: From the Longs Peak Ranger Station, allow 4 hours.

Descent: The easiest descent is to walk off Broadway to the left (south). It's several hundred feet to Lamb's Slide.

Season: Fall.

Road/Highway the climb is visible from: This climb is visible from many places in the Estes Park area, as well as from many points along Colo. 7. However, because the chimney system is relatively thin, it's hard to ascertain its condition from a distance.

63. Notch Couloir (II, AI 2, 1,000 feet) ★★

This route lies above Broadway, on the upper left side of the East Face. It is named for the prominent notch in Longs Peak's skyline to which it ascends. The couloir itself is much shorter than it looks.

To reach it, climb either Lamb's Slide or Alexander's Chimney to Broadway then traverse 1,000 feet to the bottom of the climb. There is a wildly exposed 5.2 move on this traverse. The couloir should be obvious.

The first 400 feet climb straight up, passing a chockstone and getting progressively steeper as it ascends. Then, the route jogs right for about 150 feet.

Lamb's Slide Area, Longs Peak. Left to right: Lamb's Slide Cut-Off, Lamb's Slide, Alexander's Chimney, Notch Couloir, Kiener's Route, The Window

Twenty feet into this jog is a short rock wall, often considered the crux. It is best climbed by going out right of the obvious wide dihedral in the back of the couloir, and climbing 5.3 rock to a broad flat area. The next 200 feet — which include another short rock wall — lead to the notch.

From the notch, climb the easy slabs off to the right for about 100 feet, then make a sharp left, up a steep chimney system (5.3 to 5.5, depending on the variation followed). Atop this chimney, scramble north over big blocks to the summit.

Approach time: From the Longs Peak Ranger Station, allow 4 hours.

Descent: The easiest descent is to downclimb the Keyhole (regular) Route from the summit of Longs Peak, or the North Face (Cables Route).

The Keyhole Route descends from the west side of the flat summit area and skirts around the west and north sides of the mountain.

The North Face Route follows the obvious bowl on the northeast side of the mountain. (This bowl is bounded on one side by the top, right-hand edge of the Diamond, and on the other by a ridge running directly north from the summit.) It is possible to downclimb the entire North Face but rappels are often used on the steepest sections.

From the base of the North Face (an area where both the Keyhole and North Face routes meet), the base of the east face is reached by either hiking back around Mt. Lady Washington and into Chasm Lake, or by crossing the ridge running between Mt. Lady Washington and Longs Peak and descending to Chasm Lake. The best place to cross this ridge is near the Camel, a rock formation that looks like a sitting camel. Further west (towards Longs Peak, and the descent might involve rappelling.)

Season: Summer and fall are best, as the route regularly avalanches all winter, and well into May and June.

Road/Highway the climb is visible from: This climb is visible from many places in the Front Range, the Estes Park area, as well as from many points along Colo. 7.

64. Kiener's Route (II, AI 2, 5.3, 1,000 feet) ★★★

Like the Notch Couloir, this route in generally combined with Lamb's Slide, Alexander's Chimney or some other route to produce a 2,000 foot "tour" of the East Face.

Kiener's Route officially starts just right of the Notch Couloir at two obvious belay bolts. Climb the 5.4 chimney above (Kiener's Chimney). Near the top of the chimney, go right, onto a long ledge and belay. Climb progressively easier ground up and left for two pitches, then angle up and right towards the summit, skirting the top, left-hand edge of the Diamond. The final section of the route traverse below and to the right of a large dihedral directly below the summit.

Approach time: From the Longs Peak Ranger Station, allow 4 hours.

Descent: See the descent for the Notch Couloir.

Season: Spring/Summer.

Road/Highway the climb is visible from: This climb is visible from many places in the Front Range, the Estes Park area, as well as from many points along Colo. 7.

Longs Peak. Left to right: Notch Couloir, Kiener's Route, The Window, North Face

65. The Window (I, WI 5, 5.7, 400 feet) ★

The hardest ice climb in the area, and psychologically demanding, this route sees very few ascents.

This climb follows the inside corner of the right side of a huge pillar left of the Diamond. It is named the Window because the pillar, detached from the cliff behind it, allows light (and climbers) through.

To get there, climb either Lamb's Slide or Alexander's Chimney and traverse right to a point below the base of the pillar, or climb the North Chimney (II, 5.5), the most obvious chimney system directly below the center of the Diamond, and traverse left. (The Lamb's Slide approach is recommended.)

From Broadway, at the left-hand side of the base of the pillar, climb up to the right for three pitches, until the base of the large gray slab is reached. Here, an ice runnel angles back to the left, following the inside corner of the pillar. Climb the runnel for two leads and squeeze through the Window at the top. Here, the route joins the upper part of Kiener's Route. There are a number of variations of this route, depending on conditions. Rock gear is a must.

Approach time: From the Longs Peak Ranger Station, allow at least 5 hours to get to the base of the pillar.

Descent: See the descent for the Notch Couloir.

Season: Winter and Spring.

Road/Highway the climb is visible from: None.

Wild Basin

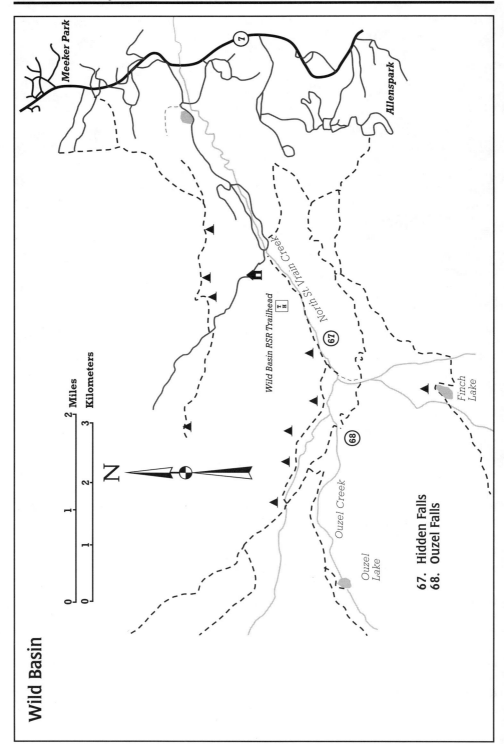

Meeker Park

Allenspark

7

North St. Vrain Creek

Wild Basin RSR Trailhead

67

68

Ouzel Creek

Ouzel Lake

Finch Lake

N

2 Miles

Kilometers

0 1 2 3

67. Hidden Falls
68. Ouzel Falls

66. North Face (Cables Route) (II, AI 2+, 5.4, 700 feet) ★★

This is one of the more popular routes on Longs Peak, and is generally the descent route for rock climbers coming off the Diamond. In the winter, the bottom of the North Face holds some easy ice climbing.

To get there, follow the description for the approach to Longs Peak. At the point where the Longs Peak trail splits, at the entrance to the Chasm, take the right branch of the trail. (There's a sign at the split, pointing to "Longs Summit 4.0 miles".) Follow this trail Around the north side of Mt. Lady Washington until the North Face comes into view.

The route starts on the left side of the face, just above the top of the right-hand side of the Diamond. Climb it to the top.

Approach time: From the Longs Peak Ranger Station, allow 4 hours.
Descent: See the descent for the Notch Couloir.
Season: Winter and Spring.
Road/Highway the climb is visible from: This climb is visible from many places in the Front Range, the Estes Park area, as well as from many points along Colo. 7.

Wild Basin
(Routes 67-68)

Wild Basin is a beautiful, pristine valley south of most of the popular areas in Rocky Mountain National Park. It offers a couple of routes that are of interest to ice climbers, the mega-classic Hidden Falls, and Ouzel Falls.

Getting There: To get to Wild Basin, drive west on Colo. 7 from Lyons for 21.1 miles (exact mileage is from the Colo. 7 - Highway 36 intersection). The turnoff to Wild Basin will be on the left. Follow this road a short way, to a parking area with restrooms on the right. Generally, this is as far as you can drive in the winter months. Park, go through the gate, and hike along the dirt road to the west. After about 3/4 of a mile, you'll reach another parking area and gate. Go through the gate and continue along the dirt road. After another mile or so, you'll reach a "Horse Unloading Station," as the sign indicates. Keep going along the road. You'll pass the Finch Lake trailhead on the left, then cross the creek and reach the Wild Basin Ranger Station. All together, this hike is about two miles. Skis are highly recommended.

From the Ranger Station, head west (further into the mountains), and cross a small footbridge. Just beyond this footbridge is a mileage sign. Continue into the woods. About 3/4 mile west of the ranger station is Upper and Lower Copeland Falls. A sign points the falls out. Continue past Upper Copeland Falls several hundred yards, and Hidden Falls will become visible off to the southwest (look left, across the drainage) among the trees. If you can't see it, it probably means you haven't walked far enough. Once you can see it, the approach is simple: leave the trail, cut left across the creek and hike up to the base of the falls.

Wild Basin. Hidden Falls

To get to Ouzel Falls, continue on the trail west past Hidden Falls. You'll pass the Pine Ridge camping area where a trail leads off to the right, cross the creek, then pass the Calypso Cascades. (From the Calypso Cascades, it's still nearly a mile to Ouzel Falls.) Continue west, up the valley, until a large knoll in the center of the valley becomes obvious. Ouzel Falls lies of the left side of the knoll, after a number of switchbacks in the trail.

67. Hidden Falls (WI 3-4, 100 feet).★★★

When its in condition, Hidden Falls offers excellent climbing. A slab of ice leads about 70 feet up to a small amphitheater below a final column of ice. There are a number of fixed rock anchors in the amphitheater. If the upper column does not form, use the fixed anchors in the rock to rappel off. If it is in condition, the fixed anchors can be used as protection as you continue up. Highly recommended.

Approach time: 1-2 hours

Descent: To descend, rappel off trees at the top.

Season: All winter.

Road/Highway the climb is visible from: None.

68. Ouzel Falls (WI 2-3, 40 feet, many variations)

Ouzel Falls is not really one waterfall, but a series of cascades, where water from Ouzel Lake splashes down over a 40-foot rock shelf and freezes to form a number of short, easy climbs. Many variations are possible.

It's recommended you ask other climbers about Ouzel's conditions before venturing out. Sometimes it's not worth the trip. And if you do go, skis are a must.

Approach time: 2-3 hours

Descent: Rappel off trees at the top, or walk left and downclimb.

Season: All winter, however, in late winter and early spring it tends to get clogged with snow.

Road/Highway the climb is visible from: None.

Rob Hering on Ouzel Falls

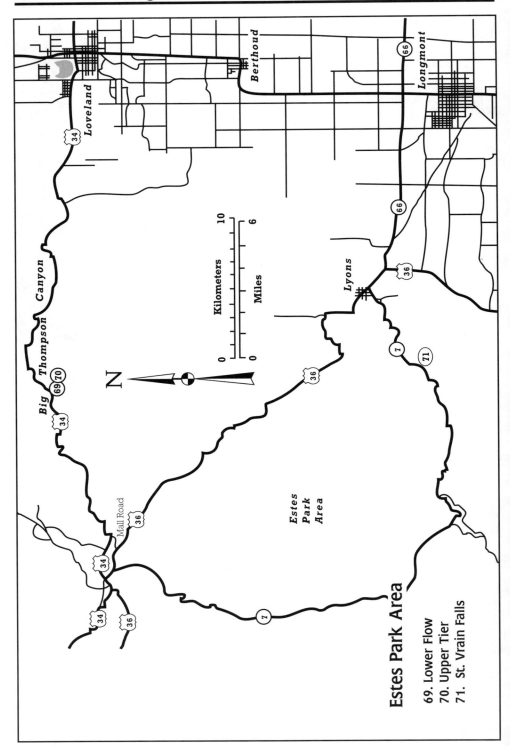

Estes Park Area

69. Lower Flow
70. Upper Tier
71. St. Vrain Falls

NORTHEAST MOUNTAINS

Front Range Areas
(Routes 69-76)

"On ice, attitude is everything,"
—Craig Luebben, Rock & Ice, 1994

The following section is devoted to several Front Range areas that lies in the Denver/Boulder/Estes Park general area. Unfortunately, the ice climbing here is limited, but it's good when it's in.

The season here is somewhat limited. Although it's not uncommon for ice to last through April, it's generally pretty sloppy that late in the season. December through March is your best bet.

Estes Park Area
(Routes 69-71)

There are two ice climbs of note in the valleys surrounding the Estes Park area and Rocky Mountain National Park.

One, the Big Thompson Canyon Ice Flow, is located in Big Thompson Canyon, east of town.

The second, St. Vrain Falls, lies along Colo. 7, between Lyons and Estes Park, in South St. Vrain Canyon. Both routes offer easy climbing, and excellent access.

Big Thompson Canyon

In reality, the Big Thompson Ice Flow is two separate climbs separated by several hundred yards of streambed.

Getting there: The flow lies on the south side of the Big Thompson River, about halfway between Estes Park and the eastern end of the canyon.

To get there from Estes Park, drive east on Highway 34 into the canyon. From the intersection of Mall Road (Larimer County Road 63) and Highway 34, which lies just east of Estes Park, the distance to the flow is 7.2 miles. The flow will be obvious on the south side of the river, opposite the Highway.

To get there from other Front Range locations, follow Highway 34 west into the canyon. From the intersection of Taft Ave. and Highway 34 in downtown Loveland, the distance to the flow is 18.8 miles. From the eastern mouth of the canyon, it's 11.2 miles.

Park on the side of the road and boulder hop across the river.

69. Lower Flow (WI 1-2, 80 feet)

The first section of the drainage that freezes up offers classic WI 2 climbing. This is an excellent place to learn to lead ice, or just have fun if you don't have time to go into Rocky Mountain National Park.

Approach time: 5 minutes
Descent: Rappel off trees or hike down to the right (west).Season: Midwinter.
Road/Highway the climb is visible from: U.S. 34.

70. Upper Tier (WI 3, 80 feet)

Several hundred yards up the drainage above the Lower Flow is an 80 section of WI 3.

Approach time: 10 minutes
Descent: Rappel off trees.
Season: Midwinter.
Road/Highway the climb is visible from: None.

South St. Vrain Canyon

St. Vrain Falls generally forms as one, stepped route, but occasionally, a smaller flow forms to its right.

Getting there The falls lie on the south side of South St. Vrain Creek, between Estes Park and Lyons. To get there from Lyons, follow Colo. 7, west up South St. Vrain Canyon. 5.4 miles west of town, the flow will be obvious on the south side of the creek, opposite the road. Park on the right hand (north) side of the road and hop across boulders in the creek.

71. St. Vrain Falls (WI 2, 100 feet) ★

A perfect place for teaching beginners or learning to lead on.
Approach time: 2 minutes
Descent: Rappel off trees or downclimb.
Season: Midwinter.
Road/Highway the climb is visible from: Colo. 7.

Vrain Falls

Boulder Canyon
(Routes 72-73)

Despite offering some of the finest rock climbing in the world, the Boulder area has precious few ice climbs.

The only local venue is a series of seeps at the upper end of Boulder Canyon, near the popular Castle Rock formation.

From the intersection of Broadway and Canyon Streets in downtown Boulder, drive west (towards the mountains) on Canyon St. for 13.1 miles. Canyon St. is also Colo. 119.

Thirteen miles from the intersection, there are three short, 70-foot ice flows, that form on the hillside south (left, as you drive up from Boulder) of the road, as the result of some frustrated climber whacking a hole in an aqueduct.

Parking is not allowed along Colo. 119 in the area, so it is necessary to park in the Castle Rock area, about a quarter mile east (back towards Boulder) of the climbs. From the parking area, you can either hike up the streambed to the climbs, or wander up the side of the road, then cross the creek, to reach the base of the climbs.

Also, during rare winters, Boulder Falls has been known to freeze (although I've never seen it happen). It lies 12.9 miles from the Canyon-Broadway intersection on the north side of the road. There is a small trail on the upcanyon side of a bridge crossing the creek that forms the falls. Follow it north for a few hundred feet, and the Falls will become obvious.

72. Boulder Falls
(WI 3, 40 feet)

The falls, when they are climbable, offer WI 2 climbing. The right side is easier. Climbers should be cautious climbing Boulder Falls as the falls generally form a shell over the rapidly running creek water and it's easy to punch through.

Approach: 5 minutes, from the parking area on the road.

Descent: Descent is made by downclimbing the falls.

Season: All winter.

Road/Highway the climb is visible from: Colo. 119

Boulder Canyon Ice Flows

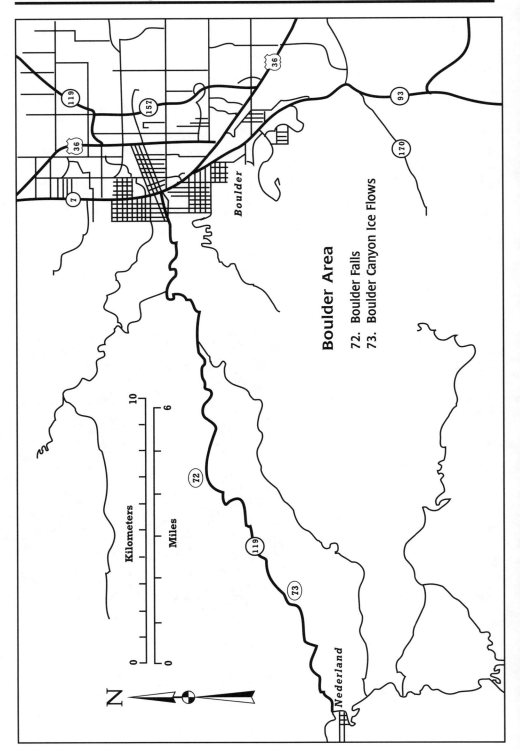

Boulder Area

72. Boulder Falls
73. Boulder Canyon Ice Flows

73. Boulder Canyon Ice Flows (WI 3, 100 feet) ★

Three separate, generally good flows, courtesy of a frustrated ice climber who took a tool to the aqueduct. The central flow is the most popular, and the most reliable.

Approach time: 5 minutes, from the parking area at Castle Rock.
Descent: To descend from the routes, rappel off trees.
Season: All winter.
Road/Highway the climb is visible from: Colo. 119
Access issues: Wintertime parking is not allowed along Colo. 119 in the area of the flows.

Clear Creek Canyon
(Routes 74-76)

Located just west of historic Golden, home of the Coors brewing empire, Clear Creek Canyon is better known for its myriad rock climbing crags. However, there are three small waterfalls located in the canyon that freeze with unflappable consistency.

Getting there The three Clear Creek Canyon routes are described in miles from the intersection of three highways, Colo. 58 and 93, and U.S. 6, on the west side of Golden, the starting point for most ice climbers headed up Clear Creek Canyon. This is essentially the start of U.S. 6 — the main thoroughfare west, through the canyon.

A note of caution: The traffic through Clear Creek Canyon can be intense. (There are a lot of half-crocked drivers coming home from the Casinos in Black Hawk and Central City.) When parking, use extreme care to get your vehicle all the way off the road, and keep walk as far off the shoulder as possible.

From the intersection of the three highways in Golden, drive west on U.S. 6 for 3.0 miles. The Beer Garden will become obvious on the south side of the canyon, across Clear Creek from the Highway. Park along the road opposite the route, then cross the creek on boulders. There is no best place for this, however, a few yards upstream or downstream are better than crossing directly opposite the climb.

1.2 miles west (upcanyon) from the Beer Garden is Coors Lite. The climb lies on the south side of the canyon, across the creek from the Highway. Park about .25 miles upstream of the climb itself, on the east end (downstream end) of a green bridge. Hike across the bridge, then follow an old road bed that goes left (east), back down the canyon on the south side of the stream. A five minute walk puts you at the base of the route.

0.3 mile west (upcanyon) from Coors Lite and west of the green bridge is Mickey's Big Mouth, a 20-foot section of ice located just a few feet off the road. Parking is difficult here, and it is best to park either further up the canyon, or in the same location for Mickey's Big Mouth.

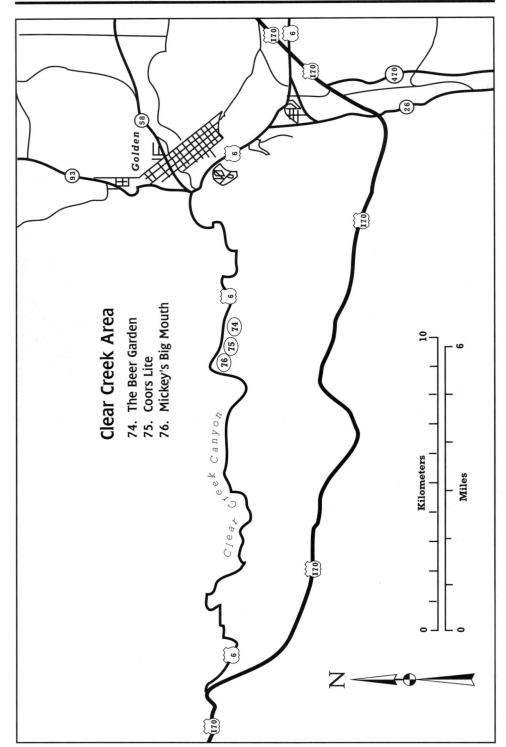

Clear Creek Area

74. The Beer Garden
75. Coors Lite
76. Mickey's Big Mouth

74. The Beer Garden
(WI 2, 60 feet)

It'll be obvious.

Approach time: 5 minutes

Descent: To descend, use a tree on the left side at the top of the waterfall. Rappel slings will be obvious at the top on the left.

Season: All Winter.

Road/Highway the climb is visible from: U.S. 6

75. Coors Lite
(WI 2-2+, 90 feet) ★

The best ice route in the canyon, offering two sections. The lower, 90-foot section is the most popular. There is a 40-foot upper step beyond the first section on this route that offers WI 2-3 climbing.

Approach time: 10 minutes

Descent: To descend, use rappel anchors on the right side at the top of the climb.

Season: All Winter.

Road/Highway the climb is visible from: U.S. 6

Coors Lite

76. Mickey's Big Mouth
(WI 2, 20 feet)

Not as reliable as the other routes, but closer to the road.

Approach time: 5 minutes

Descent: To descend this short route, downclimb.

Season: All Winter.

Road/Highway the climb is visible from: U.S. 6.

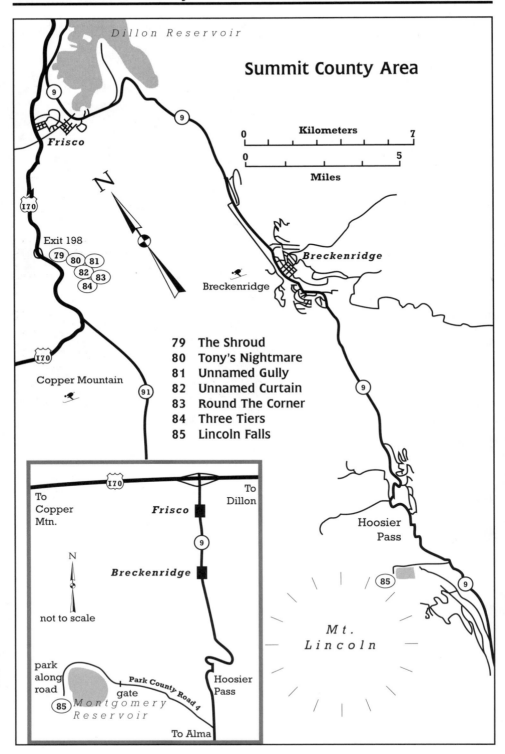

Summit County Area

Kilometers

Miles

Dillon Reservoir

Frisco

Exit 198

79 80 81
82 83
84

Breckenridge

Copper Mountain

79 The Shroud
80 Tony's Nightmare
81 Unnamed Gully
82 Unnamed Curtain
83 Round The Corner
84 Three Tiers
85 Lincoln Falls

Breckenridge

Hoosier Pass

Mt. Lincoln

To Copper Mtn.

Frisco

Breckenridge

N

not to scale

park along road

gate

Montgomery Reservoir

Park County Road 4

Hoosier Pass

To Alma

To Dillon

NORTH CENTRAL MOUNTAINS

Summit County

(Routes 77-85)

"The State of Colorado produces at least 50 percent of the avalanche deaths nationwide every year. Of these, nearly half occur in Summit County,"

—Scott Astaldi, Mike Gruber, "High Country Crags," 1993.

Although the Summit County area boasts a number of excellent ice climbs, the bulk of these routes lie in Ten Mile Canyon, a place renowned for its high avalanche danger.

These routes should be approached with a great deal of caution, and generally, only in the late fall and early winter, when the snowpack is minimal.

For those who choose to avoid the dangerous climbs in Ten Mile Canyon, there are another couple of ice climbing venues in the area that offer relatively safe climbing throughout the winter — Lincoln Falls, and the Silverplume. Ironically, Lincoln Falls lies just south of the Summit County border, in nearby Park County, and the Silverplume lies just east of Summit County, in nearby Clear Creek County.

Silverplume Area

The road cuts along I-70 through the Silverplume area boast some of the finest, most accessible ice in the state. Unfortunately climbing on these road cuts is not allowed.

However, there is one recommended ice route that isn't off limits to climbers, near the historic town of Silverplume.

The Silverplume, as some call it, is a short, noteworthy ice climb, named after the mountain on which it sits and the nearby town.

Getting there: To reach the Silverplume, exit I-70 at the Silverplume exit, Exit 226. After exiting, you'll reach a stop sign, which sits in the middle of town. From the stop sign, drive west 3/4 of a mile. There will be an old mine mill of the right. Park just below the mill, on the right side of the road. The climb cannot be seen from here, but lies up the canyon to the west of the mill. A 20 minute hike around the uphill side of the mill, then up the canyon brings one to the base of the ice.

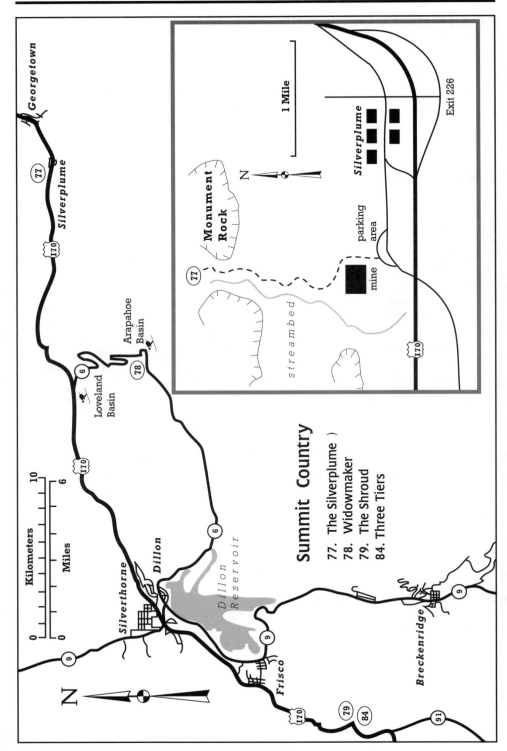

Summit Country

77. The Silverplume)
78. Widowmaker
79. The Shroud
84. Three Tiers

77. The Silverplume (WI 3, 80 feet, many variations) ★

The route usually forms as a wide curtain and offers many possible routes. This route faces south, into the sun. Caution and an early start are advised.

Approach time: 10 minutes.

Descent: To descend, walk off to the right and scramble down.

Season: Midwinter.

Road/Highway the climb is visible from: I-70, just for a few seconds west of the Silverplume exit (Exit 226).

Access issues: None.

Silverplume

Arapahoe Basin Area

One gully climb of interest — Widowmaker — forms up in a drainage near the Arapahoe Basin ski area each winter. As with the routes in Ten Mile Canyon, it should be viewed with trepidation. It got its name for a reason!

Getting there: Arapahoe Basin is east of the Dillon, Frisco, Breckenridge area, on U.S. 6. It is generally accessed from the Denver area by driving up and over Loveland Pass (on U.S. 6). It can also be reached by driving east from Silverthorne on U.S. 6.

Widowmaker, a gully climb near A Basin, lies 12.1 miles east of the I-70-U.S. 6 intersection in Silverthorne, on the left (north) side of the road.

From A Basin, it's 0.6 miles west on U.S. 6 to Widowmaker. Widowmaker lies on the right (north) side of the road, left of an obvious landslide scar 600 feet above the road. The climb trickles down from the left, in front of the scar.

78. Widowmaker (WI 1-2, 300 feet)

Named for the scary snow cornice that hangs above the route, this climb angles up and left, around the obvious rock buttress.

Approach time: 10 minutes.
Descent: Scramble off along the right side of the climb, below the scar.
Season: Fall/Early Winter.
Road/Highway the climb is visible from: U.S. 6
Access issues: None.

Ten Mile Canyon
(Routes 79-84)

Ten Mile Canyon is a large, wide valley west of Silverthorne and Frisco, through which Interstate 70 passes on its way to Copper Mountain and Vail.

The ice climbs here are similar in nature to those found in the southwestern part of the state, long snowmelt gullies that cascade over steps and boulders to produce waterfall ice.

As mentioned, the handful of routes here should be considered only in the fall and early winter, as severe avalanche dangers exist.

Getting There: To reach Ten Mile Canyon, simply drive west from the towns of Dillon, Silverthorne or Frisco, on Interstate 70. The canyon will become obvious, as it is the first major drainage west of the cities through which the highway passes.

From Exit 201 (the Main St. Frisco exit), it's 3.2 miles to the Officer's Gulch Exit, Exit 198. This is where you park for ice routes in Ten Mile Canyon, although it's possible to continue on I-70 west to check out the climbs from the comfort of your car.

The parking area isn't much, just a plowed area on the south (left side, if your coming from Frisco) of I-70. Exit at 198 and turn left, under I-70, and go straight. In summertime, road leads south to a small trailhead where a bicycle path can be accessed. In winter, however, you've got to park close to the on and off ramps for eastbound I-70.

From here, hike south up the road (crossing Ten Mile Creek) to a trailhead, and the bike path. Follow the

The Shroud

bike path, which runs along the south side of Ten Mile Creek, west, toward the ice routes. (Skis may be a good idea.)

The first ice climb of note is The Shroud, a single pitch of WI 4-4+ and a great outing. It'll be obvious, a few hundred feet above the trail.

Tony's Nightmare is situated in the first major gully west of the Shroud. The lower falls are not far off the bike path, but the upper falls are several hundred yards up the hillside.

Then, a few hundred yards west, is a complex valley with two major gullies within it. This is home to Unnamed Gully, Unnamed Curtain and Round The Corner.

These climbs are all visible from I-70, west of the Officer's Gulch Exit (Exit 198), however, the gullies are so complex, that the climbs cannot all be seen from the same location.

If you drive west of the Officers Gulch Exit, The Shroud will be on the left (south) side of the highway 0.5 miles west of Officer's Gulch. About a quarter mile on, Tony's Nightmare comes into view, along with Round The Corner and The Unnamed Curtain.

To see The Unnamed Gully, however, requires driving a few hundred feet further west (0.9 miles past the Officer's Gulch Exit), as it is tucked up in a gully left of the Unnamed Curtain.

Three Tiers will be obvious, about another quarter mile further west.

Ten Mile Canyon

79. The Shroud (WI 4-4+, 75 feet) ★★★
Climb the obvious waterfall to the top. It forms a little differently each year, but provides excellent climbing all the time.

Ten Mile Canyon.
Left to right: Tony's Nightmare, Unnamed Gully, Unnamed Curtain

Ten Mile Canyon. Left to right: Tony's Nightmare, Unnamed Gully, Unnamed Curtain, Round The Corner

Ten Mile Canyon.
Left to right: Unnamed Gully, Unnamed Curtain, Round The Corner

Approach time: 10-15 minutes.
Descent: Rappel off trees up and left of the route.
Season: Fall/Early Winter.
Road/Highway the climb is visible from: I-70
Access issues: None.

80. Tony's Nightmare (Lower Falls: WI 3, 50 feet and Upper Falls: WI 4-4+, 80 feet) ★★

This climb has two separate falls, an upper and a lower falls. The Upper Falls are the best.
Approach time: 15-25 minutes.
Descent: For the Lower falls, walk off left. For the upper falls, rappel off a tree on the right.
Season: Fall/Early Winter.
Road/Highway the climb is visible from: I-70
Access issues: None.

81. Unnamed Gully (WI 2-2+, 200-400 feet) ★★

This climb will remain hidden until your in the valley below it. It looks like it is much harder, but offers a cruise. Also, the length of the climb can vary greatly, depending on snow conditions.
Approach time: Allow 40 minutes.
Descent: Rappel off trees.
Season: Fall/Early Winter.
Road/Highway the climb is visible from: I-70
Access issues: None.

Ten Mile Canyon.
Left to right: Unnamed Curtain, Round The Corner, Three Tiers

82. Unnamed Curtain (WI 5, 75 feet)

Rarely in good condition, this thin, mixed climb ascend the rock buttress between the Unnamed Gully and Round the Corner. Rock gear is a must.

Approach time: Allow 40 minutes.
Descent: Bring rock gear for a rappel.
Season: Fall/Early Winter.
Road/Highway the climb is visible from: I-70
Access issues: None.

83. Round The Corner (WI 5, 200 feet) ★★

This climb, consisting of a spectacular 45-foot pillar, is almost hidden from view. (The top of the pillar is just visible from the Highway.) Climb the pillar, then continue on up WI 3 ground for at least a pitch. It can be longer if conditions are right.

Approach time: Allow 40 minutes.
Descent: Rappel off trees on the right side of the climb. If snow in the trees
      seems unstable, bring rock gear and rap the route.
Season: Fall/Early Winter.
Road/Highway the climb is visible from: I-70
Access issues: None.

84. Three Tiers (WI 2-2+, 400 feet) ★★

Named for the three obvious steps that form low down on this climb, it sits just west of the previous routes and is obvious from the highway. The climb can boast harder pitches above, and be longer than 400 feet, under the right conditions.

Approach time: Allow 45 minutes.
Descent: Scramble off left.
Season: Fall/Early Winter.
Road/Highway the climb is visible from: I-70
Access issues: None.

Hoosier Pass

Lincoln Falls, which goes by various names, offers the best ice climbing in the Summit County area, even though its just over the border in nearby Park County, at the foot of Mt. Lincoln. Although the falls are not steep, they boast reliable, thick blue ice as well as several variations, including some mixed climbing.

Getting there: To reach Lincoln Falls from I-70, take exit 203 and drive south on Colo. 9 through the town of Frisco. After 1.2 miles, you'll cross Frisco's Main St. Continue south 9.4 miles to the picturesque town of Breckenridge. South of town you'll climb up Hoosier Pass. From the top of the pass, Lincoln Falls will be visible to the southwest. Continue 3.75 miles south to the second entrance for Park County Road 4. (You'll pass the first entrance a couple of miles before this, but don't take it.) All told, it's 24.9 miles from I-70 to the south entrance to Park County Road 4. From the intersection of Lincoln Ave. and Colo. 9 in downtown Breckenridge, Park County Road 4 is 14. 3 miles.

   Turn right, and follow Park County Road 4 directly west for several miles until you pass through a gate. In recent winters, this gate has been closed to keep tourists from driving around the lake. Please close it after you enter.

Follow the road around the reservoir on its right side, then along its western edge to a series of small parking areas. Lincoln Falls will be obvious to the south, on the hillside above the end of the road. Use the various climbers trails to reach the base of the Falls.

85. Lincoln Falls (WI 3-5, 250 feet, various routes available) ★★★

The main falls are, obviously, on the right. They are climbed in two pitches and offer many variations and excellent, sinker ice. I'd give 'em four stars if Chockstone's recommendation system allowed it. A pillar regularly forms up and right of the main falls.

On the left, two lesser falls form, creating some interesting mixed climbing possibilities. (These climbs came about a few years ago after a couple of enterprising locals moved boulders around to change the way the ridge drains.) Bring rock gear to supplement ice screws on these routes.

Approach time: 10 minutes.

Descent: Descent for all these climbs is by rappels from trees.

Season: All winter.

Road/Highway: The climb is visible from: Colo. 9, just south of Hoosier Pass, off to the west. You can't miss this beautiful waterfall.

Access issues: None. The mining company that owns the access road has always allowed ice climbers along the road around the lake.

Lincoln Falls

Octopussy   Photo by Bill Pelander

NORTH CENTRAL MOUNTAINS

Vail
(Routes 86-102)

"The satisfaction of climbing ice is as real as that of climbing rock, and ice has one inherent advantage in that we may chop, kick, smash, pierce, mangle and mutilate our slippery friend, and no permanent harm will be done — for the substance itself is impermanent and ever changing ... If Warren Harding were an ice climber, he could do a million Walls of the Early Morning Ice and not a soul would mind."

—Jeff Lowe, Climbing Magazine, 1974

The Central Colorado resort of Vail — a two hour drive west of Denver — not only boasts some of the best skiing on the planet, but some of the best ice climbing as well. The best climbs are sprinkled along the northern slopes of Battle Mountain, which is the huge land mass on lying south of Gore Creek and I-70 as it runs through the Vail Valley. The climbs are on the eastern end of this land mass, above East Vail.

In recent years, ice climbing in Vail has tended to focus more on the rock surrounding particular icicles, than on the ice itself. The routes described here are the more popular — and better known — ice routes. Also, I've tried to use the most common names, but pretty much everyone has their own names for many of the routes.

There are really two separate areas of ice climbing, the area right (west) of the big rock buttress, and the area left (east) of it. In other words, the Designator to Pumphouse area, and the Pitkin Falls to Racquetclub area.

Tom Carr dragging a rope up Rigid Designator

Vail Area

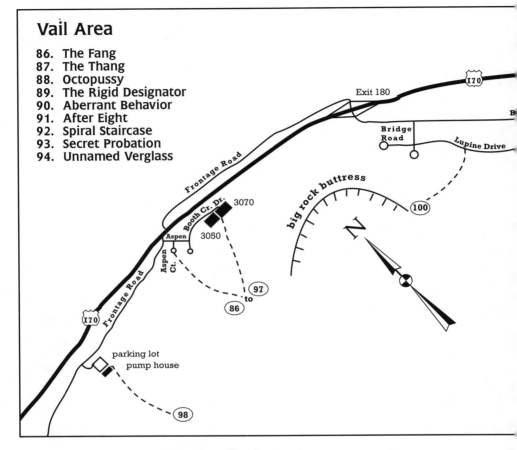

Designator/Pumphouse Area

Getting there: The best way to get to all the ice climbs in the Vail area is to exit I-70 at the East Vail exit (Exit 180), then go from there.

To reach the Rigid Designator/Fang area, 19th Green, and Pumphouse, take the Frontage Road north of I-70 west for several miles, until it passes under I-70 and runs parallel to the golf course.

To reach the Rigid Designator/Fang area, take the first street on the left (Aspen Lane) after passing under I-70. The Rigid Designator and other climbs will be visible on the hillside to the right.

The official public access to the Rigid Designator area lies at the south end of Aspen Court, the first right after you turn onto Aspen Lane. A climbers' trail at the south end of the court's cul-de-sac leads between the neighborhood's big homes, over a bridge across Gore Creek, then up the hill towards the routes.

Although the trail off Aspen Court is the official public access, the most commonly used and easiest approach involves parking on the street near the east end of Booth Creek Drive and crossing private property to reach the routes.

To reach the east end of Booth Creek Drive, continue down Aspen Lane past

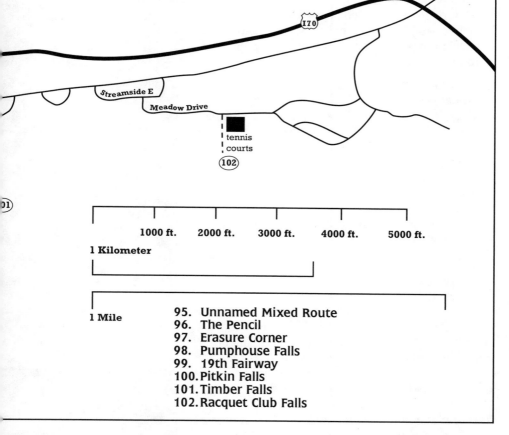

Aspen Court to a T intersection. This is Booth Creek Drive. Take a left. Follow this to the end of the street and park. (Make sure not to not block the driveway to the last house, which exits the cul-de-sac at the east end of Booth Creek Drive.)

For years, the Nystrom family in No. 3070 has allowed climbers to walk partway up their driveway and cross through the western (right, as you face the climbs) edge of their property via a small trail that can be found partway down the driveway. Indeed, family patriarch David Nystrom plows the hike for ice climbers in winter! Please respect the privacy of the family and do not litter, make noise or disturb the residence in any manner. If you ever get the chance, a note of thanks to David at P.O. Box 940 Vail, Colo. 81658 would be in order.

Near the back of the yard it is necessary to cross Gore Creek, then follow trails up to the obvious amphitheater where the ice climbs are located.

Descents from all these climbs are via rappels off slings tied around trees. Don't forget to drag a second rope as most descents require a double-rope rappel.

From right to left, the three most popular routes in the amphitheater are The Fang; The Frigid Inseminator; and The Rigid Designator.

To reach Pumphouse Falls continue west on Frontage Road from Aspen Lane. Pumphouse will become obvious on the hillside on the left. Below it, on the south side of Frontage Road, is the golf course pumphouse for which its named. Turn left into the Pumphouse's parking lot and park. A small trail will lead from the parking lot across the valley and to the base of the ice.

86. The Fang (WI 5-6, 150 feet) ★★★
The Fang is the obvious freestanding pillar that sends an immediate chill up the spine. It can form all sorts of bizarre shapes and often the mushrooms that form around the base can constitute the crux of the route.
Approach time: 10 minutes
Descent: Rappel off trees at top of the route.
Season: All winter.
Road/Highway the climb is visible from: I-70.
Access issues: See the introduction to this chapter.

87. The Thang
(WI 5-5+, 90 feet) ★★★
Originally dubbed The Thang, the exceptional smear that forms behind the Fang has been known as a number of things, including The Frigid Inseminator, The Rigid Inseminator, The Tongue, and several other names. In years where the ice formation does not reach the ground, several bolts protect the first 30 feet of rock on the route.
Approach time: 10 minutes
Descent: Descent is via rappel from bolts at the top of the route.
Season: All winter.
Road/Highway the climb is visible from: I-70.
Access issues: See the introduction to this chapter.

88. Octopussy
(MI 8, 130 feet.) ★★
This hard mixed route takes the left side of The Thang, then traverses left out the roof on pins to grapple the icicle dangling from the roof of the amphitheater. The M rating stands for "mixed."
Approach time: 10 minutes
Descent: Descent is via rappel from trees at the top of the route.
Season: All winter.
Road/Highway the climb is visible from: I-70.
Access issues: See the introduction to this chapter.

Climber starting The Fang

The Thang   Photo: Bill Pe

Left to right: After Eight, Aberrant Behavior, The Rigid Designator, Octopussy, The Thang, The Fang

89. The Rigid Designator (WI 4+/5-, 130 feet.) ★★★

The Rigid Designator is one of Colorado's all time moderate classic ice routes and is one of winter's longest lasting ice formations. Usually, the route is so well-traveled that it's generally a matter of tooling up existing placements.

However, a word of caution: I've seen up to 7 parties at once on "The Designator" and it was a mess. One fellow caught a chunk of ice in the face and had to leave for the hospital to get stitches. If you're waiting for this route, be patient. Or, better yet, go somewhere else to climb.

Approach time: 10 minutes
Descent: Descent is via rappel from trees at the top of the route.
Season: All winter.
Road/Highway the climb is visible from: I-70.
Access issues: See the introduction to this chapter.

90. Aberrant Behavior (MI 7+, 130 feet.) ★

This hard mixed route tackles the wall left of the Rigid Designator, where a prominent icicle dangles down from the left end of the obvious curtain. Two pitons protect the bulk of the route.

Approach time: 10 minutes
Descent: Descent is via rappel from trees at the top of the route.
Season: All winter.
Road/Highway the climb is visible from: I-70.
Access issues: See the introduction to this chapter.

91. After Eight (MI 8+, 130 feet.)

The current testpiece of the Vail area, this route climbs the thin dribble left of Aberrant Behavior (called "Dr. Delicate") to a huge (13 foot) roof, then cuts out across this roof to another not-so-wide curtain dangling from the lip of the cliff. Reported to be run out.

Approach time: 10 minutes

Descent: Descent is via rappel from trees at the top of the route.

Season: All winter.

Road/Highway the climb is visible from: I-70.

Access issues: See the introduction to this chapter.

92. Spiral Staircase (WI 3-4, 75 feet) ★★★

Up the left side of the Rigid Designator/Fang amphitheater is a small trail leading east. It goes around the corner and along the cliff band for several hundred feet to several more ice routes, the best of which is the Spiral Staircase, another moderate classic. The Staircase can form up very wide, offering a multitude of variations. The center line is easiest (WI 3), while the right side can be up to WI 5.

Approach time: 15 minutes

Descent: Descent is via rappel from trees at the top of the route.

Season: All winter.

Road/Highway the climb is visible from: I-70.

Access issues: See the introduction to this chapter.

93. Secret Probation (WI 5+, 50 feet)

To the right of the Spiral Staircase is a steep route with a rock start. Not always in the best shape.

Approach time: 15 minutes

Descent: Descent is via rappel from trees at the top of the route.

Season: All winter.

Road/Highway the climb is visible from: I-70.

Access issues: See the introduction to this chapter.

94. Unnamed Verglass (WI 3-4, 60 feet) ★★

Also dubbed the Spiral Staircase Smears, this bushy route lies just left of Spiral Staircase. Two ice flows regularly form up offering even more room for climbing if there's a crowd. These smears look like junk, but are excellent.

Approach time: 15 minutes

Descent: Descent is via rappel from trees at the top of the route.

Season: All winter.

Jon Butler on Spiral Staircase

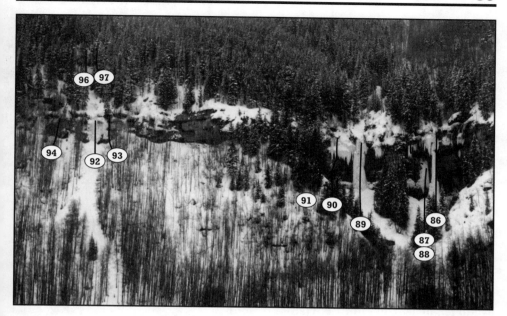

Left to right: Unnamed Verglass, The Pencil, Spiral Staircase, Erasure Corner, Secret Probation, After Eight, Aberrant Behavior, The Rigid Designator, The Rigid Designator, The Thang, The Fang

Road/Highway the climb is visible from: I-70.
Access issues: See the introduction to this chapter.

95. Unnamed Mixed Route (MI 5, 60 feet) ★★

A couple hundred feet left of the Spiral Staircase Smears is an excellent, well-protected mixed route (again, rock mostly), that climbs four bolts to a dribble of ice at the top.

Approach time: 15 minutes
Descent: There are anchors at the top of the route.
Season: All winter.
Road/Highway the climb is visible from: I-70.
Access issues: See the introduction to this chapter.

96. The Pencil (WI 4, 50 feet) ★★

Uphill, directly above the Spiral Staircase several hundred feet is The Pencil, a short pillar of vertical ice. The Pencil can range from being a thin penciled-shaped column, hence the name, or a wide curtain of vertical ice. The Pencil is hard to see from the road because of the abundant pines trees on the slope above the Spiral Staircase. To access it, climb the Spiral Staircase first.

Approach time: 30 minutes
Descent: Descent is via rappel from trees at the top of the route.
Season: All winter.
Road/Highway the climb is visible from: I-70.
Access issues: See the introduction to this chapter.

97. Erasure Corner
(WI 3+, 30 feet) ★

Right of The Pencil is a short iced corner.
Approach time: 30 minutes
Descent: Descent is via rappel from trees at the
    top of the route.
Season: All winter.
Road/Highway the climb is visible from: I-70.
Access issues: See the introduction to this chapter.

98. Pumphouse Falls
(WI 3-4, 80 feet) ★★★

Another moderate classic of the Vail area and well
worth the hike.
Approach time: 15 minutes
Descent: Descent is via rappel from trees 20 feet
    back from the top of the route.
Season: All winter.
Road/Highway the climb is visible from: I-70.
Access issues: See the introduction to this chapter.
Descent: Descent is made by rappel from trees at
    the top of the climb.

Luke Laeser on Pumphouse

99. 19th Fairway (WI 4, 40 feet) ★

A short steep step forms in the hillside above the 19th Fairway of the golf course.
It lies about a half mile west of Pumphouse Falls and is visible from the road. Park
on Frontage Road and hike to the base of the ice.
Approach time: 15 minutes
Descent: Descent is via rappel from trees.
Season: All winter.
Road/Highway the climb is visible from: I-70.
Access issues: See the introduction to this chapter.

Pitkin Falls to Racquetclub Area

Although they are not mega-classics like the Designator and the Fang, Pitkin and
Timber Falls offer superb and varied climbing and are a good alternative to the
Designator Fang and Spiral Staircase on crowded weekends. Racquetclub Falls,
just east of Columbine Falls, offers easy , low-angled ice climbing, good for inexpe-
rienced leaders or ice bouldering.

Getting there: To reach these climbs, follow Bighorn Road east from Exit 180.
Bighorn Road lies just south of I-70 and runs parallel to it.

To get to Pitkin and Timber Falls, take the first right, onto Bridge St., then the
first left, onto Lupine Drive.

Pitkin Falls, named for the creek that drains a small valley on the north side of
the valley. The Falls, however, will be visible on the hillside to the right (south).

Drive a few hundred feet along Lupine Dr. to a vacant lot. Park near the vacant lot, then hike across it to the ice.

To reach Timber Falls, continue east along Lupine Dr. to Willow Way. Turn right onto Willow Way, which is a short cul-de-sac. Park at the end of the cul-de-sac, making sure not to inadvertently block any driveways. Hike southeast, to the base of the falls.

To reach Racquet Club Falls, follow Bighorn Road east for several miles, then turn right on Streamside Circle East. Take the first right again, onto Meadow Drive, then follow this until tennis courts become visible on the right. The climb is obvious behind the tennis courts. Park near the tennis courts (in some winters the lot is plowed) and walk across the open space to the base of the ice.

100. Pitkin Falls (WI 4, 100 feet) ★★

The first route left (east) of the big rock buttress separating this area from the Designator/Pumphouse side of things.

Approach time: 5 minutes
Descent: Descent is via rappel from trees.
Season: All winter.
Road/Highway the climb is visible from: I-70.
Access issues: Just be careful where you park. (i.e. not in the street.)

101. Timber Falls (WI 4-5, 80 feet, many variations)

Timber Falls, known locally as Columbine Falls or Firehouse Falls, is unique in that at least four separate routes can form. Primarily, the waterfall is two waterfalls, and from there, there are the Left and Right sides of each waterfall.

The left side of Left Falls ("Left of the Left") offers boasts several difficult, vertical pillars (WI 5), while the right side offers easier climbing. The Right Falls are almost a mirror of the Left Falls, with the left side offering the easier climbing and columns of ice forming on the right side.

Approach time: 5 minutes
Descent: Descent is via rappel from trees.
Season: All winter.
Road/Highway the climb is visible from: I-70.
Access issues: Same as for the previous route.

102. Racquet Club Falls (WI 2-3, 60 feet)

This area offer excellent ice bouldering, solos, and easy leads.

Approach time: 5 minutes
Descent: Descent is via rappel from trees, or downclimb.
Season: All winter.
Road/Highway the climb is visible from: I-70.
Access issues: Just parking. Pick your spot carefully. Plows like to eat cars round here.

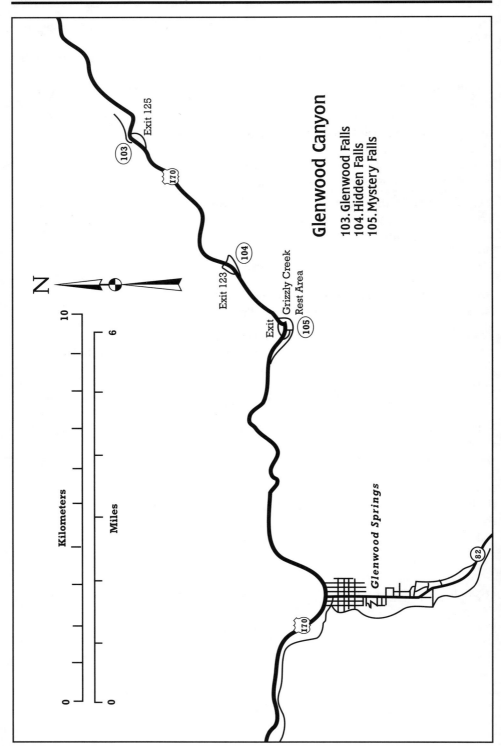

Glenwood Canyon

103. Glenwood Falls
104. Hidden Falls
105. Mystery Falls

NORTH CENTRAL MOUNTAINS

Glenwood Canyon
(Routes 103-105)

"Rationalization afforded us little comfort,"
—David Brower, For Earth's Sake, 1990

There are three noteworthy icefalls in Glenwood Canyon, Mystery Falls, Hidden Falls and Glenwood Falls. Unfortunately, the first two have very difficult approaches as they require a crossing of the Colorado River, and the third faces south, making it dangerous. However, all three offer superb climbing.

Getting There: To reach all three climbs, drive east from Glenwood Springs on I-70. 4.9 miles east of town is the Grizzly Creek Rest Area. From this rest area, Mystery Falls can be seen south, across the river, tucked back in a side canyon.

To reach Hidden Falls, continue another 1.1 miles east, to the Shoshone Exit (Exit 123). About a half mile before the exit, Hidden Falls is visible up to the right, also tucked far back in a side canyon.

To get to Mystery and Hidden Falls, exit at Shoshone from eastbound I-70. There is no exit at Shoshone for westbound traffic, so if you're coming from the Denver area, you'll need to turn around at the Grizzly Creek Rest Area, Exit 121.

At Shoshone, park in one of the several parking lots under the Interstate. There is a boat put in point just east of the parking lot, and the famed Glenwood Canyon bicycle path continues from this lot east.

Most climbers either wait until the river is frozen, in order to cross it, or walk upstream (following the bike path for about 10 minutes) and dry-hop accross the river on boulders. If the water is not frozen, or is too high to dry hop, the only other option is a cheap rubber raft. Don't laugh. It works fine. There are several very calm sections in the area.

Once across the river, hike about half a mile downstream past your car. Hidden Falls is located up a side canyon to the left, and should be visible. It is necessary to then slog up the side canyon, which can be difficult and take several hours.

To reach Mystery Falls, continue another 1.2 miles downstream (west), then follow the side canyon to the base of the route.

Glenwood Falls is located directly above the Hanging Lake exit (Exit 125) 8.9 miles east of Glenwood Springs. Like the Shoshone Exit off I-70, there is no exit for westbound traffic. If you're coming from the Denver area, you'll need to travel west to the Grizzly Creek Rest Area, Exit 121, to turn around.

After exiting I-70, drive east, under the Interstate, then across a brown box girder bridge. On the east side of this bridge there are several parking lots. Park here, then hike back west along the road to the base of the climb.

Glenwood Canyon Routes

103. Glenwood Falls
(WI 3-5, 600 feet) ★★★

Below this climb are a series of obvious metal poles. These were placed by the Colorado Department of Transportation when it built I-70 through the canyon to bust up falling ice. Because Glenwood Falls faces south, it falls apart with alarming regularity. Nearly every year it sees a climbing fatality of some kind.

The main falls are longer than they look and are usually climbed in about four pitches. The left side of the falls offers harder climbing, up to WI 5. A 50-foot column regularly forms near the top on the left side. The more popular right side follows an angling crack system in the rock and is considerably easier. (Usually WI 3-4). Bring rock gear, as ice screws are usually hard to get into the thin ice.

There are two shorter falls that form up right of the main falls and offer interesting alternatives if Glenwood Falls is crowded. Of these two, the left one is harder (WI 4) while the right one is easier.

A note of caution: Climb these routes very early in the day. You generally want to be finished by 10 a.m. as the sun begins to warm the route.

Approach time: 20 minutes.

Descent: There are rappel anchors on trees and rocks on the right side of the falls. Or, it is possible to hike down on the left side of the falls.

Season: All winter, but you should climb it mid-winter, on a cold day, and early.

Road/Highway the climb is visible from: I-70.
Access issues: None.

Glenwood Falls   Photo: Bill Pela

104. Hidden Falls
(WI 4-5, 400 feet) ★★

Hidden Falls is a wide curtain of ice that pours out of the canyon wall. It is harder on its left side and the Falls are usually climbed in several pitches. Rock climbing gear up to 4 inches is recommended.

Approach time: Allow 1-2 hours

Hidden Falls from I-70

Ann Robertson on Glenwood Falls   **Mystery Falls.**

Descent: Descent is via rappel from fixed anchors at the top of the route. Bring some old screws to leave in case these are buried.
Season: All winter.
Road/Highway the climb is visible from: I-70.
Access issues: None.

105. Mystery Falls (WI 5, 120 feet)
Reportedly only one or two ascents have been made of this route.
Approach time: Allow 2 hours
Descent: Descent is via rappel from trees.
Season: All winter.
Road/Highway the climb is visible from: I-70, barely.
Access issues: None.

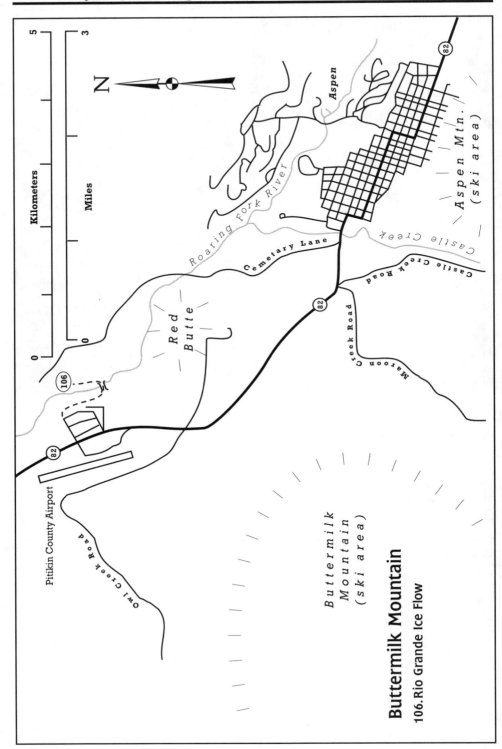

Buttermilk Mountain
106. Rio Grande Ice Flow

NORTH CENTRAL MOUNTAINS

Crystal, Roaring Fork Valleys
(Routes 106-114)

"The game was to see who could get his harness on, last. That person, by virtue of the unspoken law of how things are and always will be, would belay. The unfortunate one would have to butt heads with the rotting cuspids of sun-warmed ice dangling overhead."
—Duane Raleigh, Climbing Magazine, 1993

There are two large valleys that lie south of Glenwood Springs that are of interest to ice climbers, the Crystal River Valley, and the Roaring Fork Valley.
The first is home to many famous Colorado ice climbs and worth a day, or weekend visit. The Roaring Fork Valley, meanwhile offers only one pure ice climb that is relatively easily accessed.

Aspen
(Route 106)

While the mountains around Aspen offer countless alpine climbing possibilities, there is little in the way of waterfall ice.
   The only ice climbing of note near town lies on a small knoll, behind the Aspen Airport Business Center, where water seeps from the knoll creating a short but wide area above the Denver & Rio Grande railroad company's old, unused tracks.

Getting there: The Aspen Airport Business Center is a fairly extensive light industrial/commercial complex just west of town. To reach it, drive west from downtown Aspen on Colo. 82. (In downtown Aspen, Main St. and Colo. 82 are the same.) From the first bridge on the western edge of town (the Castle Creek bridge), it's 2.7 miles to the Business Center, which will be on the right. Take the second entrance into the center, which is at the stoplight, onto Baltic Ave. (Baltic is unmarked.)
   Follow Baltic straight, to the northern edge, or "back," of the Business Center. You'll quickly notice that parking is an issue in this area. When Baltic Ave. ends, at a single story brown wood building housing Modell & Associates and KSNO Radio, turn right.
   Drive along this street several hundred feet, until the pavement ends. Here, a sign will face you stating: "No overnight parking without written permission." In

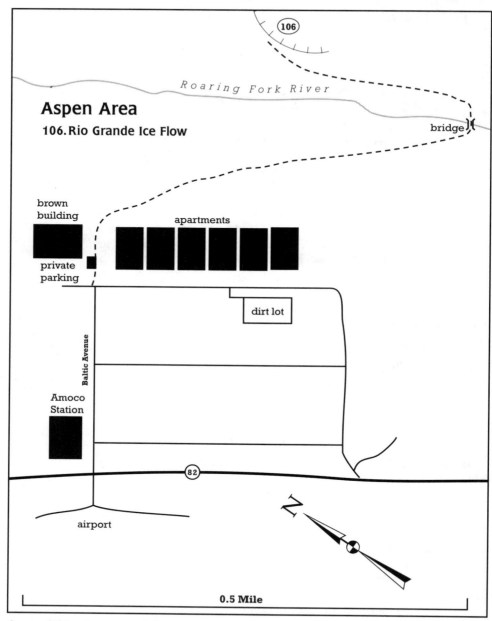

Aspen Area
106. Rio Grande Ice Flow

from of this sign, turn right, into a small dirt (in summer) parking lot. It's generally okay to park here.

To reach the ice, walk back down the street to the brown building, and skirt it on its right side (near a dumpster). A trail leading back into the valley and right (east) will become obvious. (From the top of the valley, you can see the ice climb.) Follow it down into the valley, cross the bridge, then walk back west along the opposite side of the valley to the ice.

106. Rio Grande Ice Flow (WI 1-2, 30 feet)

Also known as the Business Center Ice Flow, this is an excellent area for teaching or practice climbing. However, it faces south, and is often wet and soft. Go early on a cold day. There are also a lot of bushes.

Approach time: 15 minutes
Descent: Downclimb or walk off either side.
Season: Midwinter.
Road/Highway the climb is visible from: None.
Access issues: Although there is a public trail to the river, and a bridge across it, parking here is tough. Choose wisely.

Redstone, Marble Area
(Routes 107-114)

The Crystal River valley, which houses the funky towns of Carbondale, Redstone and Marble, offers a diverse selection of ice climbs. Unfortunately, the most dependable of these climbs are spread relatively far apart, meaning a lot of time behind the wheel. However, the drive is worth it. The regularly forming classics found here, like the Drool and The Avocado Gully, are as good as it gets.

Around Redstone, it's not uncommon for the red slabs around town to drip with thousands of possible routes during a good winter. However, these climbs are both ephemeral, very thin, and the red sandstone underneath does not offer a lot of opportunities for rock gear placements — in short, they can be really sporty. Therefore, I have tried to list only the classics, offering thunker, fat ice year after year.

Getting there: From the intersection of Colo. 82 and Colo. 133 just north of Carbondale, drive south, into Carbondale itself. Continue through town south, towards Mt. Sopris, the massive peak looming above the horizon. 13.5 miles south of Carbondale's Main St. (or 14.5 miles from the Colo. 82-133 intersection), you'll reach a section of Highway where the valley narrows, called, remarkably, The Narrows.

The Bureau of Reclamation once pondered building a dam across this tight section of valley, but fortunately for ice climbers they didn't. One of the area's mega-classics, the Avocado Gully, is located in the big, cleft on the north (right) side of the road at the southern end of The Narrows. There's a parking area on the left (south) side of the road. On the other side of the road (north, or right, as you come from Carbondale) a small, sometimes mushy trail leads north, up a hill and into the woods. In effect, you hike straight back towards the gully.

4.1 miles south of The Narrows (17.6 south of the Highway 82-Highway 133 intersection) is the South or regular entrance to Redstone. (This is the second entrance you'll pass coming from Carbondale.) To reach the classic Redstone Pillar, turn left, onto Redstone Blvd. Drive across the Crystal River, and take the first right, onto a large dirt parking lot belonging to the Redstone Inn. The Redstone Pillar is located up the private road that exits the back (south) end of the parking lot. Don't drive up this road. Your car will be removed if you do. Park

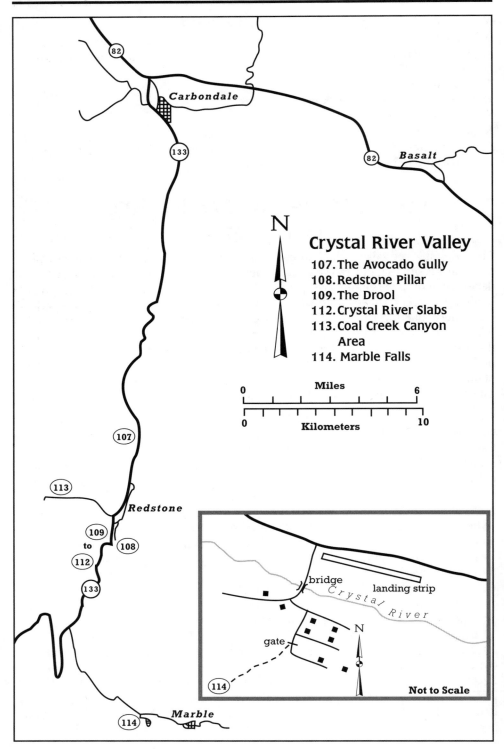

N

Crystal River Valley

107. The Avocado Gully
108. Redstone Pillar
109. The Drool
112. Crystal River Slabs
113. Coal Creek Canyon Area
114. Marble Falls

Miles
0   6

Kilometers
0   10

bridge
landing strip

Crystal River

gate

N

Not to Scale

The Narrows Area showing the location of the Avocado Gully.

wherever you think appropriate, and walk up the dirt road for 0.5 miles, until you pass a blue house. The Redstone Pillar is back to the left, in the obvious drainage. Cross a field (follow the old defunct ski lift) to reach the climb.

Coal Creek Canyon is the valley lying directly opposite (west of Colo. 133) the south entrance to Redstone. It's often closed due to big rock/snow/mush slides.

To reach The Drool, drive 0.85 miles south of Redstone's south entrance. On the right hand side of the road you'll see a line of mail boxes and a sign stating "Crystal River Park." At the southern or far end of the mail boxes, the Drool will come into view, back right, over the tops of the trees. Hike across a vacant lot and up a small stream to the base of the first column.

The Redstone Slabs are a myriad selection of ice climbs that form south of town on the massive east-facing sandstone walls that line the Crystal River Valley. To reach them, drive 1.3 miles south of the south entrance to town. The slabs will be obvious above the road. Continue on a couple of hundred feet and there'll be a parking area on the left, near a line of mailboxes and a wooden bridge going across the river. Hike up the hill on the northwest side of the road, skirting private property by going south, around the barbed wire fences.

Hays Creek Falls are on the right side (northwest) of Highway 133, 1.9 miles south of the south Redstone entrance. You can't miss them.

Just 0.5 miles beyond (south) of Hays Creek Falls is a shaded slab, the Crystal River Slabs, on the opposite side of the river from the highway that sometimes boasts a number of excellent ice slabs.

To reach Marble Falls, drive south from Redstone 5.2 miles, until you reach the turn off to Marble. Then, head south on the poorly paved Marble road for 4.4 miles, until you see a dirt road on the right, with a lot of mailboxes on its right side, and, off in the distance, Marble Falls.

Drive down the dirt road and cross a bridge. Across the bridge, take the first left. Follow this for about 0.5 miles, then take the first right, Holland Dr., which is unmarked. Drive up Holland Dr. until you reach a red gate, marking the edge of a private subdivision. Park on the right side of the road. Walk through the red gate up into the subdivision, and, when the road curves left, go right, into the woods. Usually a climber's trail marks the route. It leads to Milton Creek, which leads to the falls.

107. The Avocado Gully (WI 3, 200 feet, 3 pitches) ★★★

Climb three pitches of sinker ice and rappel off. Rock gear can be helpful.

Approach time: 15 minutes

Descent: Rappels off trees and fixed anchors.

Season: Midwinter.

Road/Highway the climb is visible from: Colo. 133, barely, although from the road it's hard to tell the route's condition.

Access issues: None.

108. Redstone Pillar (WI 4, 60 feet) ★★★

A classic pillar climb.

Approach time: 15 minutes

Descent: Descend by hiking down to the right.

Season: Midwinter.

Road/Highway the climb is visible from: Colo. 133, over the tops of the trees south of the road.

Access issues: Unfortunately, as with most climbs in this area, there is no way to access the Redstone Pillar without crossing private land. At present, this climb is closed, but hopefully in the future the landowners will allow some kind of access.

109. The Drool (WI 5, 160 feet, two pitches) ★★★

The Drool is the definitive Redstone classic, two short shafts of vertical ice separated by a sandstone shelf, there's no finer climb in the region. There are two columns, each about 80 feet.

Approach Time: 5 minutes

Redstone Pillar Photo: Bill Pelander

Descent: Walk off to the right for both columns.

Season: Midwinter. It faces south and melts out pretty easily.

Road/Highway the climb is visible from: Colo. 133, over the tops of the trees north of the road.

Access issues: This route is accessed by crossing a vacant lot that's for sale. It's not a problem, so hopefully, it won't sell.

110. The Redstone Slabs (WI 3-5, numerous variations)

The obvious slabs on the hillside to the north offer all sorts of routes and variants. It's all, generally, really thin. To add to that, it faces south. Get an alpine start!

Approach time: 5 minutes

Descent: A combination of scrambling to trees and rappelling.

Season: Midwinter. It faces south and melts out pretty easily.

Road/Highway the climb is visible from: Colo. 133.

Access issues: The slabs are accessed by crossing private land, but it does not appear to be a problem.

111. Hays Creek Falls (WI 2-2+, 60 feet) ★★

Excellent beginning ice. The right side is slightly harder.

Approach time: 30 seconds

Descent: Rappel off rock anchors on the right, at the top of the route in a cave, or pretty much any tree.

Season: Midwinter.

Road/Highway the climb is visible from: Colo. 133.

Access issues: None.

The Drool photo by Gillian Burns

The Drool photo by Gillian Burns

Marble Falls   photo by Ann Robertson

112. Crystal River Slabs (WI 3-4, 60 feet)
All sorts of stuff forms along this wall in wet winters. Not super-reliable, though.
Approach Time: 5 minutes.
Descent: Rappel off trees.
Season: Midwinter.
Road/Highway the climb is visible from: Colo. 133.
Access issues: None, except you've got to cross the river.

113. Coal Creek Canyon Area (various grades, lengths)
This is a fickle area, where one day, all sorts of smears and icicles will form, then
the next day they're gone. There are all sorts of routes, from easy slabs to stout
pillars. Be warned , though. The ice is generally thin.
Approach time: 2 minutes from your car.
Descent: Rappel off trees/downclimb.
Season: Midwinter.
Road/Highway the climb is visible from: Coal Creek Canyon Road.
Access issues: None, but keep off private land in the area.

Ann Robertson on Hays Creek Falls

114. Marble Falls (WI 4, 120 feet) ★★★

Marble Falls (known locally as Milton Creek Falls) is best known as being the scenic waterfall depicted on the Coors beer labels. It's also a classic Colorado ice route. Be warned, however, the creek underneath gushes really hard, and the ice is merely a shell over it.

Approach time: 10 minutes.
Descent: Rappel off a big anchor at the top, on the right.
Season: Midwinter.
Road/Highway the climb is visible from: The Marble Road.
Access issues: None, at the moment.

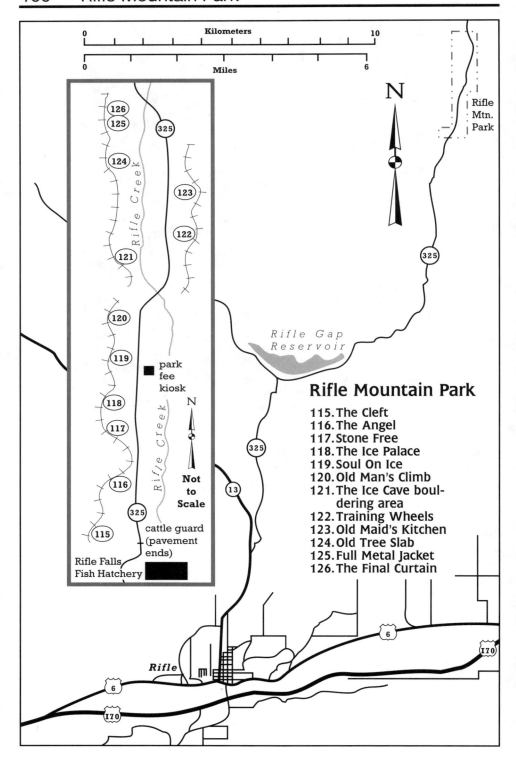

Rifle Mountain Park

115. The Cleft
116. The Angel
117. Stone Free
118. The Ice Palace
119. Soul On Ice
120. Old Man's Climb
121. The Ice Cave bouldering area
122. Training Wheels
123. Old Maid's Kitchen
124. Old Tree Slab
125. Full Metal Jacket
126. The Final Curtain

WESTERN SLOPE

Rifle Mountain Park

(Routes 115-126)

"Character Building Stuff"
—Charlie Fowler, Rock & Ice, 1992

Rifle Mountain Park is best known for it outrageously difficult rock climbs, but in the middle of winter, it plays host to a selection of excellent hard ice climbs. The ice routes in Rifle are almost all difficult, and the season here is short — expect to find the climbs melted out by early March.

Getting There: To get there, take the Rifle exit off I-70 and drive north on Colo. 13 through the town of Rifle. North of town, Colo. 13 branches. Take the right branch. Within a couple of miles, Colo. 325 will appear on the right, along with signs pointing to "Rifle Gap and Rifle Falls State Parks." Turn right onto Colo. 325. The road will wind through pretty agricultural country then pass the Rifle golf course before passing Rifle Gap, a geologic pass of sorts. About a mile further on, Colo. 325 will veer sharply right, around the Rifle Gap Dam. About 12 miles from the turn off onto Colo. 325, you'll reach Rifle Mountain Park. There is a $3 per day use fee at the park, so be prepared.

Climbs within the park are described by odometer readings starting at the physical entrance to the canyon, at precisely the point where the paved road turns to dirt. (There's a cattle guard.)

These climbs listed are not the only ones that form. During a cold wet season, numerous seeps and clefts freeze up offering many routes, especially mixed climbs. The climbs described here are those that form regularly.

The climbs are all visible from the road, the approach times are all less than five minutes (some are 30 seconds!), and there are no access issues.

115. The Cleft (WI 4-5, about 100 feet) ★★

The Cleft lies 0.3 miles into the canyon on the left (west side).

Depending on conditions, an ice flow regularly forms here. It involves a short vertical section to the roof of the cave, then a low-angled slab above.
Descent: Rappel off trees.

116. The Angel (WI 5-5+, 80 feet) ★★

The Angel lies 0.4 miles into the canyon on the left (west side). Then Angel is the obvious ice fall that forms on the south side of the prominent buttress directly above the road.
Descent: Rappel off trees.

117. Stone Free
(WI 5+, 150 feet) ★★★

Stone Free lies 0.5 miles into the canyon on the left (west side). Stone Free and The Ice Palace share an amphitheater just around the corner from the Angel. Stone Free offers dependable ice most years and is Rifle's most popular hard route.

Descent: Rappel off the small tree above the
    climb.

118. The Ice Palace
(WI 5+, 150 feet) ★★★

The Ice Palace lies 0.5 miles into the canyon on the left (west side). Just right of Stone Free, the Ice Palace is essentially a leaky cave that freezes, and all sorts of wild ice formations result. Regularly, The Ice Palace offers several thin columns that seem to defy gravity, connected at the top to a roof of ice.

Descent: Rappel off trees.

119. Soul On Ice
(WI 5+, 130 feet) ★★★

Jeff Hollenbaugh on Stone Free

Soul on ice lies 0.65 miles into the canyon on the left (west side). It is easily recognizable as the tall thin sheet that forms on the northeast facing wall above the park fee kiosk. It forms up every year and offers a stout outing. Don't miss it.

Descent: Rappel off the tree.

120. Old Man's Climb (WI 5, 90 feet) ★★

Old Man's Climb lies 0.75 miles up the canyon on the left (west side), opposite the picnic area. It regularly boasts a column in the mouth of a small cave, plus some low angled ice above the cave.

Descent: Rappel off trees.

121. The Ice Cave Bouldering Area (various grades) ★

0.25 miles upstream from Old Man's Climb, the road crosses the creek. On the left is a small trail leading to the Ice Cave, a popular tourist destination. It's also a good place for ice bouldering. A parking area lies just upstream of the bridge.

122. Training Wheels (WI 2, 25 feet)

Training Wheels lies 1.1 miles up the canyon, on the right (east side). The easiest route in the canyon, this climb does not always form. A short steep section leads to a tree on the right.

Descent: Rappel off the tree or downclimb.

123. Old Maid's Kitchen
(WI 5, 100 feet) ★★

Old Maid's Kitchen lies 1.2 miles up the canyon, on the right (east side), and forms in front of a deep cave.

Descent: Rappel off the tree above the route.

124. Old Tree Slab
(WI 5, 60 feet) ★★

The Old Tree Slab lies 1.3 miles up the canyon, on the left (west side). The old dead tree in the middle of the ice will make it obvious. It's also a lot harder than it looks, vertical all the way.

Descent: Rappel off the stump above the route.

125. Full Metal Jacket
(WI 5-6, 180 feet)

About 200 feet left of The Final Curtain, a wild mixed route occasionally forms, featuring two separate pillars at the top. Bring rock gear.

Descent: Walk off right to the rap anchors for The Final Curtain.

Old Tree Slab

126. The Final Curtain (WI 4, 60-100 feet) ★★★

The Final Curtain lies 1.4 miles up the canyon, on the left (west side). It is the huge sheet of low angled ice that is the last regularly forming ice floe in the canyon. A classic route, it offers easier, shorter routes on the left side to some hard, interesting (and sometimes bushy) variations on the right side.

Descent: Rappel anchors are on bushes and trees at the top.

The Final Curtain

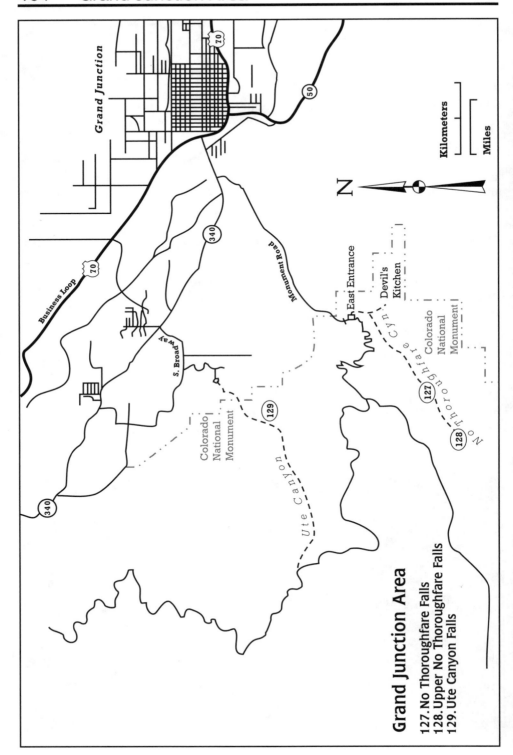

Grand Junction Area

127. No Thoroughfare Falls
128. Upper No Thoroughfare Falls
129. Ute Canyon Falls

WESTERN SLOPE

Grand Junction Area
(Routes 127-131)

"Speed can often be a decisive factor,"
—Heirich Harrer, "The White Spider"

Although the sandstone walls of Colorado National Monument don't seem like the sort of place you'd ever picture yourself ice climbing, a big waterfall in No Thoroughfare Canyon offers two excellent, reliable ice routes in the winter.

Unaweep Canyon offers a handful of ice routes; only two are documented here, Snyder Falls and Spooky Tooth.

Colorado National Monument

Getting there: To reach them, drive south of town on Colo. 340 (Redlands Parkway) towards the Monument. (If you're coming from the Denver area, exit I-70 onto the I-70 business loop, then follow it to Colo. 340.) After crossing the Colorado River, turn left onto Monument Road. Follow Monument Road south, towards the East Entrance to the Monument for nearly three miles. After entering the Monument, drive a short way up the hill to the first parking pullout on the left. This is the trailhead for the Devil's Kitchen and the No Thoroughfare Canyon trail. Park here.

Hike along the Devil's Kitchen trail towards the southeast. After about a quarter mile, it will cross No Thoroughfare Canyon, and usually a small creek trickles along the bottom of No Thoroughfare Canyon. Follow No Thoroughfare Canyon south, towards the mesas of the Monument for about 1-1.3 miles. A good trail follows the creek, regularly changing banks. No Thoroughfare Falls will be obvious, as it blocks further progress up the canyon.

About 0.75 miles up No Thoroughfare Canyon beyond No Thoroughfare Falls, simply called the Upper Falls, is a second waterfall that freezes.

The large granite cliff bands that sit below Liberty Cap also offer some ice climbing when it's cold enough. The falls, Ute Canyon Falls, face east, so they are rarely in good condition. The best thing about these falls is that you can check them out from the road, before committing to a grueling hike.

To get there, follow Colorado 340 to S. Broadway. Turn south onto S. Broadway, and drive about 1.3 miles to Willow Drive. Turn left onto Willow Dr. and follow this south for 0.4 miles, to the trailhead on the right. Park. From this point, a trail heads up towards the Monument. A few minutes of hiking leads to two forks in the trail. Take the left branch, which heads up the backside of a large, obvious, tilted rock slab. Instead of following the trail up the back side of the slab, however, skirt around the bottom of it. The falls lie at the east (left) end of the slabs and will be obvious.

To check this route's condition beforehand, drive back along Broadway to S. Camp Road and turn right. Drive along S. Camp until the back of the slab is visible. The ice should be obvious.

127. No Thoroughfare Falls (WI 3-4, 130 feet) ★★★

No Thoroughfare Falls offers a good selection of ice, from easy slabs on the left to a harder, steeper column in the center at the top. About 70 feet up the center of the falls (on an obvious shelf before the last hard section) are two bolts. These can be used for climbers who chose to lower off before the last section. The thin, mixed route to the right has also reportedly been done.

Jon Butler onNo Thoroughfare Falls
Photo by Luke Laeser

Approach time: 30-40 minutes.
Descent: In the trough above the top portion of the route are two bolts. Descend by rappelling off these.
Season: Mid-winter.
Road/Highway the climb is visible from: The condition of the ice can be checked out from East Glade Park Road.
Access issues: None.

128. Upper No Thoroughfare Falls (WI 3-3+, 120 feet) ★★

Sixty feet of WI 2 (often soloed) is capped by about 60 feet of WI 3-3+.
Approach time: 45 minutes-1 hour.
Descent: Walk off right.
Season: Mid-winter.
Road/Highway the climb is visible from: None.
Access issues: None.

129. Ute Canyon Falls (WI 3-4, 300 feet)

Can be really thin and melted out!
Approach time: 1 hour.
Descent: Descend by scrambling off right or rappelling.
Season: Mid-winter. A very cold winter

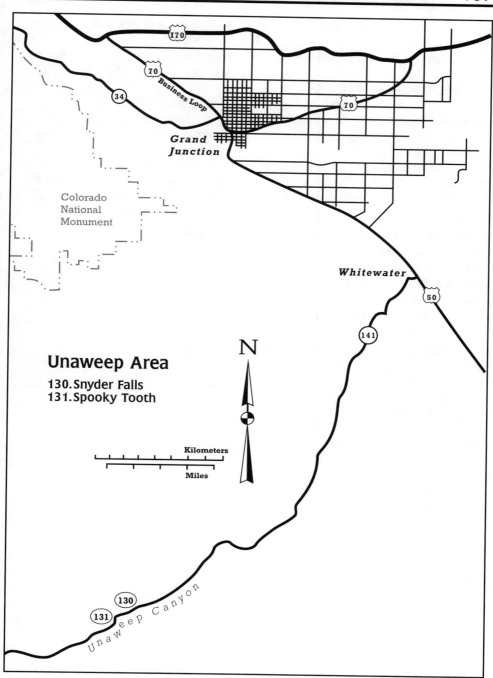

Road/Highway the climb is visible from: See notes above.
Access issues: None.

Unaweep Canyon

Getting there: To reach Unaweep Canyon, drive south of Grand Junction on U.S. 50, to the tiny pit stop of Whitewater. Here, Colo. 141 intersects U.S. 50. Turn southwest, onto Colo. 141.

Follow Colo. 141 for exactly 15.1 miles, to a pullout on the right (west) side of the road. Snyder Falls will be obvious off to the right (west). Park, duck through the fence, and approach across farmland to a gully. Ascend the gully to the base of the falls.

Spooky Tooth is located 16.6 miles down Colo. 141 from Whitewater (1.5 miles southwest of Snyder Falls). Spooky Tooth will be obvious off to the right (west). Park, hop the fence, and approach across farmland, bypassing the Sundog Wall (rock climbing area) to the left.

130. Snyder Falls (WI 3, 120 feet) ★★★

Quality sinker ice.

Approach time: 30 minutes.

Descent: Rappel off bolts at the top.

Season: Mid-winter.

Road/Highway the climb is visible from: Colo. 141.

Access issues: None, although the approach crosses private land.

131. Spooky Tooth (WI 4+/5-, 60 feet) ★

Like Snyder, but shorter and steeper.

Approach time: 30 minutes.

Descent: Rappel off a tree.

Season: Mid-winter.

Road/Highway the climb is visible from: Colo. 141.

Access issues: None, although the approach crosses private land.

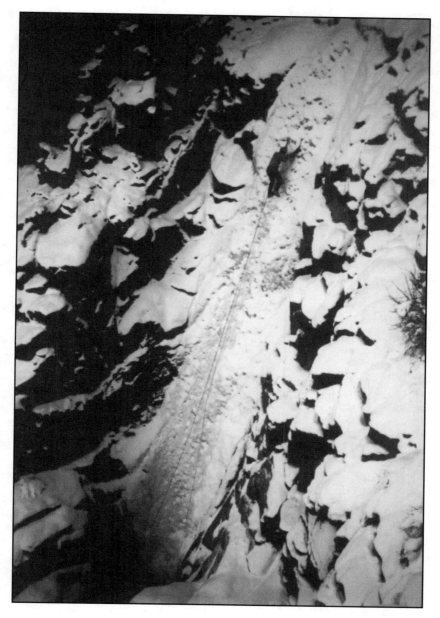

Jon Butler on Snyder Falls

Photo by Luke Laeser

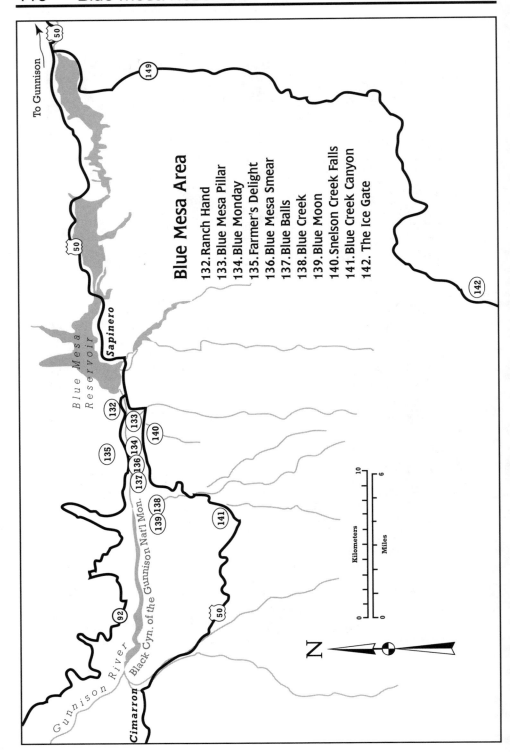

Blue Mesa Area

132. Ranch Hand
133. Blue Mesa Pillar
134. Blue Monday
135. Farmer's Delight
136. Blue Mesa Smear
137. Blue Balls
138. Blue Creek
139. Blue Moon
140. Snelson Creek Falls
141. Blue Creek Canyon
142. The Ice Gate

WESTERN SLOPE

Blue Mesa Reservoir Area
(Routes 128-137)

"There are times when one would not feel secure in relying upon the self-arrest alone,"

—Paul Petzoldt, "The New Wilderness Handbook"

Although it doesn't rank as one of Colorado's ice climbing centers, the vague, high desert area encompassing Blue Mesa Reservoir, Cimarron, and the northern end of Colo. 149 — the north-south highway running between Lake City and U.S. 50, west of Gunnison — offers some excellent ice climbing.

Indeed, it's possible to find fat, blue ice here as late as the end of April many years, and if you're an ice aficionado, this area is definitely worth a visit.

The center of ice climbing in the area is the Gunnison River canyon below the Blue Mesa Reservoir spillway. (This section of canyon actually houses the Morrow Point Reservoir, but it's easy to mistake the skinny reservoir for a river.) While this section of canyon houses a half dozen excellent routes, it is a long hike from the north, across ranchland, to reach them. The best thing to do prior to climbing in this area is to check out the condition of the routes from Colo. 92, the road between Sapinero and Hotchkiss.

A word of warning, all these routes lie on private land and/or the approach crosses private land. However, there has been little problem with climbers climbing them, so far. These routes, like the routes at Rifle Mountain Park, are described from one end of the road (in this case the south end of Colo. 92) in sequential order north.

A few routes north of the road are listed too.

Getting there: To check out the climbs first, from the intersection of U.S. 50 and Colo. 92, near the Blue Mesa reservoir, drive north on Colo. 92 for 4.5 miles to Pioneer Point. Along the way, the ice routes listed below will become obvious.

To reach the routes on foot is a different matter. A hike across empty but privately-owned ranchland to the south side of the canyon, above the Morrow Point Reservoir, is necessary.

To get to the hike-in point, from the intersection of Colo. 92 and U.S. 50, drive west on Highway 50 for about 2 miles. On the right is a small hill. Old Highway 50 skirts this hill to the north, while the new highway goes around it to the south. When the two meet again on the west side, park. The drainage to the north is

Blue Creek. Blue Creek, Blue Moon, Blue Balls and the Blue Mesa Smear can all be reached — with some work — from this point. Allow at least an hour for the walk. Skis are useful. From the canyon rim, rappel in. To reach the other routes, skirt around the edge of the mesa to the west (left, if you're skiing from the south) and rappel in. Note: It's a lot of work to reach the other routes in this area.

Snelson Creek Falls can easily been seen from U.S. 50, near Blue Mesa Point. Blue Mesa Point lies west of Blue Mesa Reservoir, on the south side of the Gunnison River.

To reach Snelson Creek Falls, drive west from the intersection of U.S. 50 and Colo. 92 for 2.4 miles. Snelson Creek Falls will be obvious, spilling off the mesa to the left (south). An old road (dirt) will loop off U.S. 50 at this point. Park in this area, and follow the loop to the creek bottom, then follow the creek up to the falls.

The Gate is a narrow spot in the valley where the Lake Fork of the Gunnison descends towards Blue Mesa Reservoir. To reach the Gate and The Ice Gate, drive south from the intersection of U.S. 50 and Colo. 149 for 29.2 miles. The area can also be reached from Lake City. It lies about 16.3 miles north of the Conoco in Lake City.

There's a sign on the western side of the road (right side, if you're coming from Gunnison/Montrose areas) designating, "The Gate."

On the other (east) side of the road, a few hundred feet up the hill, is a spectacular cascade of ice, pouring over the edge of the mesa, The Ice Gate.

Also of interest, the road cuts along U.S. 50, 13 miles east of Cimarron, in the Blue Creek Canyon area, can offer good ice bouldering, as well as a number of exceptional mixed routes, just above the road.

Ranch Hand in thin conditi

Blue Mesa Reservoir Area Routes

132. Ranch Hand (WI 5, 120 feet)

Located 1.6 miles up Colo. 92, on private property north (right) of the road, this thin cascade will be obvious. Rock gear recommended.

Approach time: 10 minutes.
Descent: Walk off either side or rappel. You might need to bring anchor materials.
Season: Mid-winter.
Road/Highway the climb is visible from: Colo. 92
Access issues: See notes above.

Blue Mesa Pillar

133. Blue Mesa Pillar
(WI 5, 80 feet) ★★

Located 1.6 miles up Colo. 92, on the south side of the Morrow Point Reservoir, this fat pillar sits on the upper left side of a large rock buttress. Rock gear is handy for belaying.

Approach time: 1 hour.

Descent: Climb up and right, in a rock corner, to reach the mesa.

Season: Mid-winter.

Road/Highway the climb is visible from: Colo. 92

Access issues: See notes above.

134. Blue Monday
(WI 4, 200 feet)

Located 4.05 miles up Colo. 92, on the south side of the Morrow Point Reservoir, this thin mixed route is rarely in condition. It sits low in the canyon, on an orange rock wall. Rock gear is a must.

Approach time: 1 hour.

Descent: Continue on up, above the climb to reach the mesa.

Season: Mid-winter.

Road/Highway the climb is visible from: Colo. 92

Access issues: See notes above.

Blue Monday

135. Farmer's Delight
(WI 5 to 6, 200 feet)

Located 4.5 miles up Colo. 92, on private property north of the road, this cascade, like Ranch Hand, will be obvious. Rock gear is necessary.

Approach time: 10 minutes.

Descent: Walk off either side or rappel. You might need to bring anchor materials.

Season: Mid-winter.

Road/Highway the climb is visible from: Colo. 92

Access issues: See notes above.

136. Blue Mesa Smear
(WI 4 to 5, 150 feet) ★

Located just under 5.0 miles up Colo. 92, on the south side of the Morrow Point Reservoir, this route is distinguished by its wide ice cur-

Blue Mesa Smear

tains. Like Blue Monday, it sits low in the canyon, in the trees. The right side tends to be hardest.

Approach time: 1 hour.

Descent: Continue on up, above the climb to reach the mesa.

Season: Mid-winter.

Road/Highway the climb is visible from: Colo. 92

Access issues: See notes above.

137. Blue Balls (WI 4-, 300 feet) ★★★

The best route in the area, this climb forms in a long, left to right (from bottom to top) angling gully. It lies 5.1 miles up Colo. 92, on the south side of the Morrow Point Reservoir. It lies fairly close to the Blue Mesa Smear.

Approach time: 1 hour.

Descent: Continue on up, above the climb to reach the mesa.

Season: Mid-winter.

Road/Highway the climb is visible from: Colo. 92

Access issues: See notes above.

Blue Balls

138. Blue Creek (WI 4, 300 feet) ★★

About 5.85 miles up Colo. 92, on the south side of the road, is Pioneer Point. From Pioneer Point, the fabulous rock spire of Curecanti Needle is obvious, directly to the south. Behind Curecanti Needle, further south, is the Blue Creek Valley. Blue Creek is a climbable series of cascades, but often has a lot of snow.

Approach time: 1 hour.

Descent: Continue on up, above the climb to reach the mesa.

Season: Mid-winter.

Road/Highway the climb is visible from: Colo. 92

Access issues: See notes above.

139. Blue Moon (WI 4, 150 feet) ★

About 3/4 of a mile down the Gunnison river valley from Blue Creek (west), on the south side of the valley, is a smear that regularly forms and offers decent climbing. It can be seen from Pioneer Point, right of Blue Creek.

Approach time: 1 hour.

Descent: Continue on up, above the climb to reach the mesa.

Season: Mid-winter.

Road/Highway the climb is visible from: Colo. 92

Access issues: See notes above.

Blue Creek Canyon

The Ice Gate

140. Snelson Creek Falls (WI 5, 120 feet) ★★
A classic waterfall.
Approach time: 20 minutes.
Descent: Rappel off a tree.
Season: Mid-winter.
Road/Highway the climb is visible from: U.S. 50.
Access issues: This approach crosses private land. Be low-key.

141. Blue Creek Canyon (WI 2-5, various lengths) ★
Just above the road. Can't miss it. The canyon below the road, which is home to
Blue Creek, also has ice at times. Helpful hint: Pick routes that won't let you
knock ice onto the highway.
Approach time: 2 minutes.
Descent: Walk off or rappel from trees.
Season: Mid-winter.
Road/Highway the climb is visible from: U.S. 50.
Access issues: None.

142. The Ice Gate (WI 4, 120 feet) ★★★
   A great outing, it boasts high quality ice for about 120 feet. The bottom can be
hollow. Rock gear is useful.
Approach time: 20 minutes.
Descent: To descend, walk off to the left (north) or rappel from trees.
Season: Mid-winter.
Road/Highway the climb is visible from: Colo. 149.
Access issues: None.

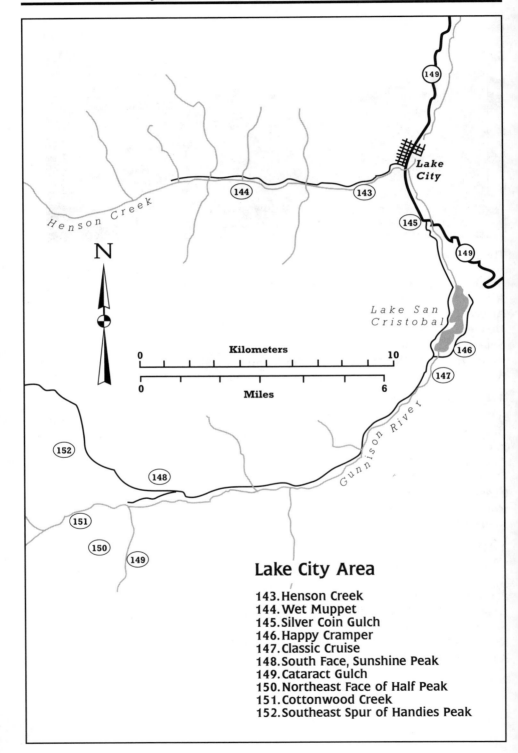

Lake City Area

143. Henson Creek
144. Wet Muppet
145. Silver Coin Gulch
146. Happy Cramper
147. Classic Cruise
148. South Face, Sunshine Peak
149. Cataract Gulch
150. Northeast Face of Half Peak
151. Cottonwood Creek
152. Southeast Spur of Handies Peak

WESTERN SLOPE

Lake City Area
(Routes 143-149)

"That Alfred Packer....what a wild dude,"
—Ice climber visiting the Alfred Packer Museum in Lake City.

Lake City is a picturesque little mining town — just like all the others — that has seen tremendous growth in recent years. It boasts a fairly good selection of cafes and hotels, restaurants and gas stations.

Ice climbing here is pretty fickle, and the best time seems to be in the middle of a cold, dry winter. Call around first, before driving all the way there.

There are three venues within the Lake City general area: Henson Creek, which is very close to town, and the Lake San Cristobal/Sherman area, a wide sweeping valley south of town, and North and South Clear Creek Falls, between Lake City and Creede.

Henson Creek

The main ice climbing in town lies along the rotten shale and limestone rock walls of Henson Creek, which lies on the southwest edge of town. Here, in a good year, the south wall of the canyon can offer hundreds of different ice routes, mostly in the WI 3-4 range, all of which are just a couple of minutes walk from the car. Further up the Henson Creek canyon, there is a big wide frozen gully, Wet Muppet, that offers thick blue ice.

Getting there: To reach Henson Creek, drive to the south end of Gunnison Ave. (Main St.) and turn west onto 2nd St. A sign points towards Engineer Pass. Henson Creek will become immediately obvious, just south of 2nd St. Follow 2nd St. west until it ends in a T intersection. Turn left onto Hinsdale County Road 20, also known as the Henson Creek Road.

From the point where the BLM signs announce the beginning of the canyon and other miscellany, it's just 0.3 miles to the first routes. (It's easy to walk here, if you're staying in town.) The myriad smears and flows continue for about a mile. Take your pick.

To reach Wet Muppet, drive 4.1 miles past the entrance signs. The route will be obvious on the south side of the canyon.

Henson Creek Routes

143. Henson Creek (WI 3-5, various routes) ★

Most of these routes tend to be thin smears, over rock. Thin pitons are a good idea, but getting one in can be hard. Most of these climbs are better done as solos or top-ropes.

Approach time: 2 minutes

Descent: There are numerous trees available as anchors.

Season: Midwinter.

Road/Highway the climb is visible from: Hinsdale County Road 20 (a.k.a. Henson Creek Road).

Access issues: The big downer with Henson Creek is that there is a lot of private land along it. Please respect it. The other downer — not so big — is that you have to boulder hop across Henson Creek to reach the climbs. Watch out for highly protective and somewhat angry dogs coming out of the various shacks.

144. Wet Muppet (WI 3-4, 200 feet)

The obvious gully. Avalanche danger is high.

Approach time: 15 minutes.

Descent: Descend by hiking off to the side, or rappelling off trees.

Season: Midwinter.

Road/Highway the climb is visible from: Hinsdale County Road 20 (a.k.a. Henson Creek Road).

Access issues: Same as for the previous route.

Lake San Cristobal/Sherman Area

The Large Valley south of Lake City, home to Lake San Cristobal and the Lake Fork of the Gunnison River, offers a variety of exceptional ice climbing. The routes in this long valley range from short frozen waterfalls near the road to long alpine mixed routes in the high country.

Getting there: To reach the entrance to this valley, drive south of Lake City on Colo. 149, towards Slumgullion Pass. About 2.3 miles south of the Henson Creek Bridge in Lake City, there'll be turn off to the right, Hinsdale County Road 30. This is the way to the Lake San Cristobol, as the huge wooden sign says, and Sherman areas.

However, of note just before you reach County Road 30, is Silver Coin Gulch. This frozen stream, offering WI 4 climbing, is tucked up on the right hand side of the road, 2.0 miles south of the Henson Creek Bridge in Lake city. There's a parking area just before (north of) the Crystal Lodge. Silver Coin Gulch lies in the small gulch to the west.

From the intersection of Highway 149, follow Hinsdale County Road 30 south for about 4.1 miles to the intersection of Hinsdale County Road 33. As you skirt Lake San Cristobal on its west side, the short pumpy ice pillar Happy Cramper will be obvious across the water. To reach Happy Cramper, turn left onto Hinsdale

County Road 33 and follow it about a mile, to the Wupperman Campground. Bypass the first couple of entrances to the campground, and turn left into Campsite No. 11. Happy Cramper lies directly below the big tree on the lake (west) side of this campsite. Rappel in and climb out. Surprisingly, this route stays in pretty good shape late into the season.

To reach the Sherman area, continue southwest on Hinsdale County Road 30, past County Road 33 and the turnoff to Happy Cramper.

The next route of interest, Classic Cruise, lies about 0.5 miles south of the intersection of County Roads 30 and 33. It's visible as you exit the south end of the small canyon, just upstream from the intersection, but as you drive further south, the route is lost behind a knoll. There's a small parking pullout on the left (east) side of the road.

To reach the Sherman area, continue south. The first few cabins of the old mining area will appear on the right, about 7.4 miles south of Classic Cruise. Above the cabins, on the south facing walls of Sunshine Peak, are numerous high quality ice climbs, ranging in difficulty and in length. As you continue west, towards Sherman, more routes will reveal themselves clinging to the cliffs above the road. Most of these routes offer excellent climbing.

0.2 miles beyond the first old cabins, the road reaches a Y intersection. The right branch heads up the hill towards Cinnamon Mountain; the left branch (Hinsdale County Road 35) leads into Sherman.

From the intersection, drive the last half mile into Sherman. There's not really anything of interest at the end of the road, except, perhaps, the BLM toilet and the parking area around it.

From this area, there are three main ice climbs nearby, Cataract Gulch, Cottonwood Creek, and the Northeast Face of Half Peak.

Cataract Gulch is the obvious drainage to the south, and the trail into the Gulch is marked by a sign. Cottonwood Creek is the obvious drainage off to the west, and offers a variety of climbs.

The Northeast Face of Half Peak looms ominously above the BLM toilet, and will be obvious. It's a short hike to the base of the peak, then straight up. Avalanche danger on this face is high.

In this area, the north side of the Southeast Spur of Handies Peak also offers a wide variety of interesting ice routes. These routes come into condition in the spring. To reach this area, take the right-hand branch of the intersection, half mile east of Sherman. Drive up the narrow winding road about 1.9 miles beyond the intersection. Across the valley, the Southeast Spur will come into view, and the ice will be obvious. The approach — across the narrow valley — is from hell!

Northeast Face of Half Peak

Lake San Cristobal/Sherman Area Routes

145. Silver Coin Gulch (WI 4, 70 feet)
A frozen stream, offering WI 4 climbing, tucked up on the right hand side of the road.
Approach time: 5 minutes
Descent: Rappel off a tree.
Season: Midwinter.
Road/Highway the climb is visible from: None, quite.
Access issues: Park carefully!

146. Happy Cramper (WI 5, 60 feet) ★★
When it's in shape, this is a killer ice pillar. You can top-rope it off your bumper.
Approach time: 5 seconds
Descent: Rappel off the big tree or your bumper.
Season: Midwinter.
Road/Highway the climb is visible from: Hinsdale County Road 30, across the lake from the route.
Access issues: None.

147. Classic Cruise (WI 4, 250 feet) ★★
A long, stepped waterfall.
Approach time: 15 minutes.
Descent: Rappel off trees.
Season: Midwinter.
Road/Highway the climb is visible from: Hinsdale County Road 30, just south of the intersection of County Roads 30 and 33. It's visible as you exit the south end of the small canyon, just upstream (southwest) from the intersection.
Access issues: None, at the moment.

148. South Face, Sunshine Peak
(WI 2-5, 200-700 feet) ★★★

Pick a line! Most of them are pretty good. Bring much rock gear!
Approach time: 15 minutes.
Descent: Descents can be tricky however, so taking a handful of pitons and rap slings is advised. Rappel off trees where you can.
Season: Midwinter. They face south, remember.
Road/Highway the climb is visible from: Hinsdale County Road 30.
Access issues: None.

149. Cataract Gulch (WI 4-5, 160 feet) ★★

High quality climbing in the obvious gulch.
Approach time: 20 minutes.
Descent: Rappel off trees.
Season: Midwinter. Avalanche danger can be high.
Road/Highway the climb is visible from: None.
Access issues: None.

150. Northeast Face of Half Peak (WI 3, 600 feet)

The big thick blue waterfall bisecting the face of the mountain.
Approach time: 20 minutes.
Descent: Rappel off trees.
Season: Fall. Avalanche danger can be EXTREME!!
Road/Highway the climb is visible from: Pretty much any road in the Sherman area.
Access issues: None.

151. Cottonwood Creek (WI 2-5, various lengths) ★

Various sections of the creek freeze up offering many climbable lines.
Approach time: 20 minutes.
Descent: Rappel off trees.
Season: Midwinter. Avalanche danger can be high.
Road/Highway the climb is visible from: None.
Access issues: None.

152. Southeast Spur of Handies Peak (WI 3-5, 400 feet)

A wide variety of interesting ice routes, from WI 3 to 5, and 300-400 feet long.
Bring rock gear and rap slings.
Approach time: 2 hours.
Descent: Rappel off trees.
Season: Spring.
Road/Highway the climb is visible from: The Sherman-Cinnamon Mountain Road.
Access issues: None, 'cept it's a bitch.

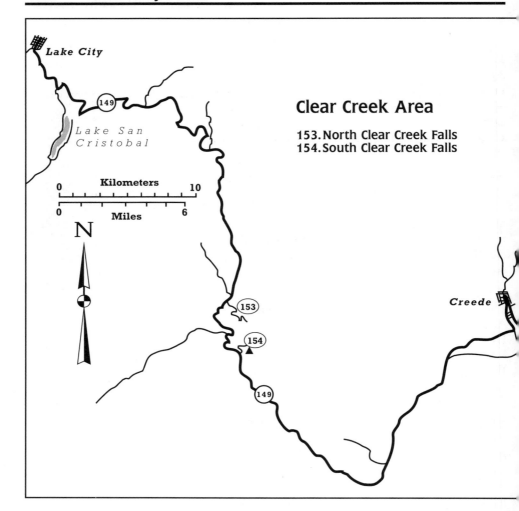

Lake City

149

Lake San
Cristobal

Kilometers

Miles

N

Clear Creek Area

153. North Clear Creek Falls
154. South Clear Creek Falls

153

154

149

Creede

North and South Clear Creek Falls

These two waterfalls, located between Lake City and Creede, are popular tourist attractions. Indeed, North Clear Creek Falls is one of the most photographed waterfalls in the state, and in recent years has appeared on the covers of numerous books. The two falls also offer excellent ice climbing.

Getting there: To reach North Clear Creek Falls from Lake City, drive south on Colo. 149 for about 24 miles, into the wide flat valley of the Rio Grande. From Creede, it's about 27 miles. On the east side of the road (the left side if you're coming from Lake City), is well built road, leading the about 0.5 miles or so to a parking lot and viewing area above the falls. Rappel in.

Oftentimes, this road is closed, due to snow. Brings skis, just in case. It's a flat, easy ski all the way.

South Clear Creek Falls lies about 3 miles south of North Clear Creek Falls, on Colo. 149. From Creede it's about 24 miles.

Southeast Spur-Handies

At a bend in the road, a turn off leads east into the U.S. Forest Service's Silver Thread Campground. At the back of the campground, a trail leads 900 feet to the base of the falls.

Also of note, a number of excellent ice slabs form up on the west side of a large field, 9.3 miles south of the Silver Thread campground. They are visible from the road. It's a long flat ski to these 80-foot slabs, and it's necessary to cross private property, and the Rio Grande to get there.

153. North Clear Creek Falls (WI 3-5, 90 feet) ★★★
A classic waterfall.
Approach time: 5 minutes.
Descent: None. You walk off the top.
Season: Winter.
Road/Highway the climb is visible from: The road leading to the parking lot and viewing area.
Access issues: None, although you might want to bring skis in case the road is closed due to snow.

154. South Clear Creek Falls (WI 4-5 70 feet) ★★
Another clas sic waterfall.
Approach time: 5 minutes.
Descent: None. You walk off the top.
Season: Winter.
Road/Highway the climb is visible from: None.
Access issues: None.

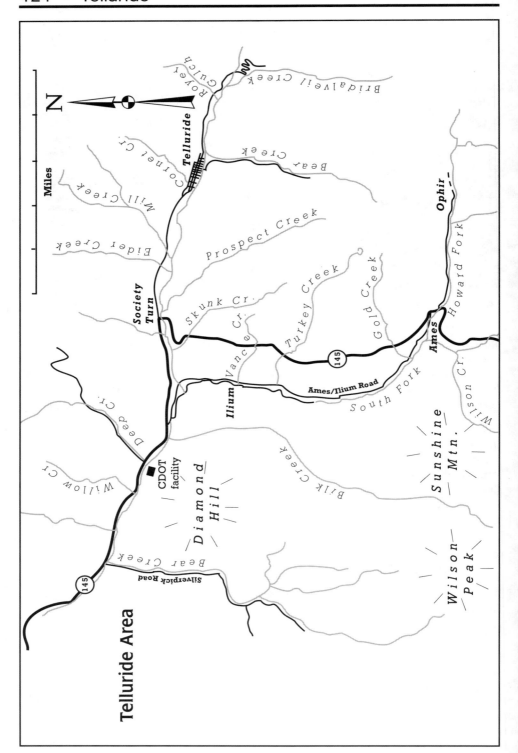

Telluride Area

SOUTHWESTERN MOUNTAINS

Telluride
(Routes 155-214)

"For hardmen seeking strenuous, multi-pitch waterfall climbs, Telluride is the place,"
—Charlie Fowler, San Juan Ice Climbs, 1991

Telluride is not only one of the prettiest ski resorts in the world, it's one of the three biggest ice climbing centers in Southwest Colorado (along with Ouray and Silverton).

It boasts such mega-classic hardman routes as the Ames Ice Hose and Bridalveil, but a lot of exceptional-yet-relatively-unknown climbs as well.

There are, in reality, about a dozen separate ice climbing areas within the general Telluride area, from areas lying within a couple of blocks of downtown to the more remote mountain valleys west of Telluride.

For ease, this section has been divided into a number of areas, starting with climbs in the area east of Telluride, then moving west, to Ilium and Placerville, then south to Ames, Ophir and Dunton.

Access issues, which are fairly big around Telluride, are discussed in each individual section.

In terms of lodging, drinking, gear, etc., Telluride's a ritzy ski resort now, so everything's pretty expensive. You can stay in Ridgway cheaper, or, better yet, camp. Dining out's pretty steep, but a brief visit to a restaurant at the end of the day is a nice break before a cold night in the back of the truck. There are also several shops in town that sell ice climbing gear (see list at back of book).

Telluride East
(Routes 155-163)

Bridalveil Falls is undoubtedly one of the great ice climbs of North America, but there are a number of excellent, lesser known routes in this area that are well worth a visit, such as Upper and Lower Royer Gulch, and Ingraham Falls.

Unfortunately, the area is a complex patchwork of old mining claims, private and public lands, making climbing here no simple affair.

The Mine Road, which leads into the Bridalveil Creek Basin, is now a public right of way. The lands on the sides of the road, however, are mostly private. To make the issue more complex, some of the cliffs around the basin are on public land.

Ingraham Falls, Ingraham Creek and Bridalveil Creek, have generally not seen access disputes and climbers on them report few, if any, problems.

Bridalveil Falls is still open for debate. According to some, the falls and the streambed above are public. According to others, they're not.

What is definitely not public is the power plant above the falls and wooden deck at the top of the falls on the left. In other words, should you venture up Bridalveil and tie off to the deck, or walk across the deck to get back to the road, you're trespassing, and you'll likely (and justly) feel the wrath of the landowner. (There are reports of ice tools tossed off the cliff and other such retributions.) If you decide to climb the falls, stay in the streambed, using your axes/screws to belay, even though it's not as convenient as clipping into the deck.

Above the falls, you must stay in the streambed and hike southeast, up the streambed to reach the road. Once on the road, it's a half mile or so back down to the base of the falls.

Perhaps more important than access, ice climbers should be aware of the avalanche potential in this area, which can be pretty extreme after even a small snowfall. In short, the entire basin area can be pretty dangerous in midwinter.

Getting there: While all the climbs east of Telluride are pretty straightforward to reach, Upper Royer Gulch is reached from downtown.

To get to Upper Royer Gulch, follow Oak St. north, towards the red cliffs of the Cornet Creek Canyon. It is important to note that Oak St. does not intersect with Colorado Ave. (Main St.) in Telluride. Oak St. is the street where the Sheridan Opera House sits, and the block in front of the Opera House has been turned into a park. However, it's easy to get to upper Oak St. simply by going around the block on Fir St. or Aspen St., which lie west and east of Oak, then cutting back over to Oak. Follow Oak St. to its northern (uphill) end. Park without blocking any of the Oak St. driveways.

From here, Tomboy Road leads out east (right), across the hillside, to Royer Gulch. The road is closed to vehicular traffic in the winter, so you have to ski or hike. It's 2.2 miles to the ice climbs, which lie right above the road in a small amphitheater.

To reach Bridalveil and the Fang drive east (towards the mountains) on Colorado Ave. (Main St.). Colorado Ave is the same thing as Colo. 145 in downtown.

At the east end of the built up area, you'll pass Town Park, on the right (south) side of the road. There's a big sign. This is a good place to reset your odometer to 0.0.

From Town Park, it's exactly 1.0 mile to Lower Royer Gulch. A stream draining the gulch trickles down from the left (north) side of the road and under the road. There's a parking pullout on the right (south) side of the road. Park, and walk up the drainage to Lower Royer Gulch.

To reach the Fang, continue east on Colo. 145, for another 0.3 miles past Lower Royer Gulch (1.3 miles from Town Park). The Fang will be off to the right (south) across the valley and will be obvious.

1.6 miles east of Telluride, you'll reach the Pandora Mill and the start of the disputed territory. As mentioned, the road — which goes up into the basin, but is gated off in the winter — is public and there are no access issues involved with traveling up it.

Anyway, after skirting the gate at the Pandora Mill, ski or hike the twisting Mine Road up 1.2 miles. Ingraham Creek flows in from the left (east) and leads to Ingraham Falls. Grunt up the streambed (which is often considered a route in itself) to reach the base of Ingraham Falls.

The Fang

The base of Bridalveil is another 0.6 miles up the road, and spills out of the cliff just right of the power plant atop the cliff. Bridalveil Creek offers a number of short falls between the base of the falls and the Pandora Mill which can be accessed from various points on the Mine Road.

Telluride East Routes

155. Upper Royer Gulch Left (WI 4-4+, 300 feet)
Not climbed very often as it gets nailed by the sun. A stream trickles down from the left. Done as three or four pitches, the first slab is often hollow and rotten.
Approach time: From the top of Oak St., allow 40-60 minutes, by ski or boot.
Season: Midwinter.
Descent: Descend by walking off right, around the top of Upper Royer Gulch
    Right, then descending an easy gully back to the road.
Road/Highway the climb is visible from: None.
Access issues: Tomboy Road is a public right of way, however, much of the land
    around Tomboy Road is private. Stay on the road!

156. Upper Royer Gulch Right (WI 4-4+, 250 feet) ★★★
This is the classic route for which climbers visit the Upper Royer area. It lies right of the previous route, and climbs easy ground (WI 3) to a platform, about 80 feet up. Then, another lead tackles the crux (WI 4-4+), which climbs a steep wall into the gully above.
Approach time: From the top of Oak St., allow 40-60 minutes
Season: Midwinter.
Descent: Descend by walking off right, then descending an easy gully back to the
    road.
Road/Highway the climb is visible from: None.
Access issues: Tomboy Road is a public right of way, however, much of the land
    around Tomboy Road is private. Stay on the road!

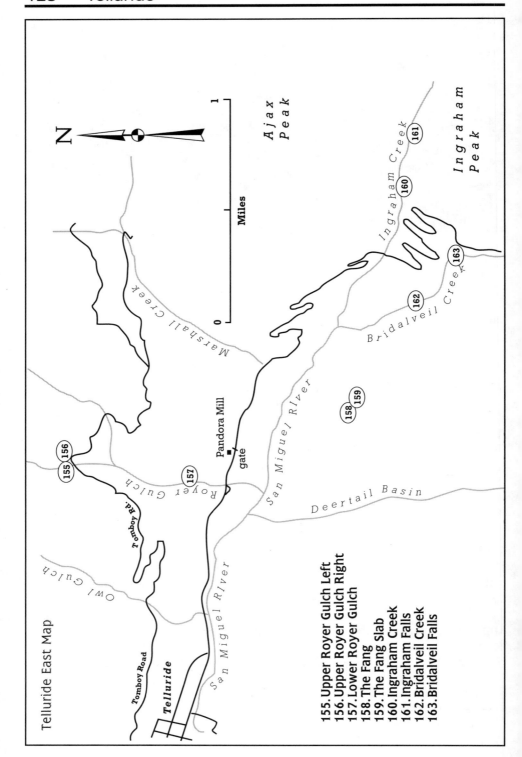

Telluride East Map

155. Upper Royer Gulch Left
156. Upper Royer Gulch Right
157. Lower Royer Gulch
158. The Fang
159. The Fang Slab
160. Ingraham Creek
161. Ingraham Falls
162. Bridalveil Creek
163. Bridalveil Falls

157. Lower Royer Gulch
(WI 3-4, 120 feet) ★★

This route actually consists of two 60-foot pillars, both about the same: Big cones leading to 10 feet or so of vertical climbing.

Approach time: 5 minutes
Season: Midwinter.
Descent: Walk off right.
Road/Highway the climb is visible from: Colo. 145, through the trees.
Access issues: Stay in the creek on the hike up to it.

Lower Royer Gulch
Photo: Doug Berry

158. The Fang (WI 5, 100 feet) ★★★

The approach is pretty straightforward. From a parking spot on the road, hike across the valley to the route. Snowshoes are a must. A freestanding pillar leads to a stance on the right, then it's a short way to the top.

Approach time: 30 minutes
Season: All winter. The route is in good shape for a long time, but snow conditions above the route should help you decide when to climb it.
Descent: Rappel off a tree.
Road/Highway the climb is visible from: Colo. 145.
Access issues: The approach crosses private land, but this does not appear to be a problem for anyone.

159. The Fang Slab (WI 2-3, 80 feet) ★

The obvious slabs, a couple hundred feet left of the Fang.

Approach Time: 30 minutes.
Season: All winter. The route is in good shape for a long time, but snow conditions above the route should help you decide when to climb it.

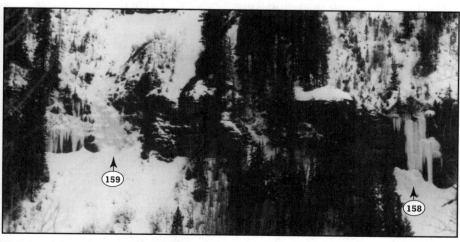

Left to right: The Fang Slab, The Fang

Pandora Mill. Left to right: Ingraham Falls, Ingraham Creek

Descent: Walk off left.
Road/Highway the climb is visible from: Colo. 145.
Access issues: The approach crosses private land, but it's not a problem.

160. Ingraham Creek (WI 3-4, 500 feet) ★
The streambed, leading to Ingraham Falls.
Approach time: From the gate at the Pandora Mill, allow an hour.
Season: All winter. Avalanche potential should be considered.
Descent: Walk off right. A county road leads back down into the basin.
Road/Highway the climb is visible from: Colo. 145, and many places in the
      Telluride area.
Access issues: None, so far.

161. Ingraham Falls (WI 5, 200 feet) ★★★
The obvious falls, high above the road.
Approach time: From the gate at the Pandora Mill, allow an hour and a half.
Season: All winter. Avalanche potential should be considered.
Descent: Walk off right and down the road.
Road/Highway the climb is visible from: Colo. 145, and many places in the
      Telluride area.
Access issues: None, so far.

162. Bridalveil Creek (WI 4, various lengths) ★
The creek draining the famed falls offers a number of short steps. They're spread
out in the drainage right of the road.
Approach time: From the gate at the Pandora Mill, allow an hour.

Bridalveil Falls

Season: All winter. Avalanche potential should be considered.
Descent: Walk off left.
Road/Highway the climb is visible from: Colo. 145, and many places in the east Telluride area.
Access issues: The approach crosses private land, but it does not seem to be a problem.

163. Bridalveil Falls (WI 5, 400 feet) ★★★

The famed falls, which looks like a series of splattered cauliflowers on the cliffside, below and just right of the power plant.
Approach time: From the gate at the Pandora Mill, allow an hour.
Season: All winter. Avalanche potential should be considered.
Descent: Walk up the drainage above the falls, until you reach the road. Follow the road back down to the base of the falls.
Road/Highway the climb is visible from: Colo. 145, and many places in the east Telluride area.
Access issues: See the introduction above. Also, the ice climbs that form left and right of Bridalveil are definitely off limits to climbers. Verboten. No. Nada.

Bear Creek Falls Area
(Routes 164–171)

The Bear Creek valley is a dramatic canyon with towering pinnacles and mountains surrounding it, the Bear Creek Valley offer several fine climbs. Like the Bilk Creek Valley, a trip to Bear Creek is easily worth the lengthy, but easy approach.

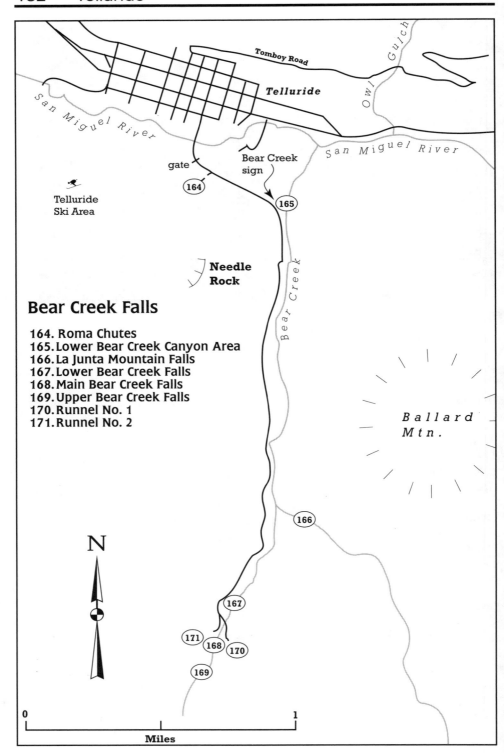

Bear Creek Falls

164. Roma Chutes
165. Lower Bear Creek Canyon Area
166. La Junta Mountain Falls
167. Lower Bear Creek Falls
168. Main Bear Creek Falls
169. Upper Bear Creek Falls
170. Runnel No. 1
171. Runnel No. 2

Getting there: Bear Creek lies in the valley just left (east) of the Telluride ski area, when viewed from town. An old dirt road follows the valley all the way up to the falls, although the dirt road is closed to vehicular traffic. (You've gotta ski or walk.)

From downtown Telluride, follow South Pine Street south, as it crosses the San Miguel River and begins climbing into the woods. A gate, closing off cars to Bear Creek, is soon reached. From the gate, it's about 1.75 miles to the Main Bear Creek Falls, although it seems like less. (A friend clocked it on his mountain bike.) Bypass the gate and hike up the road.

After five minutes of hiking, a small chute will open up on the right, allowing you to see a small amphitheater on the hillside above the road. This is the Roma Chutes area.

Continue up the road to the big bend where the road curves south, into the valley itself. There's a new Bear Creek sign on the left side of the road, a colorful description of the valley. Down in the canyon behind the sign (it takes a little trial and error to get there) is the Lower Canyon area, where the Bear Creek Canyon wall ices up.

To reach the main Bear Creek area, continue up the road. About a half mile past the Bear Creek sign, a subsidiary valley joins the Bear Creek valley from the east (left). A waterfall, dubbed La Junta Mountain Falls, can offer some early season climbing. The approach is straightforward. Cross Bear Creek (a hassle) and hike up the base of the falls.

Bear Creek Falls is another half mile up the road, and consists of a Lower Falls (near the massive boulder next to the road), a Main Falls, and a rarely climbed Upper Falls. To either side of the Main Falls are thin runnels, occasionally offering climbable ice.

164. Roma Chutes
(WI 4, 50 feet)

The chute above the road on the hike into Bear Creek offers a brief detour.

Approach time: Allow 15 minutes from the gate.

Descent: Rappel off trees.

Season: All winter.

Road/Highway the climb is visible from: Pretty much everywhere in the Telluride area.

Access issues: None.

La Junta Mountain Falls

165. Lower Bear Creek Canyon Area (WI 4-5, 80 feet) ★★

Behind the Bear Creek sign, a number of top-ropable routes for up. To reach the base of the routes, walk north (left as you look into the canyon from above) and find an easy place to downclimb, or simply rappel.

Approach time: 25 minutes from the gate.
Descent: Walk off.
Season: All winter.
Road/Highway the climb is visible from: None.
Access issues: None.

166. La Junta Mountain Falls (WI 2-3, 200 feet)

A series of cascading steps, La Junta Mountain Falls sits in a rock band just above Bear Creek. Rarely climbable; it fills with snow.

Approach time: Allow 45 minutes from the gate.
Descent: Rappel off trees next to the falls, or down-climb.
Season: Late fall/early winter. Avalanche danger in this area is high.
Road/Highway the climb is visible from: None.
Access issues: None.

Main Bear Creek Falls

167. Lower Bear Creek Falls (WI 2, 70 feet) ★

Located just downstream of the point where the Bear Creek road intersects Bear Creek and dies out are two short steps.

Approach time: Allow an hour from the gate.
Descent: Walk off either side.
Season: All winter.
Road/Highway the climb is visible from: None.
Access issues: None.

168. Main Bear Creek Falls (WI 3-4, 120 feet) ★★★

The main attraction, many lines are possible.

Approach time: Allow an hour from the gate.
Descent: Walk off right.
Season: All winter.
Road/Highway the climb is visible from: None.
Access issues: None.

169. Upper Bear Creek Falls (WI 2-3, 80 feet)

Located several hundred feet above the Main Falls.

Approach time: Allow an hour from the gate.
Descent: Walk off.

Season: All winter.
Road/Highway the climb is visible from: None.
Access issues: None.

170. Runnel No. 1 (WI 2-3, 100 feet)
Located just left of the Main Falls.
Approach time: Allow an hour from the gate.
Descent: Walk off left.
Season: Late fall/early winter, before snows cover it.
Road/Highway the climb is visible from: None.
Access issues: None.

171. Runnel No. 2 (WI 3-4, 150 feet)
Located just right of the Main Falls, this runnel climbs into the trees..
Approach time: Allow an hour from the gate.
Descent: Rap off trees is best, or downclimb to the left.
Season: Late fall/early winter, before snows cover it.
Road/Highway the climb is visible from: None.
Access issues: None.

Cornet Falls, Butcher Creek Falls
(Routes 172-174)

Cornet Falls, located nearly in town, is one of the more classic hard pillar climbs of the Telluride area. A stunning creation, it pours from a small notch in a picturesque canyon on the north side of town.

On the other hand, Butcher Creek Falls, which offers decent climbing, is often overlooked because the approach requires a 20 minute hike.

Getting there: Cornet and Butcher Creek Falls lie in two parallel red sandstone canyons on the north side of Telluride.

To reach them from downtown Telluride, follow Aspen Street north until the street ends. There are a couple of boulders blocking the road from cars, and a steep, strenuous trail continues into the canyon. Just beyond the boulders the trail branch-

Cornet Falls   Photo: Doug Berry

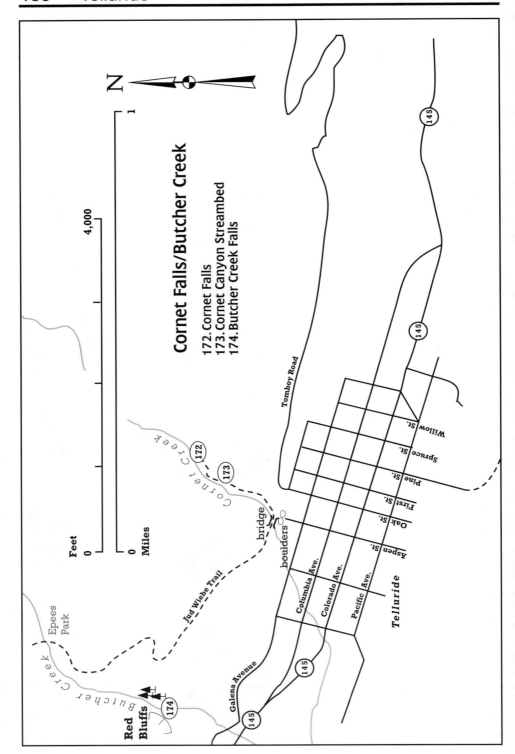

Cornet Falls/Butcher Creek

172. Cornet Falls
173. Cornet Canyon Streambed
174. Butcher Creek Falls

Mill Creek Falls

es, and the left branch crosses Cornet Creek.

To reach Cornet Falls and the Cornet Canyon Streambed, stay on the trail and hike directly north, into the canyon. Within a couple of minutes, the streambed will appear on the right, tucked in a steep corner. Cornet Falls lie just a couple of hundred feet beyond the streambed and are impossible to miss.

To reach Butcher Creek, go left over the bridge and follow the Jud Weibe Trail as it climbs across the broad open slope above town. (There's no sign announcing the trail, but it's the only one there.) After 10 minutes of hiking, the trail makes its first switchback. 100 feet before the crest of the switchback, there's an almost imperceptible gap between a couple of Aspen tree stumps. Down and to the left (sort of east south east) is an open field, bounded on the far side by a cluster of pine trees. Behind the pine trees, the top of a red cliff is just visible. Butcher Creek Falls tumble through that cliff band, behind the pines trees. A small trail skirts around the top of the falls to the right.

Admittedly, Butcher Creek falls are hard to find, but they offer a nice alternative when Cornet's all booked up.

172. Cornet Falls (WI 5, 120 feet) ★★★

The stunning, obvious pillar. Because it faces south, it has a short season. Also, the top can melt out. Bring some rock gear (medium stoppers) to supplement ice screws.

Approach time: Allow 5 minutes from the end of Aspen Street (where the boulders block the street).

Descent: Rappel off trees next to the falls, or walk off to the right.

Season: Mid-winter, when it's cold.

Road/Highway the climb is visible from: Not quite visible from town.

Access issues: None.

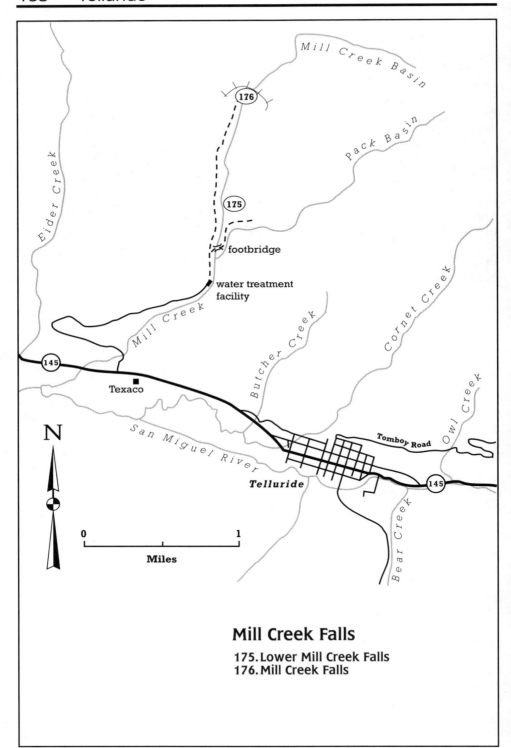

Mill Creek Falls

175. Lower Mill Creek Falls
176. Mill Creek Falls

173. Cornet Canyon Streambed (WI 2, 100 feet) ★★

A great beginner's route, tucked up in a corner on the right side of the canyon.
Approach time: Allow 5 minutes from the end of Aspen Street.
Descent: Rappel off trees next to the falls, or scramble down to the left.
Season: Mid-winter.
Road/Highway the climb is visible from: None.
Access issues: None.

174. Butcher Creek Falls (WI 4, 120 feet) ★★

A worthwhile endeavor, this waterfall is shaded by trees, and has a longer life than Cornet Falls. Most parties rappel off the big tree above the falls to get into it, the walk off.
Approach time: Allow 20 minutes from the boulders at the end of Aspen Street.
Descent: Rappel in. Walk off.
Season: All winter.
Road/Highway the climb is visible from: None, trees block the view.
Access issues: None.

Mill Creek Falls Area
(Routes 175-176)

The Mill Creek drainage near Telluride boasts a number of interesting ice routes, however, like Bear Creek, the approach is a solid mile and a half. If snows close the road to the trailhead, another mile and a half can be added onto the hike.

Getting there: Mill Creek lies west of Telluride, on the north side of Colo. 145. To reach it, drive 0.1 miles west of the big Texaco station west of town. Turn right (north) onto a dirt road, and drive 1.6 miles up the road to the water treatment plant. Park a few hundred feet back from the plant or you might be towed, as the signs warn.

The Deep Creek trailhead is on the left (west) side of the road. Follow the trail (skis and or snowshoes are a must) up the valley for about a half mile. Just before reaching a footbridge, the trail cuts up the hill to the left and switchbacks through the forest. This trail is easy to lose, but the goal on the approach is to follow the drainage another 3/4 or mile to a large rocky cirque, into which several waterfalls drain. The most prominent of these, directly at the back of the cirque, is Mill Creek Falls.

Lower Mill Creek Falls lies on the approach to Mill Creek Falls, just upstream of the footbridge described above.

175. Lower Mill Creek Falls (WI 4 to 5, 60 feet) ★★

Often, a wide curtain of quality ice forms to the right of the falls themselves, offering good climbing without too much approach wallowing. This curtain is just visible from the bridge.
Approach time: 15 minutes.
Descent: Rappel off a tree.
Season: Mid-winter.
Road/Highway the climb is visible from: None.
Access issues: None.

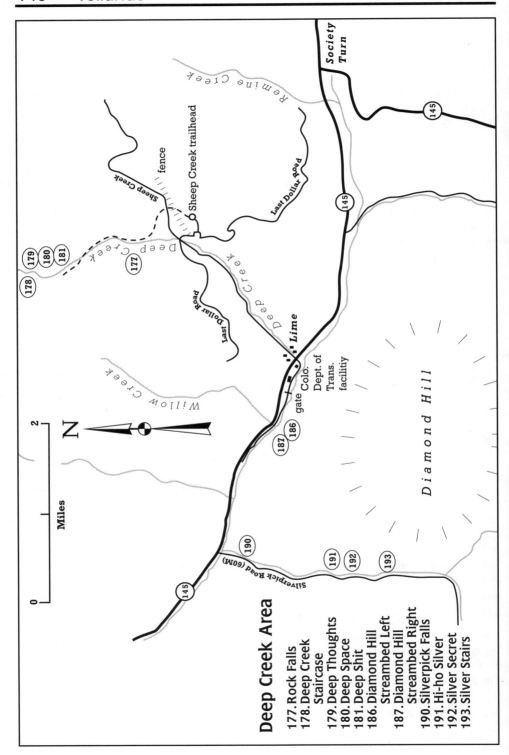

Deep Creek Area

177. Rock Falls
178. Deep Creek Staircase
179. Deep Thoughts
180. Deep Space
181. Deep Shit
186. Diamond Hill Streambed Left
187. Diamond Hill Streambed Right
190. Silverpick Falls
191. Hi-ho Silver
192. Silver Secret
193. Silver Stairs

176. Mill Creek Falls (WI 4, 180 feet) ★★★

A classic waterfall climb.

Approach time: Allow 30-45 minutes.
Descent: Rappel off a tree.
Season: Mid-winter.
Road/Highway the climb is visible from: None.
Access issues: None.

Deep Creek
(Routes 177-181)

The Deep Creek area is, basically, just one of many high valley areas in the mountains surrounding Telluride containing a handful of ice climbs. The difference between Deep Creek and other Telluride areas — like Cornet Falls, Mill Creek and other areas — is its somewhat more remote. On the good side, that equates to fewer people. On the down side, the approach is longer than many other areas mentioned in this guide. Skis are a must for this approach. (I learned this the hard way.) And while it's a relatively flat approach, allow 45 minutes or more.

Getting there: To reach the trailhead for Deep Creek, follow the Deep Creek. This dirt road lies 3.5 miles west of Society Turn, on Colo. 145.

(Society Turn is west of town, and is where Colo. 145 makes a sharp turn as it intersects the spur road leading into Telluride. This spur is also Colo. 145, but technically, the route number is S-145.)

Follow the road north (the only way you can go) for about 2.0 miles, to the intersection of Last Dollar Road.

There are two points of interest along the Deep Creek Road for ice climbers. About 0.3 miles (from the intersection of Colo. 145) up this road on the right (east) side is an ice cave, with okay ice bouldering, and 1.55 miles up the road, also on the right, is a small seep (WI 4, 40 feet) under some bushes that offers okay climbing.

Deep Creek Area. Left to right: Deep Thoughts, Deep Space, Deep Shit

About 2.0 miles up the Deep Creek Road, there's a T intersection, with Last Dollar Road. Turn right, crossing Sheep Creek almost immediately, and drive 1.1 miles to a turn off to the left, where the Sheep Creek Trailhead lies.

From the trailhead, hike northwest, sort of up the hill towards a fence on the left. Follow the fence for a few hundred feet, until you reach a gate with an old road running across the slope. Follow the old road through the fence, then around the corner, into the Sheep Creek Valley. Cross Sheep Creek again, and continue west, into the next valley, the Deep Creek Valley. The road peters out when it meets Deep Creek, near an irrigation diversion gate and becomes somewhat hard to follow. It actually crosses the stream and follows the left (east) bank of Deep Creek for about half a mile, to the rocky cirque where the Deep Creek ice routes are located. As you ascend this last half mile up the creek, there are a number of ice routes on the right wall of the canyon. While mostly ice covered rock slabs, with a few pillars here and there, they do offer decent ice. To reach the main Deep Creek climbing area, continue up the valley about half a mile from the road to a rocky cirque. You'll know you're there when you see the stunning blue ice pillars and curtains of Deep Space, and Deep Shit.

The Deep Creek area is climbable throughout the winter, however, mid-season should be avoided as some of these routes form the bottoms of avalanche chutes. Early and late season are recommended, and the area is often climbable into early May.

177. Rock Falls (WI 4, 200 feet)
On the left-hand side of the valley, just above the point where the old roadbed intersects the creek, is a frozen cascade on the left side of the canyon.
Approach time: 40 minutes
Season: Early winter, late winter.
Descent: Descend by rappelling off trees.
Road/Highway the climb is visible from: None.

178. Deep Creek Staircase (WI 4, 200 feet) ★
Toward the back of the cirque is a stream that forms a series of short waterfalls as it cascades into the valley. Climb it.
Approach time: 45-60 minutes
Season: Early winter, late winter.
Descent: Descend by walking off right, then halfway down, cross the route and walk down off to its left side.
Road/Highway the climb is visible from: None.

179. Deep Thoughts (WI 4, 150 feet) ★★
An interesting route, it looks as though it could be mixed at times (though I've never experienced that). Bring some rock gear just in case.
Approach time: 45-60 minutes
Season: Early winter, late winter.
Descent: Walk off or rappel.
Road/Highway the climb is visible from: None.

180. Deep Space (WI 4 to 5, 80 feet) ★★
A slab to a pillar or curtain.
Approach Time: 45-60 minutes
Season: Early winter, late winter.
Descent: Rappel off a tree.
Road/Highway the climb is visible from: None.

181. Deep Shit (WI 4 to 5, 80 feet) ★★
A stunning blue pillar or pillars makes this route obvious.
Approach Time: 45-60 minutes
Season: Early winter, late winter.
Descent: Rappel off a tree.
Road/Highway the climb is visible from: None.

Ilium Area
(Routes 182-185)

The Ilium area, technically called Vance Junction on the maps, is the northern end of the valley that is home to the South Fork of the San Miguel River. The upper, southern, end of this valley is where the small community of Ames lies.

Getting there: To reach the Ilium, drive west from Telluride on Colo. 145. to South Fork Road. At the intersection, turn left or south, onto South Fork Road, and pass the big gravel operation, cross the river and continue south on this dirt road.

About 1.6 miles from the intersection of Colo. 145 and South Fork Road, on the left, is the Ilium Slabs, a massive sheet of ice visible for miles around.

On the opposite side of the valley from the Ilium Slabs, high up on the hillside, is the Short Curtain.

About 2.2 miles from the intersection of Colo. 145 and South Fork Road, the road to Bilk Creek Falls and Sunshine Mesa intersects South Fork Road. Just south of this intersection, along the South Fork Road, is Vance Creek Falls, hidden in the trees on the hillside to the left (east). Hike through the woods to the falls.

About 1.1 miles south of the intersection of the South Fork and Sunshine Mesa Roads (about 3.3 miles south of the Colo. 145 and South Fork Road intersection) is Turkey Creek Falls. Like Vance Creek Falls, Turkey Creek Falls is tucked up against the mesa to the east (left). It is easily found by locating the blue-roofed house and the two brown roofed houses — Turkey Creek flows between them. Hike through the woods to the falls.

182. Ilium Slabs (WI 3 to 5, 300 feet)
The left side is harder and sometimes boasts WI 5 pillars.
Approach time: Allow 15 minutes from the road.
Descent: Rappel off trees next to the falls, or scramble down.
Season: Mid-winter.
Road/Highway the climb is visible from: The route is visible from both Colo.
      145 and the South Fork Road.
Access issues: None.

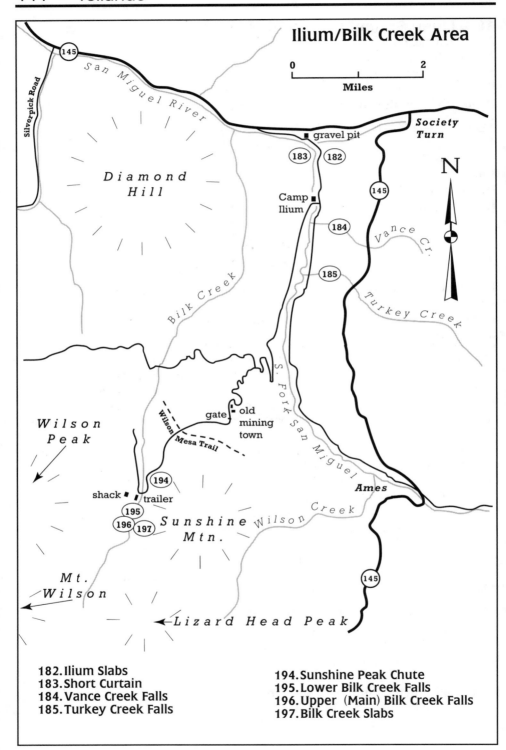

Ilium/Bilk Creek Area

182. Ilium Slabs
183. Short Curtain
184. Vance Creek Falls
185. Turkey Creek Falls

194. Sunshine Peak Chute
195. Lower Bilk Creek Falls
196. Upper (Main) Bilk Creek Falls
197. Bilk Creek Slabs

183. Short Curtain (WI 5, 40 feet)
Not worth the hike.
Approach time: Allow 15 minutes from the road.
Descent: Rappel off trees next to the falls, or scramble down.
Season: Mid-winter.
Road/Highway the climb is visible from: The route is visible from the South Fork Road.
Access issues: None.

184. Vance Creek Falls (WI 4, 100 feet)
A small waterfall.
Approach time: Allow 15 minutes from the road.
Descent: Rappel off trees next to the falls.
Season: Mid-winter.
Road/Highway the climb is visible from: None.
Access issues: None.

185. Turkey Creek Falls (WI 4, 80 feet)
Like Vance Creek Falls..
Approach time: Allow 15 minutes from the road.
Descent: Rappel off trees next to the falls.
Season: Mid-winter.
Road/Highway the climb is visible from: This route is visible from the Sunshine Mesa road.
Access issues: None.

Placerville Area
(Routes 186-193)

The downvalley area lies, essentially, down the San Miguel River Valley west of Telluride. Although pretty much everything west of Telluride qualifies as downvalley, in this case downvalley includes a handful of climbs located around Placerville and Sawpit, two tiny towns strung out along Colo. 145.

There are five four climbs in the area — The Diamond Hill Streambeds, The Bone, The Elephant, and Silverpick Falls (a.k.a. The Sword). The routes are described from east to west, down the valley, with the exception of the Sword. Even though it lies halfway between Diamond Hill and the Bone/Elephant area, it is described in a brief section devoted to Silverpick Road.

Getting there: To reach the first climb in this area, drive 3.5 miles west of Society Turn on Colo. 145.

(Society Turn is west of town, and is where Colo. 145 makes a sharp turn as it intersects the spur road leading into Telluride. This spur is also Colo. 145, but technically, the route number is S-145.)

On the right (north) will be Last Dollar Road and the way into Deep Creek. On the left will be a Colorado Department of Transportation facility (trucks, plows, road maintenance stuff). Turn left onto a small road that passes left (east) of the white dome and circles around behind it. Drive a few hundred yards to a gate.Park.

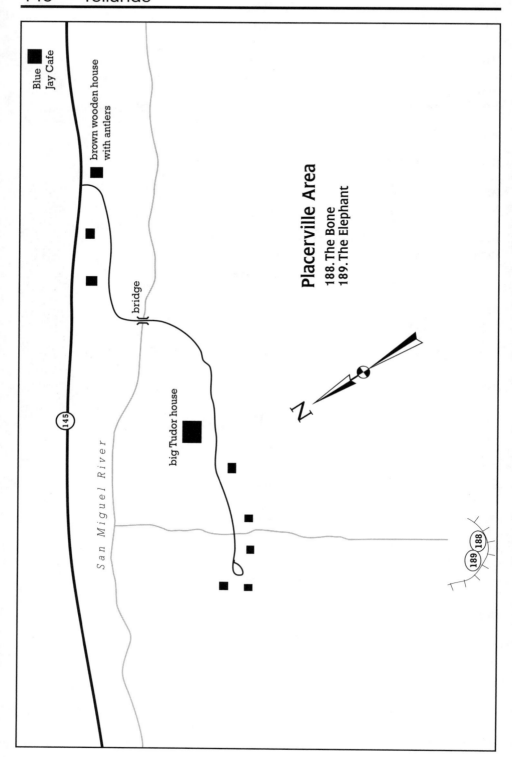

Blue
Jay Cafe

brown wooden house
with antlers

bridge

145

San Miguel River

big Tudor house

N

Placerville Area

188. The Bone
189. The Elephant

189 188

To reach the two Diamond Hill Streambeds, it's necessary to walk or ski from here. Follow the road down the right (north bank of the river). The two climbable streambeds will soon be obvious. (It's best to check them out from Colo. 145 before you hike.) Cross the river to reach the base of the routes.

To get to The Bone and The Elephant, continues west on Colo. 145, past Sawpit and Fall River Road, to a small dirt road leading off left (south), across the river. There's no great way to describe this unmarked road, except to say it lies 0.7 miles west (downvalley) of the Blue Jay Cafe or 1.8 miles east of the intersection of Colo. 145 and Colo. 62. There's a brown, wooden house with antlers over the front door on the left, as you turn into the road. Follow the road 0.5 miles, over a bridge, past a pond (on the right) and a big, Tudor-style home (also, on the right). Exactly 0.5 miles from the highway (Colo. 145) the road crosses a stream, which drains the obvious gulch to the left (south). Park on the road and follow the stream for 15-20 minutes into the gulch. The Bone and The Elephant will be obvious.

Diamond Hill Streambed Right

186. Diamond Hill Streambed Left (WI 2-3, 400 feet) ★

This is the first streambed west of the Colorado Department of Transportation facility. Check it from your car before making the stomp.

Approach time: 30 minutes
Season: All winter.
Descent: Rappel off trees.
Road/Highway the climb is visible from: Colo. 145, very easily.
Access issues: None.

187. Diamond Hill Streambed Right (WI 2-3, 400 feet) ★★

This streambed, a better outing than the left streambed, is another few hundred feet downvalley. Often, it is in good nick through May.

Approach time: 35 minutes
Season: All winter.
Descent: Rappel off trees.
Road/Highway the climb is visible from: Colo. 145, very easily.
Access issues: None.

188. The Bone (WI 5, 100 feet) ★★★

A Classic pillar dripping off the roof of a cave.

Approach Time: 15-20 minutes
Season: Midwinter.
Descent: Walk off right.
Road/Highway the climb is visible from: Colo.
    145, barely, through the trees.
Access issues: None, so far.

189. The Elephant (WI 5, 100 feet) ★

Right of The Bone and similar to The Bone, but less
reliable and the ice isn't as high quality. It faces into
the sun more.
Approach Time: 15-20 minutes
Season: Midwinter.
Descent: Walk off right.
Road/Highway the climb is visible from: None.
Access issues: None, so far.

Silverpick Road

In his excellent guide, "San Juan Ice Climbs,"
Charlie Fowler mentioned that the bulk of the
routes around Telluride are on the hard side. True,
but Silverpick Road offers several easy outings for
beginners. Avalanche danger along Silverpick Road
is low, and the following routes all form up throughout the winter although they can be thin, hollow, or
snow-covered at times.

The Bone   Photo: Doug B[

Getting there: Silverpick Road (Road 60M), runs
south, off Colo. 145, 6.1 miles west of Society Turn,
near Telluride. These climbs are described with odometer readings from the intersection of Colo. 145, and Silverpick Road.

Located just south of the river, on the left (east) side of the road, Silverpick Falls
drains the major bowl above the valley.

To reach it, drive 0.3 miles from Colo. 145, and park. There's a small pullout on
the left side of the road. Ford the creek and hike up to the climb. Hi-ho Silver is
located 1.5 miles up Silverpick Road, on the left.

1.9 miles up Silverpick Road, tucked up in a right-angling slot and not visible from
the road, is Silver Secret.

Plainly visible from Silverpick Road, 2.6 miles from Colo. 145, is Silver Stairs.

190. Silverpick Falls (WI 5, 80 feet).★★★

A Classic pillar dripping off the roof of a cave.
Approach time: 15-20 minutes
Season: Midwinter.
Descent: Rappel off a tree.
Road/Highway the climb is visible from: The route can be seen over the tops
    of the trees from both Silverpick Road, and Colo. 145.
Access issues: None.

191. Hi-ho Silver (WI 2-3, 200 feet)

This low-angle stream boasts 100 feet of WI 1 climbing, followed by a section of canyon that is choked with debris and, usually, snow. Bypass this debris-filled section, and gain the upper part of the creek for two steep steps of WI 2-3 climbing. The lower part of the route is visible from the road. The upper part is only partially visible from the road.

Approach time: 2 minutes
Season: Midwinter.
Descent: Rappel off trees and downclimb.
Road/Highway the climb is visible from: Silverpick Road.
Access issues: None.

192. Silver Secret (WI 2-3, 200 feet) ★★★

It boasts a couple of steep steps, the second being the hardest.
Approach time: 2 minutes
Season: Midwinter.
Descent: Rappel off trees and downclimb.
Road/Highway the climb is visible from: None.
Access issues: None.

Charlie Fowler on SilverpickFalls

Photo: Doug Berry

193. Silver Stairs (WI 2-3, 200 feet) ★

More WI 3 climbing (at the top). There's another step up high.
Approach time: 2 minutes
Season: Midwinter.
Descent: Rappel off trees and downclimb.
Road/Highway the climb is visible from: Silverpick Road.
Access issues: None.

Bilk Creek Falls Area
(Routes 194-197)

The Bilk Creek valley is one of the most beautiful ice climbing venues around. A high valley that drains the west side of Sunshine Peak and the east side of Wilson Peak, climbing the several frozen waterfalls that form here are worth the rather lengthy, but easy approach.

Getting there: Bilk Creek lies up on the mesa west of Ilium. To reach Bilk Creek, drive West on Highway 145 from Telluride to the South Fork Road.

Turn south (left if you're coming from Telluride) onto South Fork Road. Follow it

Bilk Creek Slabs is on the left; Lower Bilk Creek Falls is on the extreme right

for 2.2 miles, to Camp Ilium (a collection of buildings west of the road), then turn right, onto 63J Road (the road immediately south of Camp Ilium).

From this intersection — South Fork Road and 63J Road — it's 5.55 miles to the trailhead for Bilk Creek. Follow 63J Road up the hill west of the camp. The road cuts across the slope, then makes one switchback before reaching the top of Wilson Mesa. 3.85 miles from the intersection is a large ranch on the right. (A U.S. Forest Service sign stating "Wilson Mesa Trail, Lizard Head Trail" will become obvious.)

Often, the road is only passable to this point. Then it's necessary to ski the remaining 1.7 miles to the trailhead. If it is possible to continue, drive along the road another 0.3 miles (that's 4.15 from the South Fork Road and 63J Road inter-section) to a fork in the road. Follow the left fork for 1.4 miles, until the end of the road (which consists of a closure gate across the road) is reached. (1.2 miles past the fork you'll pass an old mining town, consisting of several shacks.) You'll know you're there when you see a sign declaring :"Wilson Mesa Trail No. 421. Bilk Creek 2. Lizard Head Trail 2." At this point, skis or snowshoes are generally a good idea.

From the closure gate, an old dirt road leads into the woods. It traverses the northern side of Sunshine Peak and leads into the huge Bilk Creek Valley. Hike along the road. About 10 minutes into the hike, the Wilson Mesa Trail will branch off right, into the trees. Stay on the road as it emerges from the woods into the upper Bilk Creek Valley.

In recent years, the road has been washed away, so be careful crossing the nar-row, remaining sections.

Another 10 minutes of hiking will put you below Sunshine Peak Chute, an avalanche chute that boasts a creek. There are no real landmarks here, but the chute, is on the left (east) side of the road, about 200 yards above the road, and can hold climbable ice.

To reach Bilk Creek, continue along the old road as it winds down to Bilk Creek. The trail crosses the creek, then goes left, between an old, red construction trailer and an old, semi-crushed shack. From this little mining community, it's another 20 minutes to the climbs up the valley.

Follow the trail through the trees. Upper and Lower Bilk Creek Falls will soon come into view, as will the Bilk Creek slabs off to the left, about 200 yards up the slope on a subsidiary creek. As the trail emerges onto an open talus field, Lower Bilk Creek Falls can be accessed by traversing down and left to the creek. To reach the upper falls, there are two options: 1. Climb the lower falls then follow the streambed for several hundred yards to the base of the Upper Falls, or 2. stay on the trail for another quarter mile. It passes within a few hundred feet of the base of the upper falls.

To reach the Bilk Creek slabs, merely wander across the main branch of Bilk Creek and over to them.

194. Sunshine Peak Chute (WI 4, 50 feet)

Early in the season, a chute above the road on the way to Bilk Creek freezes up. Most of the year it's too snow-filled to climb (not to mention way too dangerous), but very early in the season it can be climbable.

Approach time: Allow 25 minutes from the closed gate. Longer if snows close the road further down.

Descent: Walk off left or right of the route.

Season: Late fall. This climb sits in the middle of an avalanche chute. Don't climb it in winter. You'll get clobbered.

Road/Highway the climb is visible from: None.

Access issues: None.

195. Lower Bilk Creek Falls (WI 3, 60 feet) ★★

A classic, easy pillar forms in the small rock band that squirts Bilk Creek to the west (right as viewed from the trail).

Approach time: Allow an hour from the closed gate. Longer if snows close the road further down.

Descent: Walk off either left or right.

Season: Late fall/early winter. Avalanche danger in this area is extreme, so get these climbs in before things get dicey.

Road/Highway the climb is visible from: None.

Access issues: None.

196. Upper (Main) Bilk Creek Falls (WI 4, 200 feet) ★★★

A beautiful series of cascading steps, Bilk Creek's Upper or Main Falls are a must-do for any ice climber.

Approach time: Allow an hour from the closed gate. Longer if snows close the road further down.

Descent: Rappel off trees next to the falls.

Season: Late fall/early winter. As mentioned, avalanche danger in this area is
extreme.
Road/Highway the climb is visible from: None.
Access issues: None.

197. Bilk Creek Slabs (WI 4-5, 120 feet) ★★

Although not actually on the main stem of Bilk Creek, a big, wide slab forms on the
hillside east of the Bilk Creek. It has many possible lines, including some thin,
mixed variations.
Approach time: Allow an hour from the closed gate. Longer if snows close the
road further down.
Descent: Walk off or rappel
Season: Late fall/early winter. Beware! This slab sits in the middle of an avalanche
chute.
Road/Highway the climb is visible from: None.
Access issues: None.

Ames Area
(Routes 198-203)

Ames is one of the smallest most inconspicuous communities in the state. Tucked
in the crook of Colo. 145, as it circles around the junction of the Howard and South
Forks of the San Miguel River, the dozen or some homes are barely noticeable to
passing motorists.

In sharp contradiction is one of the state's most notorious routes, the Ames Ice
Hose. A 150-foot wide swath of ice teetering on a steep, 600-foot cliff west of town,
the Ames Ice Hose is one of Colorado's legendary ice routes. But the Ice Hose isn't
the only game in town. Remarkably, Ames offers as many easy routes as it does
hard routes.

Getting there: To reach Ames, drive south of Telluride on Colo. 145 to the
Ames/Ilium Road, which descends into the valley to the west. Follow this road a
short way, then turn left. Ames lies down this road a half mile. The parking for
most routes in the area is at the "Ames Station" power plant, the first building in
town, on the left.

Ames Falls, Upper Ames Falls, and the Ames Falls Practice Areas are accessed by
hiking southwest from the power plant, passing an old green house on its right,
then an old shed on its left. Cut through the trees towards the low point in the valley. The Ames Falls Practice Area is located on the north-facing slope of hill, just a
few hundred feet southwest of the shed.

From the practice area, continue southwest a couple of hundred feet to reach
Ames Falls. It's best to rappel into the base of the falls.

Upper Ames Falls is reached by following the river upstream several hundred yards.

To reach the Ames Ice Hose, park at the power plant and at the old shed, cut left,
following the power lines, until an old railroad grade is reached. Follow the railroad
grade all the way around the valley to the base of the Ames Wall, and the Ice Hose.

The Howard Fork Canyon lies just downhill from the Colo. 145-Ames/Ilium Road

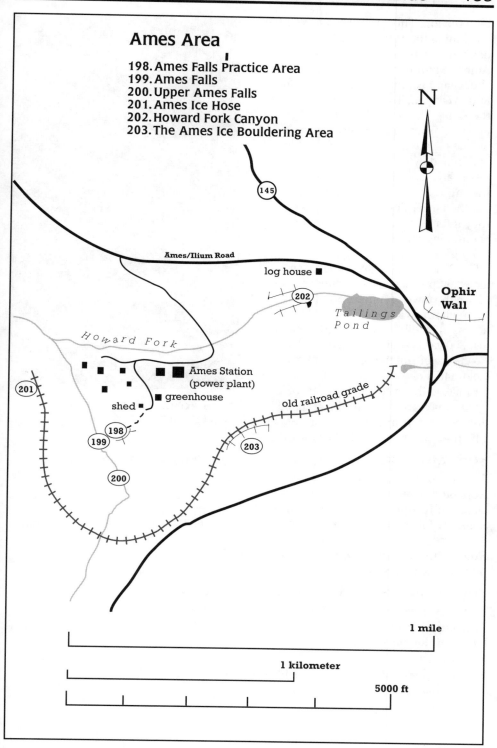

Ames Area

198. Ames Falls Practice Area
199. Ames Falls
200. Upper Ames Falls
201. Ames Ice Hose
202. Howard Fork Canyon
203. The Ames Ice Bouldering Area

intersection. The narrow slot of a canyon containing the Howard Fork River suddenly deepens as it plunges towards Ames. A number of exceptional pillars, sheets and columns — all hard — form in this canyon. To reach it, drive down the Ames/Ilium Road 0.4 miles. Just downhill from a big log house, the ice will be visible through the trees. Park and hike down.

This area can also be accessed from the Ames Ice Bouldering area, by following the power lines to the point where they intersect with the canyon, then scrambling down a steep ramp or rappelling.

The Ames Ice Bouldering Area, an excellent practice and teaching area lies above the town of Ames, sort of halfway between Ames and Colo. 145. It is accessed by hiking from a parking area just 200 yards south of the Ames/Ilium Road turn off, on the right (west) side of Colo. 145. Follow the old grade for a quarter mile, to the exceptional sheets of ice.

The Ames area can also be reached by driving west from Telluride, on Colo. 145, then south, on South Fork Road.

Ames Access. Left to right: Ames Falls Practice Area, Ames FAlls

198. Ames Falls Practice Area (WI 3 to 4, 70 feet) ★
A small bowl holding ice.
Approach time: Allow 5 minutes.
Descent: Rappel off trees or walk off left.
Season: All winter. This area is often in good shape long after Ames Falls is runny and wet.
Road/Highway the climb is visible from: Colo. 145.
Access issues: None.

199. Ames Falls (WI 4-5, 90 feet) ★★★
The classic waterfall climb of the area. Easily top-roped off trees.
Approach time: Allow 10 minutes.
Descent: Rappel in. Walk off.
Season: All winter.
Road/Highway the climb is visible from: Colo. 145, barely.
Access issues: None.

200. Upper Ames Falls
(WI 4, 50 feet)

Approach time: Allow 20 minutes.
Descent: Rappel in. Walk off.
Season: All winter.
Road/Highway the climb is visible from:
None.
Access issues: None.

201. Ames Ice Hose
(WI 5, 600 feet) ★★★

The classic hard route of the area. Usually done in four pitches, the first two are generally thin and/or mixed. Bring rock gear. Atop the first pitch, belay off to the left side, to avoid being hit by falling ice from the second lead. Pitch two follows the chimney. Pitches three and four are steep, high-quality ice. Avalanche danger is moderate.
Approach time: Allow 30-40 minutes.
Descent: To descend, rappel the route or
    walk off to the left.
Season: All winter. It often stays good
    through to early May.
**Road/Highway the climb is visible
    from:** This route is visible from most
    roads in the area.
Access issues: None.

Ames Ice Hose Photo: Doug Berry

202. Howard Fork Canyon
(WI 5 to 5+, 100 feet) ★★

Pillars, curtains ... the works. Go nuts! Although it's possible to downclimb into the canyon, it's easier to rappel. The best routes are on the south (north-facing) side of the canyon, but some routes form up on the north (south-facing) wall as well. Good top-roping.
Approach time: 5 minutes.
Descent: Rap in, climb out.
Season: All winter. It often stays good
    through to early May.
**Road/Highway the climb is visible
    from:** This route is visible from the Ames/Ilium Road, near the house.
Access issues: The access route might cross private land. Be low-key.

Howard Fork Canyon

Ames Overview. Left to right: Ames Falls Practice Area, Ames Falls

203. The Ames Ice Bouldering Area (WI 2-4, 60 feet) ★★★
Killer bouldering on big, thick, wide sheets of ice.
Approach time: 5 minutes.
Descent: Walk off.
Season: All winter. It often stays good through to early May.
Road/Highway the climb is visible from: This route is visible from throughout
the area.
Access issues: None.

Ophir Area
(Routes 204-209)

The Ophir area includes everything along the Ophir Road in the Howard Fork valley, the valley east of Colo. 145 as it encircles the Ames area.

Getting there: The first ice climbs of note in this area form on the large southwestern corner of the Ophir Wall above the intersection of Colo. 145 and the Ophir Road.

0.5 miles up the Ophir Road from Colo. 145, on the left (north) side of the valley, is Cracked Canyon. Tucked up in this narrow mountain cleft, about a quarter mile from the Ophir Road, is the Cracked Canyon Ice Fall.

1.5 miles up the Ophir Road from Colo. 145, on the left (north) side of the valley, is a long staircase of very low-angled ice, Ophir of Flying. The route is visible from the Ophir Road, unless it is covered by snow.

The historic town of Ophir lies 2.3 miles up the road from Colo. 145. To the south (right), is Waterfall Canyon. To reach it and the several ice climbs in the canyon, continue east, to East Ophir, 0.4 miles beyond Ophir. it might be necessary to park here, if snow cover the road.

From East Ophir, an old road skirts the southeast side of the valley and cuts along the hill side into Waterfall Canyon. Hike it into the canyon.

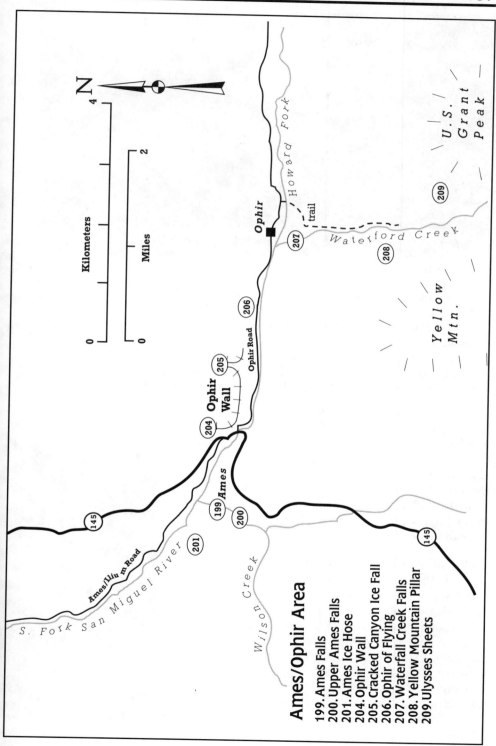

Ames/Ophir Area

199. Ames Falls
200. Upper Ames Falls
201. Ames Ice Hose
204. Ophir Wall
205. Cracked Canyon Ice Fall
206. Ophir of Flying
207. Waterfall Creek Falls
208. Yellow Mountain Pillar
209. Ulysses Sheets

Ophir of Flying

The first big falls reached in this canyon are Waterfall Creek Falls. They rarely freeze, but in cold winters can offer a challenging outing.

Further up the valley, on the lower slopes of Yellow Mountain on the right, a prominent short pillar regularly forms, the Yellow Mountain Pillar, along with a number of other seeps and smears.

The Ulysses Sheets are further up the valley, on the left, on the slopes of U.S. Grant Peak. None of the routes up Waterfall Canyon are visible from the road.

204. Ophir Wall (various)

Several routes form on the left end of the Ophir Wall. These routes — and their dozens of variations — are generally thin, hard (WI 4 to 6) and require extensive mixed climbing.

Approach time: 5 minutes.
Descent: Rappel off fixed anchors and scramble left.
Season: Mid-winter.
Road/Highway the climb is visible from: Colo. 145.
Access issues: None.

205. Cracked Canyon Ice Fall
(WI 5+, 250 feet) ★★★

The first pitch can either be a steep ice column or rock, depending on conditions. The second pitch is a ramp (WI 4), with a steep finish (WI 5). Rock Gear is thoroughly recommended. You'll use it more than ice gear.Approach time: 10 minutes.

Descent: Rappel off fixed anchors left of the route.
Season: Mid-winter.
Road/Highway the climb is visible from: The route is visible from the Ophir Road.
Access issues: None.

Cracked Canyon Photo: Dou

206. Ophir of Flying (WI 1, 200 feet)

A good place to show someone how to place ice screws. Not a good warm-up for the Cracked Canyon icefall. Check it out in late or early season.

Approach time: 2 minutes.
Descent: Walk off.
Season: Mid-winter.
Road/Highway the climb is visible from: The route is visible from the Ophir Road.
Access issues: None.

207. Waterfall Creek Falls (WI 4, 130 feet)

The falls rarely freeze, but in cold winters can offer a challenging outing.

Approach time: 20 minutes.
Descent: Walk off or rappel.
Season: Mid-winter during a cold winter.
Road/Highway the climb is visible from: The route is visible from the Ophir Road and the town of Ophir.
Access issues: None.

208. Yellow Mountain Pillar (WI 5, 60 feet)

Approach time: 30 minutes.
Descent: Walk off or rappel.
Season: Mid-winter, although avalanche danger is high.
Road/Highway the climb is visible from: None.
Access issues: None.

209. Ulysses Sheets (WI 3, 60-80 feet)

Easy sheets.

Approach time: 40 minutes.
Descent: Walk off or rappel.
Season: Mid-winter, although avalanche danger is high.
Road/Highway the climb is visible from: None.
Access issues: None.

Dunton/Rico Area
(Routes 210-214)

Dunton is a small, former mining town that sits at the top of the West Dolores River. The small town itself was bought in 1994 by a couple of Telluride investors who have turned it into something of a high-dollar resort, available only on a weekly basis. (The small cabins, renovated inside, run about $350 a night, in case you're wondering.)

There are also a few ice climbs of note in the Dunton area, the best of which is Eagle Creek Falls.

To reach Dunton from the Telluride area, drive south on Colo. 145 about 24.0 miles. (From the south, drive north on Colo. 145 from Dolores.) From just south of the community of Stoner, take Forest Road 535.

From the intersection of the two roads (Colo. 145 and Forest Road 535) drive it's 21 miles to Dunton.

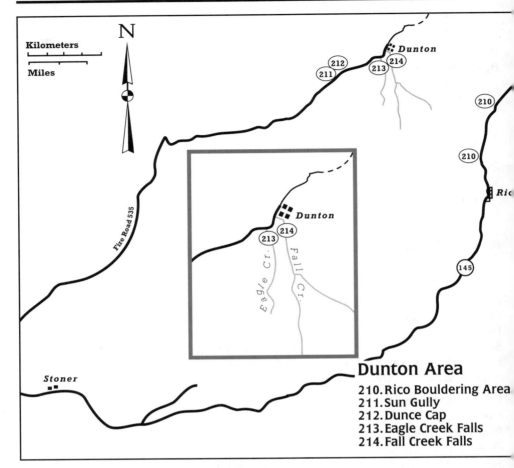

Dunton Area
210. Rico Bouldering Area
211. Sun Gully
212. Dunce Cap
213. Eagle Creek Falls
214. Fall Creek Falls

About 20 miles up Forest Road 535, on the left, are a series of red cliffs. Two routes of note form up here, although the approaches to them lie on private property.

Sun Gully is 20.3 miles from the intersection of Colo. 145 and Forest Road 535, and sits on the hillside behind a ranch with an obvious wooden fence. Dunce Cap, a gully similar to Sun Gully, sits upvalley about 0.3 miles beyond Sun Gully, behind a large metal ranch building.

Eagle Creek Falls is located 21.6 miles north on Forest Road 535. It sits on the right-hand (east) wall of the valley, back behind the Emma Mine Co. property, in the obvious drainage.

Fall Creek Falls is located in the heart of Dunton, this short waterfall lies on public land but to reach it requires crossing privately-owned Dunton. To get permission, call Bernt Kuhlmann, one of the owners of Dunton, and ask permission. His phone number in Telluride is 970-728-4840. If you're interested in getting a beer at the saloon in town, forget it. It's available for private functions only.

Also, there are a couple of ice bouldering areas along the west side of the road near Rico that are of note.

From Rico, the two areas are 1.9 miles and 4.0 miles north on Colo. 145 respectively. The first area is a series of cascades that form just south of a road cut. The second area is tucked back in a small (50-foot high) cirque. Both are visible from the road, although to find the second area requires a keen eye.

Dunton/Rico Area Routes

210. Rico Bouldering Areas
Good in a cold winter.
Approach time: 10 seconds.
Descent: Downclimb.
Season: Mid-winter.
Road/Highway the climb is visible from: Colo. 145.
Access issues: None, but don't fall on a car..

211. Sun Gully (WI 3, 200 feet)
Rarely, if ever, forms well. Often thin and rotten. At least you can check it out from the road first.
Approach time: 10 minutes.
Descent: Rappel off trees.
Season: Mid-winter.
Road/Highway the climb is visible from: Forest Road 535.
Access issues: The access and the climb are on private land.

212. Dunce Cap (WI 3, 250 feet)
Fickle and rarely forms.
Approach time: 10 minutes.
Descent: Rappel off trees.
Season: Mid-winter.
Road/Highway the climb is visible from: Forest Road 535.
Access issues: The access and the climb are on private land.

213. Eagle Creek Falls (WI 4, 100 feet) ★
The best route in the area, Eagle Creek Falls ain't much compared to other San Juan ice climbs.
Approach time: 10 minutes.
Descent: Rappel off trees.
Season: Mid-winter.
Road/Highway the climb is visible from: Forest Road 535.
Access issues: None.

214. Fall Creek Falls (WI 3, 40 feet)
Not worth the trip, or the effort.
Approach time: 2 minutes.
Descent: Rappel off trees.
Season: Mid-winter.
Road/Highway the climb is visible from: Forest Road 535.
Access issues: See introduction above.

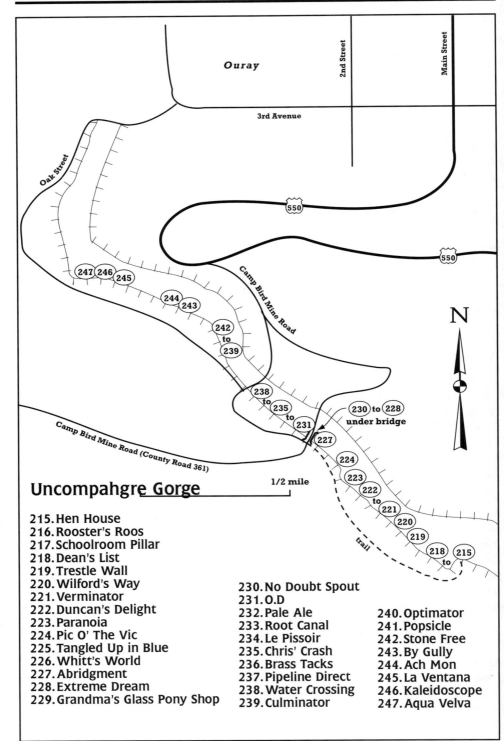

Ouray

2nd Street

Main Street

3rd Avenue

Oak Street

550

550

Camp Bird Mine Road

247 246 245

244 243

242 to 239

238 to 235 to 231

230 to 228
under bridge

227

224

223

222 to 221

220

219

218 to 215

N

Camp Bird Mine Road (County Road 361)

trail

1/2 mile

Uncompahgre Gorge

215. Hen House
216. Rooster's Roos
217. Schoolroom Pillar
218. Dean's List
219. Trestle Wall
220. Wilford's Way
221. Verminator
222. Duncan's Delight
223. Paranoia
224. Pic O' The Vic
225. Tangled Up in Blue
226. Whitt's World
227. Abridgment
228. Extreme Dream
229. Grandma's Glass Pony Shop

230. No Doubt Spout
231. O.D
232. Pale Ale
233. Root Canal
234. Le Pissoir
235. Chris' Crash
236. Brass Tacks
237. Pipeline Direct
238. Water Crossing
239. Culminator

240. Optimator
241. Popsicle
242. Stone Free
243. By Gully
244. Ach Mon
245. La Ventana
246. Kaleidoscope
247. Aqua Velva

SOUTHWESTERN MOUNTAINS

Ouray
(Routes 215-284)

"The best way to learn? Do it! Make mistakes; really screw up. This about describes my early climbing career."
— Warren Harding, Downward Bound

Ouray makes one believe God is an ice climber.

And, the sheer amount of fat, blue, plastic ice around this tiny town in the San Juans will make you think you're in heaven.

Nowhere else in North America, or perhaps the world, can you get so much superb quality climbing so close to the road, hotels, bars, hot-tubs and other elements of civilization.

There's the Uncompahgre Gorge (a.k.a. the Box Canyon), with its hundreds of routes and variations (most of which are excellent), there's the Skylight Area, where you can literally belay from the driver's seat. Then there's Red Mountain Pass with its long, mixed cruises.

If you're an ice climber living in Colorado, you ain't seen nothing until you've seen Ouray.

In more practical terms, Ouray lies along U.S. 550, about halfway between Grand Junction and Durango. It's not as expensive as its neighbor, Telluride, because there's no ski resort in Ouray, but things can be pricey.

If you're looking for lodging, ask around. Many hotels, like the Victorian Inn, offer discounts to ice climbers (the owners of the Vic are ice climbers).

There are several good restaurants, and a couple of gas stations, a couple of stores sell ice gear, but shopping for groceries is pretty limited. Best to pickup those Pop Tarts and weiners in Durango or Montrose, before heading into Ouray.

The biggest winter attraction in Ouray (after the ice climbing), is the Hot Springs Pool. A long soak with a gently falling snow is a great way to relax after a hard day on the ice ... or in the bar. (Don't forget to bring your shorts, though. They don't rent bathing suits.)

The routes in this guide are divided up into areas of Ouray, with the Uncompahgre Gorge being described firs. Then, it moves on to Ouray North (Dexter Creek Slabs, Skyrocket, etc.), the Camp Bird Mine Road Area, and, finally, Red Mountain Pass.

Uncompahgre Gorge
(Routes 215-247)

The Uncompahgre Gorge, also known as the Box Canyon, is the centerpiece of Ouray ice climbing. With its short approach, ease of access, great ice and lack of avalanche danger, the area upvalley (south) of the County Road 361 bridge has long been one of the most popular ice climbing venues in the world. It has also served for three decades as a teaching area, where top-ropes are easily set up and the ice is sinker and plastic.

In 1994, town leaders in Ouray recognized the importance of ice climbing to Ouray's winter economy, and allowed a group of local ice climbers to install, essentially, an irrigation system, bringing water to all parts of the canyon is controllable amounts.

As soon as all that water starting flowing, a hardcore group of locals began devising new and interesting routes and dozens of variations.

Today, the Uncompahgre Gorge boasts reliable ice from late November until late April, as well as dozens of established routes and hundreds of variations. More hoses, spickets and piping is planned for the coming years, so the park is destined to grow considerably. The best aspect of the Canyon is that it is close to town, and cars can be left at your hotel.

Getting there: To reach the Gorge by foot from Ouray, head, basically to the southwest corner of town. More specifically, walk south to 3rd Ave., then west to Oak St., then south. The Gorge will become obvious.

By car, it's best to drive south on U.S. 550 (towards Silverton and Durango), then take County Road 361 (a.k.a the Camp Bird Mine Road) to the bridge over the Gorge, and park. There are numerous parking areas on both sides of the bridge.

The routes are described from the top of the canyon downhill, in sections. Because the routes are literally only a few feet apart, the best reference is a map of the Gorge.

As far as all the details go, none of these routes have access issues, they're good all winter long, the approach is five minutes or less, and many of the routes can be seen from County Road 361 or Oak St. Descents are either by rappel off established anchors, off trees, or by walking off.

All the routes in the Gorge are a ropelength (160 feet) or less. In other words, you need two ropes to top-rope most of them. Also, every route here has about a hundred variations. You can't get bored.

Rooster's Roost

Upper Gorge Area

While it's pretty easy to rappel into the Gorge just about anywhere, there's is a trail leading into the Upper Gorge Area from the west (uphill) side of County Road 361 bridge. It takes three minutes walk to reach the bottom of the Gorge at its upvalley end.

215. Hen House (WI 2, 60 feet) ★★
An easy slab, upstream from the trail that leads into the top of the Gorge. (It's to the right, as you descend the last few feet into the Gorge).

216. Rooster's Roost (WI 3-4) ★★★
A long slab just downstream of the trail. On the left as you descend into the Gorge.

217. Schoolroom Pillar (WI 4-4+) ★★★
Just downstream (climber's right) from Rooster's Roost. Excellent short pillar over a roof to a long slab above.

218. Dean's List (WI 4, 5.11)
Steep bolted wall downstream from the Schoolroom Pillar. 4 bolts.

219. Trestle Wall (WI 3+/4-) ★★
Below the old trestle. Many variations.

220. Wilford's Way (MI 6/7) ★
A mixed route on the right side of the alcove below the trestle.

221. Verminator (WI 4) ★★★
There are two arêtes in the area upstream of the bridge. This route is on the upstream side of the upstream arête. It tackles a hanging pencil then leads to easier ground above.

222. Duncan's Delight (WI 5) ★★★
A smear on the downstream side of the upstream arête. (Got it?)

223. Paranoia (WI 4) ★★
The scary, brown-walled area between the two arêtes.

224. Pic O' The Vic (WI 4) ★★★
The long sheet visible from the bridge. There's a small tree halfway up the route.

Tangled Up in Blue

225. Tangled Up in Blue (WI 4-5) ★★★
A series of columns and stances, just upstream from the bridge.

226. Whitt's World (WI 4) ★
Start on the slab, then wander up to the top.

227. Abridgment (WI 4) ★★
The first route upstream from the bridge. It starts directly under the uphill edge of the bridge.

Under the Bridge Area
The following three routes are under the County Road 361 bridge. Rapping in is easiest.

228. Extreme Dream (WI 5) ★★
Under the left (upstream) side bridge next to Abridgment.

229. Grandma's Glass Pony Shop (WI 6) ★
A desperate route up the chadeliered pencil under the center of the bridge.

Abridgment

230. No Doubt Spout (WI 5) ★★★
Under the right (downstream) edge of the bridge.

New Faithful Area
This area lies just downstream from the County Road 361 Bridge, and is identified due to the yellow ice in the area. There are four separated routes here.

231. O.D.On Ice (WI 5)
Leftmost of the four routes. Cauliflowered ice.

232. Pale Ale (WI 5+)
Just right of O.D. Steep, thin climbing.

233. Root Canal (WI 6)
Like Pale Ale, but right (downstream of it). Steep, brittle, hard to protect.

234. Le Pissoir (WI 5) ★★
The right-hand (downstream) of the four routes.

Between the Bridges Section

These climbs are between the County Road 361 Bridge, and the second bridge crossing the gorge, which lies downstream. In other words, these climbs are just downstream from the New Faithful Area.

235. Chris' Crash (WI 5)
Large, hanging slab just downstream from the New Faithful area. There's a fixed pin in the cave at the bottom.

236. Brass Tacks (WI 4-5)
An old classic.

237. Pipeline Direct (WI 4) ★★★
Under the trestle where the pipe crosses the gorge.

238. Water Crossing (WI 4) ★★
A couple of feet downstream from Pipeline Direct.

Lower Gorge Section

This are lies below the lower bridge (which is closed) in the Gorge.

239. Culminator (WI 5)
The first route downstream from the lower bridge.

240. Optimator (WI 5)
Downstream from the Culminator.

241. Popsicle (WI 5-6) ★★
Steep chandaliered ice.

242. Stone Free (WI 5) ★★★
Thin at the top.

243. By Gully (WI 3) ★
Mixed gully right of Stone Free.

244. Ach Mon (WI 3) ★
Mixed gully right of By Gully.

245. La Ventana (WI 5+) ★★★
A thin, steep pillar.

246. Kaleidoscope (WI 4) ★★★
Left side of Aqua Velva.

247. Aqua Velva (WI 4) ★★
The big blue slab below the obvious mushroom.

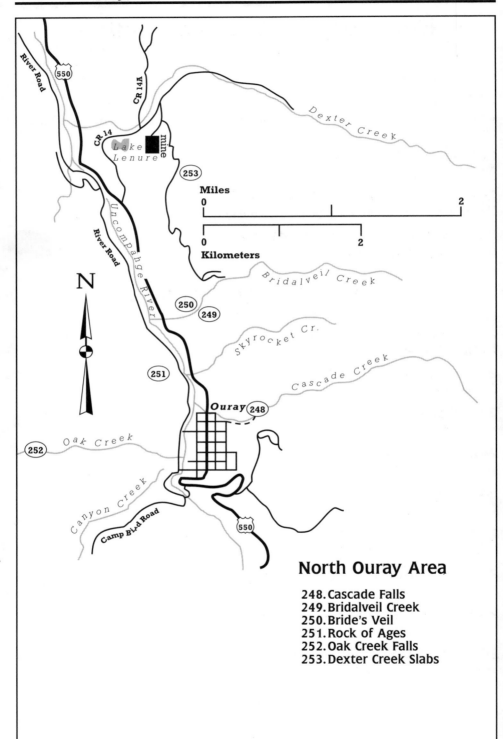

Miles

Kilometers

North Ouray Area

248. Cascade Falls
249. Bridalveil Creek
250. Bride's Veil
251. Rock of Ages
252. Oak Creek Falls
253. Dexter Creek Slabs

North Ouray Area
(Routes 248-253)

Ouray is tucked up in the mountains so well that a number of waterfalls pour directly into town. There are all close to town, but unlike the Uncompahgre Gorge, they lie on the outskirts of the metro Ouray area and either require driving or a long walk to reach.

Quickly, the specific routes are: Cascade Falls, Bridalveil Creek (better known as Skyrocket Creek) and Bride's Veil, Rock Of Ages, and Oak Creek Falls.

While these routes are all classics, they form with less reliability than other ice flows in the area. Still, if it's a cold year, check 'em out.

Note: Lower Dexter Creek Canyon, which houses a number of excellent hard ice routes has been closed to ice climbing by the property owner. Big, yellow steel signs that are hard to vandalize and impossible to move have been placed all around the lower canyon, warning ice climbers away. The landowner has reportedly had ice climbers arrested on numerous occasions for trespassing. Hence, the excellent climbs of Lower Dexter Creek Canyon are not included in this edition of this guidebook.

Getting there: To reach Cascade Falls from Main St., take 8th Ave. east (up the hill) until the end of the street. There's a fence across the road, and a massive sign describing Cascade Falls. Park here and hike the quarter mile or so to the falls.

Bridalveil Creek has long been known by climbers as Skyrocket Creek, something of a geographic error that has persisted through the ages. (After all, Skyrocket's a really cool name.) Skyrocket Creek is actually a low-angled stream of no interest to ice climbers that lies just south of Bridalveil Creek.

Bride's Veil is one of two spectacular waterfalls that drain into a tight, yellow/orange canyon on the north side of town, and often, this route in particular is still called the Skyrocket.

Anyway, to reach Bridalveil Creek and Bride's Veil, drive north of town on Highway 550.

Located 0.6 miles north of the hot springs pool (and just a few hundred feet north of the Red Mountain Lodge, Timber Ridge Motel sand Texaco Station) is a big, old brown wooden sign, touting Ouray's Hot Springs pool and Box Canyon Falls. Park at the sign. Bridalveil Creek is to the east (right, if you're coming from Ouray). Hike up the drainage, following the creek that drains the two falls. Bride's Veil — steeper and longer — will be on the left wall of the canyon, while Bridalveil Creek drains the back wall of the canyon.

Oak Creek Falls is located in the narrow canyon on the west side of town, Oak Creek Falls has difficult access and is rarely in good form.

The official public access follows a trail from high on the hillside above Ouray. To reach the trailhead, drive west to Oak St. in downtown Ouray. Then, turn west onto Queen, then left on Pine Crest. Follow Pine Crest up the hill until the street steepens. There's a number of 'no trespassing' and 'private property' signs here, making it seem as though you're entering private property. You are, but the road is a public thoroughfare. Drive up it as far as you can. It makes several switchbacks before reaching the trailhead. Then follow the trail into the falls.

Left to right: Bride's Veil, Bridalveil Creek

The Dexter Creek Slabs is one of the best easy routes in the Ouray area, despite its distant location from town. To reach it, drive north out of Ouray. (Go about 1 .7 miles from the north edge of town.) Dexter Creek Road, (County Road 14), a dirt road, will diverge off to the right, up a hill. Follow this onto the mesa, passing Lake Lenore on the lake's left side. 1.0 miles up County Road 14, County Road 14A will branch off left. Stay on County Road 14 and go straight. About a quarter mile later, the road will fork again. (The left branch goes into the National Forest.) Veer right. Bypass the mine to the left, and drive as far as the snow allows. Park. From just about anywhere, the Slabs should be visible, high on the hillside to the southeast. Wander up gullies to the base of the ice.

Occasionally, several routes form on the Rock of Ages, the west (east-facing) walls of the valley, just north of town, a few hundred yards north of the hot springs pool. To access them, drive north from the big wooden sign for about 3 miles, until you reach a bridge going west, across the Uncompahgre River. Drive over to the west bank, and follow Ouray County Road 17 ("River Road") back towards town until you're under the cliff.

248. Cascade Falls (WI 4 to 5, 300 feet) ★★

Cascade Falls is rarely in good condition, due to its location up against is a large south-facing cliff, but when it is reported to be a very classic climb. In recent years, the town of Ouray has made Cascade Falls into something of a park.

Approach time: 15 minutes by foot; 5 by car.
Descent: Descent is by rappel, off a tree.

Season: A cold winter.

Road/Highway the climb is visible from: This climb is visible from the south side of town. The best way to check it out without hiking anywhere first is to drive south, out of Ouray, up towards Red Mountain Pass for a mile or so.

Access issues: None.

249. Bridalveil Creek (WI 3 to 4, 100 feet)

The creek in the back of the drainage. Rarely in good condition.

Approach time: 15 minutes.

Descent: Descent is by rappel, off a tree.

Season: Winter.

Road/Highway the climb is visible from: The best way to check out the condition of this climb from your car is to drive north from the big wooden sign for about 3 miles, until you reach a bridge going west, across the Uncompahgre River. Drive over to the west bank, and follow Ouray County Road 17 ("River Road") back towards town until the climbs are visible over the tops of the trees.

Access issues: None.

250. Bride's Veil (WI 5, 120 feet) ★★★

The classic route of the area. Still called Skyrocket by most climbers.

Approach time: 15 minutes.

Descent: Rappel off trees.

Season: Winter.

Road/Highway the climb is visible from: Same as for the previous route.

Access issues: None.

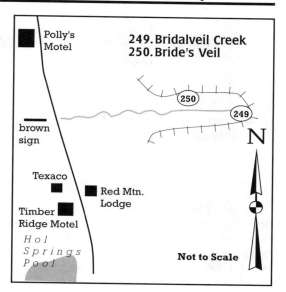

Bride's Veil   Photo: Doug Berry

251. Rock of Ages
(WI 4 to 5, 250 feet)
Rarely, if ever, in.
Approach time: 5 minutes.
Descent: Descent is by rappel, off trees.
Season: A cold winter.
Road/Highway the climb is visible from:
This climb is visible from throughout the area.
Access issues: None.

252. Oak Creek Falls
(WI 4 to 5, 200 feet) ★
Approach time: 20 minutes.
Descent: Descent is by rappel, off trees.
Season: Winter.
Road/Highway the climb is visible from:
None.
Access issues: None.

253. Dexter Creek Slabs
(WI 3, 250 feet) ★★★
High quality slabs, for much of the winter.
Approach time: 20 minutes.
Descent: Rappel off trees, or walk off to the left.
Season: Winter.
Road/Highway the climb is visible from:
The slab is visible from Highway 550, north of the Dexter Creek Road.
Access issues: None.

251. Rock of Ages

252. Oak Creek Fall

Camp Bird Mine Road Area
(Routes 254-273)

The Canyon Creek Valley, which extends southwest out of Ouray, contains some of the finest ice routes in the state. From long classics like The Ribbon to short gymnastic workouts like The Skylight, the valley is a veritable six-pack sampler of Colorado ice climbing.

Fortunately, Camp Bird Mine Road follows the valley to the best ice climbs and pressure from Ouray merchants who support the ice climbing industry keeps the road plowed all winter long. Despite the plowing, 4-wheel drive is highly recommended (two-wheel drives often won't make it) along with a keen awareness. When the ice is good, this road can sport a traffic jam.

Because they lend themselves to it, the areas along Camp Bird Mine Road are

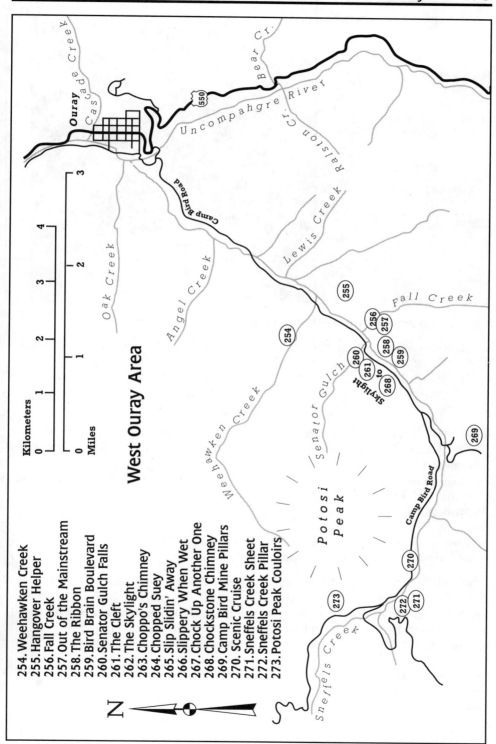

West Ouray Area

254. Weehawken Creek
255. Hangover Helper
256. Fall Creek
257. Out of the Mainstream
258. The Ribbon
259. Bird Brain Boulevard
260. Senator Gulch Falls
261. The Cleft
262. The Skylight
263. Choppo's Chimney
264. Chopped Suey
265. Slip Slidin' Away
266. Slippery When Wet
267. Chock Up Another One
268. Chockstone Chimney
269. Camp Bird Mine Pillars
270. Scenic Cruise
271. Sneffels Creek Sheet
272. Sneffels Creek Pillar
273. Potosi Peak Couloirs

The Ribbon Area. Left to right: Fall Creek, The Ribbon, Bird Brain Boulevard

described in mileages from the start of County Road 361 (Camp Bird Mine Road). The road starts just south of Ouray on Highway 550, after the first switchback on Highway 550. A sign indicates the road goes to Yankee Boy Basin and Camp Bird Mine. From the start of the road, drive up the hill and over the bridge, passing over the Uncompahgre Gorge's walls of ice.

254. Weehawken Creek (WI 3 to 5, various lengths) ★

About 2.0 miles up County Road 361, the road crosses a bridge. A few hundred feet beyond this bridge, on the right side of the road will be a small sign, designating the Weehawken Creek Trail. Weehawken Creek offers a number of pillars and cascades (WI 3 to 5) not far from the road.

Approach time: 20 minutes
Descent: Rap off trees.
Season: Winter, although avalanche danger can be high.
Road/Highway the climb is visible from: None.

255. Hangover Helper (WI 5, 100 feet) ★★

About 2.85 miles up County Road 361, the road crosses another bridge. Directly south, across the valley, is a small waterfall that regularly forms as several pillars on the obvious band of red sandstone. It stays in all season and offers plastic blue ice. To reach it requires crossing the valley, a snow slog of hefty proportions, but the climb is exceptional.

Approach time: 30 minutes
Descent: Rap off trees.
Season: Winter.
Road/Highway the climb is visible from: County Road 361 (Camp Bird Mine Road).

256. Fall Creek (WI 4, 1,000 feet)

About 3.5 miles up County Road 361, the road passes along a cut into a steep red cliff. On the opposite side of the valley is Fall Creek. It offers two separate routes, the main creek itself, which goes up the center of the drainage, and Out of the Mainstream, the creek that angles up and right from the main creek. (It'll be obvious when you see it.) The main creek is mostly low-angled climbing (WI 2) with a short step or two of WI 4.

Approach time: 45 minutes
Descent: Rap off trees and downclimb.
Season: Fall.
Road/Highway the climb is visible from: County Road 361 (Camp Bird Mine Road).

257. Out of the Mainstream (WI 4 to 5, 1,200 feet) ★★

Basically a variation of Fall Creek. About halfway up Fall Creek, Out of the Mainstream cuts off right, into the trees, and climbs the steep hill to the right. At it gets higher, it steepens and can offer some decent climbing.

The better of the two routes, by far, is Out of the Mainstream. Generally, both are so covered in snow they aren't worth the massive snow wallow required to get there. (Also, during a normal year, avalanche danger here is outrageous.) However, during a dry year, or early in the season, both routes can be worth the trouble.

Approach time: 45 minutes
Descent: Rap off trees and downclimb.
Season: Fall.
Road/Highway the climb is visible from: County Road 361 (Camp Bird Mine Road).

258. The Ribbon (WI 4, 600 feet) ★★★

About 3.6 miles up County Road 361 (0.2 miles past Fall Creek), the road crosses yet another bridge, this time over Senator Gulch. On the opposite wall of the valley, to the right of Fall Creek, is a 1,000-foot gray, rock wall. Breaking up this cliff, about half a mile right of Fall Creek, is The Ribbon, a spectacular waterfall that cascades out of a narrow canyon.

Park at the big pullout, just down canyon from the Senator Gulch bridge. Hike across the valley to the base of the route.

The Ribbon is a pure ice climb, and only screws are usually needed.

Approach time: 30-40 minutes
Descent: Descend by rappelling the route. Bring extra rock gear in case the anchors are buried under snow.
Season: Avalanche danger on it is super extreme, so do it early in the season or during a dry year.
Road/Highway the climb is visible from: County Road 361 (Camp Bird Mine Road).

259. Bird Brain Boulevard (WI 5 to 6, 1,000 feet) ★★

To the right of The Ribbon a couple of hundred yards, is a thin cleft, where Bird

Brain Boulevard lies.

Bird Brain Boulevard is a mixed route, and is best done in the mid-to-late part of the season. Also, the emphasis should be placed on rock gear, not on ice gear. A dozen thin pitons are highly recommended. Gear placements are limited, so the route is pretty run out. Forty to eighty foot falls have been reported on this route, so be prepared.

Approach time: 30-40 minutes

Descent: Descent for Bird Brain Boulevard is by rappel from trees left of the route.

Season: Mid to late winter.

Road/Highway the climb is visible from: County Road 361 (Camp Bird Mine Road).

260. Senator Gulch Falls (WI 4 to 5, 100 feet) ★★★

Senator Gulch Falls is just upstream from the parking area for The Ribbon and Bird Brain Boulevard. It's best reached by parking in the same pull out as for the two previous climbs, then walking up the road for a few hundred yards, to the upper switchback. At the crook of this switchback, a small trail leads around the corner to the north, into the small valley housing Senator Gulch Falls. The falls will be obvious. The left side is generally easier. The right side offers steep pillars.

Left to right: The Ribbon, Bird Brain Boulevard

Approach time: 5 minutes

Descent: Rappel from rock anchors above the falls, to the right.

Season: Winter.

Road/Highway the climb is visible from: None.

Access issues: Though this route is currently closed, it gets climbed all the time.

The Skylight Area

The skylight area lies approximately 4.0 miles from the start of County Road 361. It is basically a long gray, shale cliff on the right (north) side of the road that houses a number of high-quality, naturally forming ice routes that can be climbed (and scoped) from the car. The road passes directly under them. Avalanche danger can be high in this area, and there are no access issues to contend with.

Although all sorts of odd seeps and smears can form up along this cliff during a really wet winter, tøhere are seven routes that form consistently every season. They are described here from right to left.

261. The Cleft. (WI 3, 250 feet) ★

The Cleft looks like its namesake, a big cleft, 300 feet high. The WI 3 ice requires a pitch of snow wallowing first. There are a couple of routes that form up down canyon a few hundred feet from the cleft, the most reliable being a 60-foot pillar right above the road.

Approach time: 10 seconds.

Descent: To descend, traverse out left onto the left wall, and rappel off the obvious tree.

Season: All winter.

262. The Skylight.
(WI 4 to 5, 250 feet) ★★★

The Skylight is easily identified by the big boulder capping the first 25 feet of the route. It lies about 300 feet uphill from The Cleft. The upper section (the big chimney for which the route is named) should be done as one long pitch. Bring rock gear.

Approach time: 10 seconds.

Descent: Rappel off trees near the route.

Season: All winter.

Choppo's Chimney

263. Choppo's Chimney
(WI 4 to 5, 190 feet) ★★★

The best pitch of ice in the area! Located 100 feet uphill from the Skylight. Climb an easy pitch to the cave at the bottom of the steep section, and belay here, out of the way of falling ice. Then, it's a 160 foot lead to the top. More demanding than it looks.

Approach time: 10 seconds.

Descent: Rap off trees.

Season: All winter.

264. Chopped Suey (WI 5-, 170 feet) ★★★

Located in the same cleft of rock as and just a few feet left of Choppo's Chimney, this excellent moderate mixed route shares the same approach as Choppo's, then moves left on 5.6 rock, and climbs straight up to the icicles capping the cliff below the obvious tree. Protection is sparse. Bring thin pitons, a couple of small friends, and a #3 friend.

Approach time: 10 seconds.

Descent: Rappel off the tree.

Season: All winter.

Slip Slidin' Away

265. Slip Slidin' Away (WI 4, 180 feet) ★★★

Located 40 feet left of Choppo's Chimney, this route follows a left trending ramp with hard pillars to the right. The little tree on the left side distinguishes the climb. A good first WI 4 lead as the steep section is short.

Approach time: 10 seconds.
Descent: Rap off trees.
Season: All winter.

266. Slippery When Wet (WI 5, 180 feet) ★★★

Located 60 feet left of Slip Slidin' Away, Slippery When Wet trends up and left, up a narrow slot. Done as two pitches. Other, hard mixed routes often form right of this route.

Approach time: 10 seconds.
Descent: Rappel off trees.
Season: All winter.

267. Chock Up Another One (WI 3 to 4) ★★★

This prominent cleft, located 150 feet uphill from Slippery When Wet, features two distinct lines. The left line is a cascade of WI 3 ice, while the right side takes a narrower part of the cleft and climbs short pillars (WI 3-4).

Approach time: 10 seconds.
Descent: Rappel off trees.
Season: All winter.

Slippery When Wet

Chock Up Another One

Chockstone Chimney

268. Chockstone Chimney (WI 3 to 5, 90 feet) ★★★

Located 150 feet uphill of Chock Up Another One, this, the last regularly occurring route in the Skylight area, is discernible by the massive tilted block lodged in the back of the gully. The main flow of ice forms just left of the block, and is WI 3. Sometimes, steeper ice forms left of that flow, WI 5.

Approach time: 10 seconds.
Descent: Rappel off trees.
Season: All winter.

Camp Bird Mine Area

269. Camp Bird Mine Pillars (WI 4-5, 90 feet) ★★

Located just upcanyon from the Skylight area are several pillars on the far side (southwest) side of the canyon.

Approach time: 15 minutes.

Descent: Rappel off anchors at the top. You might want to bring some screws, in case you can't find the anchors.

Season: All winter.

Access issues: These climbs are reportedly on private land (owned by the mine) but access has not been a problem.

Sneffels Creek Canyon Area

One of my favorite areas, and a good place to escape the hordes at the Skylight, is the narrow canyon housing Sneffels Creek as it plunges down to meet Canyon Creek near the Mine.

To reach Sneffels Creek Canyon, continue up County Road 361 past the Skylight area. (Go about 1.4 miles past Chockstone Chimney). En route you'll pass numerous seeps and smears that form up on the cliffs to the north. All these can, obviously be climbed, but very few of them form continuous routes and they all require a snow wallow approach.

After passing under a rock overhang with icicles, the road bends around to the left, then back right. Generally, it's possible to park on this corner.

270. Scenic Cruise
(WI 4, 120 feet) ★★★

Directly below the parking spot on the corner is a route called the Scenic Cruise. Rappel into it. Numerous other WI 4 routes form in this area.

Approach time: 10 seconds.

Descent: Climb out.

Season: All winter.

271. Sneffels Creek Sheet
(WI 4, 100 feet) ★★★

To reach this two climb, drive about a quarter mile past the curve above the Scenic Cruise. There's a pullout on the left and a trail leading down into the canyon. The broad sheet of ice across the creek is known as the Sneffels Creek Sheet.

Approach time: 5 minutes.

Descent: Rappel off trees.

Season: All winter, although avalanche potential should be considered.

Jon Butler on Sneffels Creek Sheet

Road/Highway the climb is visible from: County Road 361 (Camp Bird Mine Road), barely.

272. Sneffels Creek Pillar (WI 5, 50 feet) ★★

Just to the right of the Sheet is an obvious stout pillar. Rappel off trees. Note: Numerous other unnamed routes form up in this little canyon which can't be seen from the road.

Approach time: 5 minutes.

Descent: Rappel off trees.

Season: All winter, although avalanche potential should be considered.

Road/Highway the climb is visible from: County Road 361 (Camp Bird Mine Road), barely.

273. Potosi Peak Couloirs (WI 4 to 5, 1,000 feet)

About 0.3 miles up the road from the Scenic Cruise, on the right, is a waterfall, Potosi Falls. It is just visible from the road, via an avalanche path that has cleared out all the trees. The falls are climbable and lead to two 800-900 foot couloirs. The falls are about a half mile from the road. Avalanche danger is high.

Approach time: 20 minutes.

Descent: Walk off to left. Rappels may be necessary.

Season: Late fall/early winter is safest.

Road/Highway the climb is visible from: County Road 361 (Camp Bird Mine Road), barely.

Red Mountain Pass
(Routes 274-284)

The climbs in the Red Mountain Pass area aren't really atop the pass, as the title to this section might suggest. Rather, they lie along Highway 550 as it climbs out of Ouray, south, towards Silverton. For the most part, the Highway follows the Uncompahgre River as it twists and turns through the tight gorge like a teenager's muddled excuses for wrecking dad's pickup.

The routes here tend to be longer than many other places, and 300-500 feet is the norm. They also tend to be somewhat fickle, as many of them face south, meaning Red Mountain Pass needs to be caught during a cold, wet snap. Then again, too wet, and avalanche danger goes up.

There are no access issues associated with any of the routes listed, however, there are some routes not mentioned here because they lie above the road, and to climb them would be to court disaster.

All the routes described in this section lie between Ouray and Engineer Pass Road, 3.7 miles to the south. The climbs are described from north to south, using odometer measurements from the south edge of town (Ouray).

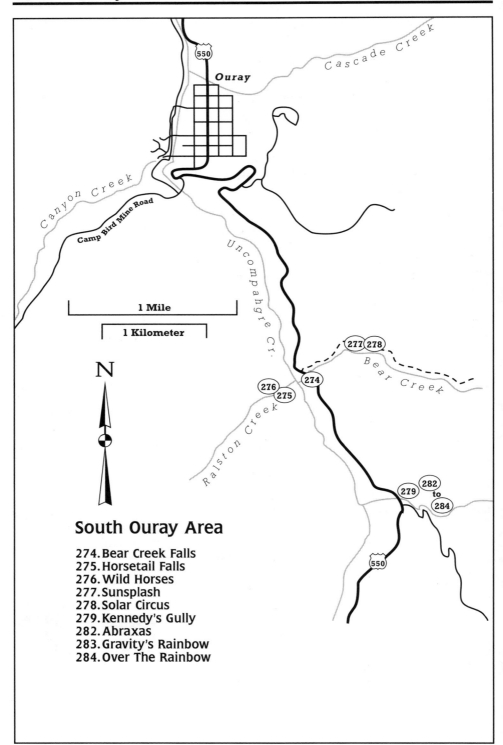

South Ouray Area

274. Bear Creek Falls
275. Horsetail Falls
276. Wild Horses
277. Sunsplash
278. Solar Circus
279. Kennedy's Gully
282. Abraxas
283. Gravity's Rainbow
284. Over The Rainbow

Bear Creek Area

2.7 miles south of Ouray is the Bear Creek area, where Bear Creek comes spilling out of the mountains to the east, and crosses under Highway 550, before cascading down the hill into the Uncompahgre River.

There are several parking pull outs here, both above and below Bear Creek.

274. Bear Creek Falls (WI 4 to 5, 160 feet).

Despite its rapid flow, Bear Creek often freezes enough to be climbable, just below the bridge. The best approach is to rappel right off the bridge, or, if the climbing looks questionable, get a partner to lower you. The ice is often very wet, hollow and very dirty, so be prepared.

Approach time: 5 minutes.

Descent: None. Climb it out.

Season: Midwinter.

Road/Highway the climb is visible from: This route can be checked out from Highway 550, downhill (north) of the creek itself at the obvious sweeping corner.

275. Horsetail Falls (WI 4 to 5, 500 feet) ★★★

An all-time classic, this route lies directly across the valley from Bear Creek. It sometimes gets the grade of WI 5, however, the WI 5 section (the second pitch) can be bypassed by going left, up easier ground. To reach the climb, walk south (uphill) of the Highway 550 bridge over Bear Creek, and along a wire fence until it's possible to scramble down into the canyon. There's usually a trail already stomped out. Cross the river, and begin climbing. Pitch 1, is often a snowy ramp, and therefore not really part of the climb. The second lead's the crux.

Approach time: 15 minutes.

Descent: To descend, walk off to the left about 150-200 feet and downclimb. Some sections of the descent require rappelling.

Season: Midwinter.

Road/Highway the climb is visible from: The route can be easily seen from Highway 550, at Bear Creek.

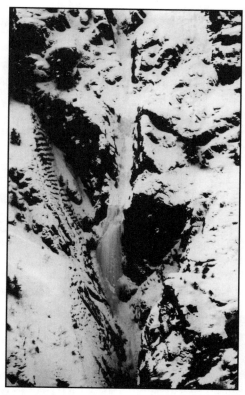

Horsetail Falls

276. Wild Horses. (WI 3, 600 feet) ★

The large, rounded, low-angled buttress on which Horsetail Falls sits boasts another route, Wild Horses, climbable during the early season. Although avalanche danger prompts one to want to do this route earlier rather than later, snow is a greater factor, and often by January this climb is covered.

Approach time: 15 minutes.

Descent: Rappel off trees..

Season: Early winter.

Road/Highway the climb is visible from: Like Horsetail Falls, the route can be easily seen from Highway 550, at Bear Creek.

277. Sunsplash (WI 5, 500 feet) ★

Sunsplash and Solar Circus lie up Bear Creek, above Highway 550, and are generally in good shape during mid to late winter, if it's cold. To reach them, scramble up the rock rib that lies just left (north) of Bear Creek, on the east side of the Highway, to a trail that follows a large ledge. Follow the trail a short way and watch for the two climbs below. Rappel into them.

Sunsplash lies to the left (north), as viewed from below, and tackles a corner/gully system for five pitches. Solar Circus lies to the right (south).

Approach Time: 25 minutes.

Descent: Climb it out.

Season: Late winter.

Road/Highway the climb is visible from: None.

278. Solar Circus (WI 4, 300 feet) ★★★

The easier of the two, to the right (south) of Sunsplash. Three pitches.

Approach time: 25 minutes.

Descent: Climb it out.

Season: Late winter.

Road/Highway the climb is visible from: None.

Engineer Pass Road Area

The Engineer Pass Road Area lies around the intersection of Highway 550 and Engineer Pass Road, a summer 4x4 road that leads east, out of the Uncompahgre Valley. The intersection is 3.7 miles south of Ouray.

A number of excellent routes form in this area, all of which are exceptionally fickle, as they face south. An early start is highly recommended. None of these routes have access issues, and all these routes can more or less be checked out from Highway 550.

279. Kennedy's Gully (WI 5, 1200 feet) ★★

Kennedy's Gully is the huge, prominent gully system that rises directly above Highway 550, about 150 feet north of Engineer Pass Road.

It rarely ever forms into an ice climb, and when it does, most parties climb only the first two leads (WI 3 and WI 5) before rapping off. Bring rock gear.

Approach time: 3 minutes.

Descent: Rappel off fixed anchors.

Season: Mid-winter.
Road/Highway the climb is visible from: Highway 550.

280. Mixed Emotions (WI 5, 150 feet) ★
Mixed Emotions is the obvious huge, right-facing corner that angles up left from the base of Kennedy's Gully. Bring rock gear.
Approach time: 5 minutes.
Descent: Rappel off fixed anchors. Bring some spares.
Season: Mid-winter.
Road/Highway the climb is visible from: Highway 550.

281. Blue Condition (WI 5, 200 feet)
Blue Condition is a 200-foot variation of Kennedy's Gully that takes off right, after the first pitch of Kennedy's Gully, and rejoins Kennedy's Gully above the steep cliff. Bring rock gear.
Approach time: 5 minutes.
Descent: Rappel off fixed anchors. Bring some spares.
Season: Mid-winter.
Road/Highway the climb is visible from: Highway 550.

282. Abraxas (WI 5 to 6, 300 feet)
This thin, mixed route rarely forms. It lies just right of the large rock buttress right of Kennedy's Gully, in the first obvious drainage. Bring rock gear.
Approach time: 5 minutes.
Descent: Rappel off fixed anchors and trees. Bring some spare webbing.
Season: Mid-winter.
Road/Highway the climb is visible from: Highway 550.

Abraxas, Gravity's Rainbow, Over the Rainbow

283. Gravity's Rainbow (WI 5 to 6, 500 feet) ★★

A Ouray classic, Gravity's Rainbow lies in the next gully right of Abraxas, and forms regularly in mid-to-late winter. The four-pitch route boasts continuous WI 4 to 5 climbing, which is often mixed. Bring rock gear.

Approach Time: 5 minutes.

Descent: Rappel fixed anchors just left of the climb.

Season: Mid-winter.

Road/Highway the climb is visible from: Highway 550.

284. Over The Rainbow (WI 4-5, 300 feet) ★★

Over The Rainbow lies in the next big gully right of Gravity's Rainbow, and forms regularly in mid-to-late winter with a steep, thick pillar. Bring rock gear. Avalanche danger can be high.

Approach time: 8 minutes.

Descent: Rappel fixed anchors and trees.

Season: Mid-winter.

Road/Highway the climb is visible from: Highway 550.

Note: Several other ice climbs form up Engineer Pass Road in the Over the Rainbow Area. They offer WI 4 climbing and are one to two pitches long.

Also, ice forms up all over the western side of the Uncompahgre River Valley (across the valley from Highway 550) and numerous routes are regularly climbed there. To reach requires crossing the valley on foot, an approach that ranks up there with the Bataan Death March.

Some easier to-get-to-routes can be accessed by driving south (uphill) from the Engineer Pass Road 1.4 miles to the snowshed covering Highway 550. From the uphill side of the snowshed, it's much easier to cross the valley. In this area, most of the routes are short (30-60 feet) and occur as seeps under bushes and trees, however, downstream, the routes get quickly bigger.

Dexter Creek SLabs

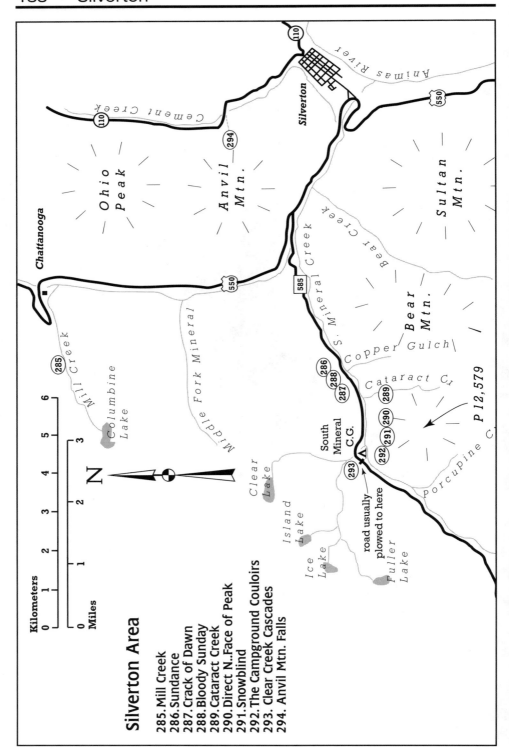

Silverton Area

285. Mill Creek
286. Sundance
287. Crack of Dawn
288. Bloody Sunday
289. Cataract Creek
290. Direct N. Face of Peak
291. Snowblind
292. The Campground Couloirs
293. Clear Creek Cascades
294. Anvil Mtn. Falls

SOUTHWESTERN MOUNTAINS

Silverton
(Routes 285-316)

"Beware of snow that talks to you!"
—Ed LaChapelle, The ABCs of Avalanche Safety

Silverton is still a relatively undiscovered area, as far as ice climbing goes. But that's okay with most regulars who climb there. The long alpine-type routes in Eureka and South Mineral Creek are as good as anything in the state, and at this writing, there's never ever a line.

The only drawback to climbing here is that avalanche danger is extreme in pretty much all the Silverton area venues. Late fall/early winter is the time to climb here — after that, you're pushing the envelope. Besides, the routes get covered with snow.

Of the three big ice climbing centers in the San Juans (Ouray, Telluride and Silverton) Silverton is the least overrun (or expensive) in the winter. Some of the local merchants are warming to the idea of ice climbing becoming a popular sport here, so check with motels for an ice climber's discount.

For Silverton, the routes are divided up north to south, with Mill Creek, between Ouray and Silverton first, and Eureka climbs last. Routes along U.S. 550 south of Silverton are in the section on Durango.

Mill Creek, Chattanooga
(Route 285)

Mill Creek, a 1,000-foot streambed featuring WI 3 climbing lies along Highway 550 north of Silverton, about 7.5 miles, (about 5.5 miles north of South Mineral Creek Road, and 2.5 miles south of the crest of Red Mountain Pass), near the one-home town of Chattanooga.

Just north of Chattanooga, the highway makes a deep wide curve, across a fairly wide valley, before it continues its climb towards Red Mountain Pass. Mill Creek drains the valley.

285. Mill Creek (WI 3, 1,000 feet) ★★

Early in the season, before avalanche danger becomes serious, Mill Creek can be climbed. The climbable portions of the stream lie about a half mile west of the road.
Approach time: 20 minutes.
Descent: Scramble down or rappel.
Season: Early winter.

Road/Highway the climb is visible from: The route is visible from Highway
    550.
Access issues: None.

South Mineral Creek
(Routes 286-293)

Although Eureka offers a far greater number of routes and tends to be the focus
of Silverton area ice climbing, the South Mineral Creek Valley offers a handful of
ice routes, nearly all of which are high quality.

Like other areas around Silverton, avalanche danger is generally high to extreme
in this area, so early season ascents are heavily advised.

All the routes in South Mineral Creek are visible from Forest Road 585, have no
access problems, require only 5-15 minutes to approach, and should be climbed in
the late fall/early winter.

Getting there: To reach South Mineral Creek, drive north from Silverton on
Highway 550, for 2.0 miles. Turn left (west) onto Forest Service Road 585.

For clarity, and because there are so many routes in South Mineral Creek, routes
will be described in mileages from the intersection of Forest Service Road 585 and
Highway 550.

At 1.0 mile, cross a small bridge. Beyond the bridge, on the left (south side of
the valley) are a number of obvious snow chutes that often offer blue ice. Because
these chutes vary dramatically with each season, they will not be listed individual-
ly. However, they obviously offer some easy climbing.

At 2.3 miles, there's a small waterfall on the hillside to the right that sometimes
freezes up. WI 3, 30 feet. Walk off right. At 2.5 miles, there's a campground.

Sundance

Crack of Dawn, Bloody Sunday

286. Sundance (WI 5, 180 feet) ★★★

2.9 miles along Forest Road 585. Sundance is the obvious, spectacular waterfall above the road on the right (north). Hard mixed routes sometimes form a few hundred feet to either side of Sundance.
Descent: Walk off right.

287. Crack of Dawn (WI 5-5+, 170 feet)

3.1 miles along Forest Road 585. Crack of Dawn takes the obvious vertical chimney, up wild pillars. Rock Gear (pitons) is very useful.
Descent: Scramble down, or rappel.

288. Bloody Sunday (WI 4-5, 170 feet) ★

3.1 miles along Forest Road 585. Bloody Sunday is the wide, bowl-shaped cascade right of Crack of Dawn, that forms a series of thin curtains. Numerous lines are often possible. Rock Gear (pitons) is very useful.
Descent: Scramble down, or rappel.

289. Cataract Creek (WI 3-4, 600 feet)

3.5 miles along Forest Road 585. The snow-choked gully to the left (south) side of the road. Much of it is walking between steep steps.
Descent: To descend, rappel off trees and downclimb the route.

Kent Robinson on Cataract Creek

290. Direct N..Face of Peak 12,579
(WI 4-5, 1500 feet) ★★★

3.9 miles along Forest Road 585. An outstanding long route with varied climbing. The cruxes are, obviously, the steep steps. Do it early in the season. Often, a major variation forms up a couple hundred feet to the right, offering 400 feet of steep climbing in a big, left-facing red corner. **Descent:** Scramble down to the left (east).

291. Snowblind (WI 5, 1000 feet) ★★★

4.2 miles along Forest Road 585. The obvious huge cleft in the red cliff (WI 5) leads to easier climbing above.
Descent: Descend by walking and rappelling down to the left side of the climb.

292. The Campground Couloirs (WI 4, 1,000 feet) ★★★

4.3 miles along Forest Road 585. Three couloirs dominate the south wall of the canyon, above the Forest Service campground. They all meet, more or less, about 500 feet up and continue up easier ground for several hundred feet. The left and central couloirs are obvious. The right-hand couloir is in the trees.
Descent: Descend by rappelling off trees, or walking down to the right.

293. Clear Creek Cascades (WI 4, 40 feet) ★★

4.4 miles along Forest Road 585. At the end of the plowed road a couple of thick little flows form on the west wall of Clear Creek, as it flows across the end of the road. Walking or driving in, they'll be visible up the stream 100 feet to the right.
Descent: Rap off trees or downclimb.

Direct North Face of Peak 12,57•

Snowblind

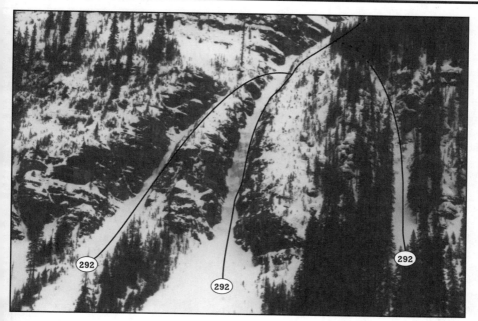

The Campground Couloirs

Cement Creek Valley
(Route 294)

Although the Cement Creek Valley northwest of Silverton has only one route of interest to ice climbers — Anvil Mountain Falls — this stunning pillar is worth the visit.

Getting there: To reach the falls, drive north out of Silverton on Colo. 110.

Colo. 110 road runs between Eureka, and Gladstone. Instead of turning right, the route to Eureka, go straight, up a couple of switchbacks, and into the Cement Creek Valley. Follow the road for about 2 miles from town. The falls will become very visible off to the southwest.

Park upstream from a small bridge, then ski in.

294. Anvil Mountain Falls (WI 4-5, 100 feet) ★★★

A stunning waterfall that tumbles over a large rock wall on the north side of Anvil Mountain. When it's in good shape, the pillar can be 50 feet around. However, often it's not, since it faces southeast. The top can get slushy, like Cornet Falls in Telluride. Wait for cold weather. Not to be missed!

Approach time: The approach takes about 30 minutes on skis. Much longer if you posthole. (In other words, bring skis or snowshoes.)

Descent: Walk off far to the right side and scramble down a gully. Rappelling off trees would also work.

Season: Midwinter, although if there's a lot of snow, avalanches can pose a threat.

Road/Highway the climb is visible from: Colo. 110.

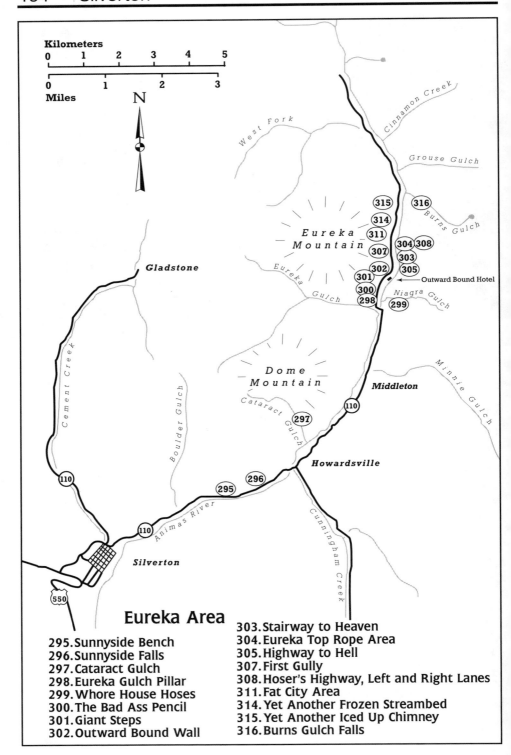

Eureka Area

295. Sunnyside Bench
296. Sunnyside Falls
297. Cataract Gulch
298. Eureka Gulch Pillar
299. Whore House Hoses
300. The Bad Ass Pencil
301. Giant Steps
302. Outward Bound Wall
303. Stairway to Heaven
304. Eureka Top Rope Area
305. Highway to Hell
307. First Gully
308. Hoser's Highway, Left and Right Lanes
311. Fat City Area
314. Yet Another Frozen Streambed
315. Yet Another Iced Up Chimney
316. Burns Gulch Falls

Eureka Gulch Pillar

Eureka
(Routes 295-316)

Eureka, an almost non-existent historic mining town north of Silverton, offers enough high quality ice climbing that it is generally considered its own area.

Ironically, however, Eureka routes aren't concentrated in one small area. They are spread up and down the entire Animas River Valley, from the north side of Silverton to the ghost town of Animas Forks. (Eureka simply sits near the largest concentration of routes.)

This broad, wide valley is not only beautiful, it's a dangerous place. In mid-winter, avalanches rip down the walls of the valley making climbing here a scary proposition. Nearly all the climbing that is done in this valley is done in November, before the threat of avalanches gets too high.

Colorado Highway 110 runs the length of the valley, meaning you can drive almost to the base of many routes. However, in mid-winter the road is generally only passable as far as Stairway to Heaven, the ultra-classic route of the area. To reach climbs further up the valley when snows close the road requires a short ski or walk.

Perhaps the best thing about climbing in this area is the fact that even if you can't drive the whole way up the road, there are enough routes along the road to keep you entertained.

Getting there: To get to Eureka and the Animas River Valley, drive north through the town of Silverton on Greene St. (a.k.a. Main St.), to the north side of town. Just past the courthouse (on the left), Colo. 110 branches off to the right.

Turn onto Colo. 110, and, for the sake of accurately finding routes, set your odometer to 0. I'll describe the routes — and other significant landmarks — in terms of their distance from the Colo. 110-Greene St. intersection.

295. Sunnyside Bench (WI 3-4, 60 feet)

2.3 miles up Colo. 110. This not really a route but a short cliff band about a quarter mile up the hill on the left side of the road. (It's 600 feet right of the Sunnyside Gold Mine, just for reference.)

Approach time: 10 minutes from the car.
Descent: Walk off or rappel down the cliff.
Season: Late fall.
Road/Highway the climb is visible from: Colo. 110.
Access issues: None.

296. Sunnyside Falls (WI 2-3, 60 feet)

3.2 miles up Colo. 110. Located 0.3 miles upvalley of a nice brown house, this small waterfall sits just 100 yards off the road and cascades over a short cliff band.

Approach time: 5 minutes from the car.
Descent: Walk off or rappel from trees.
Season: Late fall.
Road/Highway the climb is visible from: Colo. 110.
Access issues: None.

297. Cataract Gulch (WI 2-2+, 800 feet)

4.65 miles up Colo. 110. (For reference, it's 0.95 miles past the first bridge over the Animas River.) Cataract Gulch drains the massive valley on the south side of Dome Mountain that enters the Animas River Valley from the left. Early in the season, the creek is climbable. Mostly, it's a hike.

Approach time: 20 minutes from the car.
Descent: Walk off.
Season: Late fall.
Road/Highway the climb is visible from: Colo. 110.
Access issues: None.

298. Eureka Gulch Pillar (WI 5, 60 feet) ★

7.9 miles up Colo. 110. 7.9 miles up Colo. 110, you cross the Animas River a second time, on the Eureka Gulch Bridge. (This bridge will be a reference point for climbs, along with the Colo. 110-Greene St. intersection.) On the upvalley side of the bridge, and off to the left, a major gulch — Eureka Gulch — will be obvious. It sits left of a large set of concrete stairs, a remnant of Eureka's mining days. The Eureka Gulch Pillar is not in the gulch itself, but just off to the right of the gulch, in a sort of amphitheater. Hike up the hill right of the gulch and rappel into the pillar.

Approach time: 10 minutes from the car.
Descent: Walk off right.
Season: Late fall/early winter.
Road/Highway the climb is visible from: Colo. 110.

Access issues: None.

299. Whore House Hoses (WI 5, 500 feet) ★★★

8.0 miles up Colo.110. A stunning sight when you first see it, the Whore Houses Hoses fills the massive chimney on the right (east) side of the valley, opposite Eureka Gulch. (Whore House Hoses fills a gulch named Niagra.) Three hard, strenuous leads bring you to easier climbing.

Approach time: 20 minutes from the car.
Descent: Rappel off.
Season: Late fall/early winter.
Road/Highway the climb is visible from: Colo. 110.
Access issues: None.

300. The Bad Ass Pencil (WI 5, 100 feet) ★★

8.1 miles up Colo. 110. (0.2 miles past the Eureka Gulch Bridge.) The aptly named pencil lies on a small, unlikely cliff band on the hillside to the left (west). If it's in condition, you can't miss it.

Approach time: 5 minutes from the car.
Descent: Rappel off or scramble down.
Season: Late fall/early winter.
Road/Highway the climb is visible from: Colo. 110.
Access issues: None.

301. Giant Steps (WI 5, 170 feet)

8.3 miles up Colo. 110. (0.4 miles past the Eureka Gulch Bridge.) A two-pitch climb located high on the hillside to the left (west), above the road.

Approach time: 30 minutes from the car.
Descent: Rappel off or scramble down.
Season: Late fall/early winter.
Road/Highway the climb is visible from: Colo. 110.
Access issues: None.

302. Outward Bound Wall (WI 5, 500 feet)

8.5 miles up Colo. 110. (0.6 miles past the Eureka Gulch Bridge). There's a hotel owned by Outward Bound on the right. On the left side of the road is a major rock wall that boasts a number of ice and mixed routes. Rock gear's a really good idea.

Approach time: 15 minutes from the car.
Descent: Rappel off or scramble down left.
Season: Late fall/early winter.
Road/Highway the climb is visible from: Colo. 110.
Access issues: None.

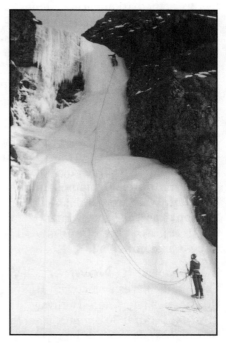

Stairway to Heaven

303. Stairway to Heaven
(WI 4, 900 feet) ★★★

8.8 miles up Colo. 110. (0.8 miles past the Eureka Gulch Bridge. Stairway to Heaven is the mega-classic of the area. It lies on the right (east) side of the valley, and is the most visible climb in the area where the road bends around a large rock buttress on the left.

There's also a good parking area on the right side of the road. Often, snows close the road from this point on, so you might have to walk ski to get any further.

Approach time: 20 minutes from the car.
Descent: Wander off to the left and scramble down. A rappel may be necessary.
Season: Late fall/early winter.
Road/Highway the climb is visible from: Colo. 110.
Access issues: None.

304. Eureka Top Rope Area
(WI 3-5, 80 feet)

This area is located upstream a few hundred feet from the parking area mentioned in the Stairway to Heaven description.

Stairway to Heaven

Approach time: 2 minutes from the car.
Descent: None.
Season: Late fall/early winter.
Road/Highway the climb is visible from: Colo. 110, sort of.
Access issues: None.

305. Highway to Hell (WI 4+, 800 feet) ★

This climb lies 500 feet right of Stairway to Heaven and ascends discontinuous ice up several rock bands. It shares a start with Road to Nowhere, then goes right, while Road to Nowhere goes left. Bring some rappel stuff.
Approach time: 30 minutes from the car.
Descent: Walk around the top of Stairway to Heaven to descend.
Season: Late fall/early winter.
Road/Highway the climb is visible from: Colo. 110.
Access issues: None.

306. Road to Nowhere (WI 4+, 800 feet)

This climb shares a start with Highway to Hell and is very similar to Highway to Hell. It goes left, where Highway to Hell goes right.
Approach time: 30 minutes from the car.
Descent: Walk around the top of Stairway to Heaven to descend.

Eureka Area Ice Climbs. Left to right: First Gully, Second Gully, Goldrush, Fat City Area, Just Another Gully Climb, Tempered By Fire, Yet Another Frozen Streambed

Season: Late fall/early winter.
Road/Highway the climb is visible from: Colo. 110.
Access issues: None.

307. First Gully (WI 4-4+, 800 feet) ★★★

8.9 miles up Colo. 110. (1.05 miles past the Eureka Gulch bridge.) This is the first climb located in the upper section of the valley, just after you pass around the large rock buttress on the left. It lies, literally, above the road, and follows a series of cascades up the cliff band. The ice is often thin, so bring rock gear.
Approach time: 5 minutes from the car.
Descent: Rappel the route.
Season: Late fall/early winter.
Road/Highway the climb is visible from: Colo. 110.
Access issues: None.

308. Hoser's Highway, Left and Right Lanes (WI 5-5+, 1,000 feet)

8.95 miles up Colo. 110. (1.05 miles past the Eureka Gulch Bridge.) These two wild climbs follow clefts in the large rock wall that lies several hundred feet left of Stairway to Heaven. (For reference, it's about opposite Hoser's Highway.) The two clefts are obvious, and lie about 200 feet apart. Both routes get progressively harder As they get higher. Bring lotsa rock gear!
Approach time: 10 minutes from the car.

Descent: Walk way left from the top of the routes. Descend using a combination of rappelling and scrambling.
Season: Late fall/early winter. Can be thin and scary.
Road/Highway the climb is visible from: Colo. 110.
Access issues: None.

309. Second Gully (WI 4-4+, 800 feet) ★★★
9.1 miles up Colo. 110. (1.2 miles past the Eureka Gulch bridge.) This route is located 500 feet upvalley from the First Gully and is similar in nature, except even closer to the road! (Bring rock gear.)
Approach time: 2 minutes from the car.
Descent: Rappel the route.
Season: Late fall/early winter.
Road/Highway the climb is visible from: Colo. 110.
Access issues: None.

310. Goldrush (WI 4-5+, 500 feet) ★★★
9.1 miles up Colo. 110. (1.2 miles past the Eureka Gulch bridge.) This route is located 300 feet upvalley from the Second Gully and is obvious due to the huge rock corner it follows, which you cannot miss. Conditions on this outstanding route vary greatly. (Bring rock gear.)
Approach time: 10 minutes from the car.
Descent: Rappel the route.
Season: Late fall/early winter.
Road/Highway the climb is visible from: Colo. 110.
Access issues: None.

311. Fat City Area (WI 3-5+, various lengths) ★★★
9.2 miles up Colo. 110. (1.3 miles past the Eureka Gulch bridge.) Fat City is a popular pillar that forms in a small alcove/amphitheater 200 yards above the road. In all, there are three routes in this amphitheater, although two form with regularity. The right-hand route is Fat City (WI 5-5+, 500 feet), a obvious route boasting a steep pillar/column. Left of that is are two runnels that form up. From left to right they are the Fat Slabs (WI 3, 500 feet) and the Fatter Slabs (WI 4, 500 feet). Rock gear is helpful on all these routes, but on Fat City especially.
Approach time: 10 minutes from the car.
Descent: Rappel the routes, carefully. Pick your line well.
Season: Late fall/early winter.
Road/Highway the climb is visible from: Colo. 110.
Access issues: None.

312. Just Another Gully Climb (WI 3-4, 500 feet) ★★
9.35 miles up Colo. 110. (1.4 miles past the Eureka Gulch bridge. Like Fat City, Just Another Gully Climb sits in an alcove on the hillside above the road, a few hundred feet right of the Fat City area, and the alcove actually boasts two separate routes, Left and Right. Both are mostly WI 3, but the right-hand gully can be WI 4.
Approach time: 10 minutes from the car.
Descent: Rappel off trees next to the routes.
Season: Late fall/early winter.

Road/Highway the climb is visible from: Colo. 110.
Access issues: None.

313. Tempered By Fire (WI 4+, 120 feet) ★★★
9.45 miles up Colo. 110. (1.55 miles past the Eureka Gulch bridge. Tempered By Fire sits right above the road on the left, in a left leaning chimney. The first lead climbs the chimney; the second climbs the pillar above. Don't miss it.
Approach time: 3 minutes from the car.
Descent: Walk off right.
Season: Late fall/early winter.
Road/Highway the climb is visible from: Colo. 110.
Access issues: None.

314. Yet Another Frozen Streambed (WI 3, 1,000 feet) ★
9.55 miles up Colo. 110. (1.65 miles past the Eureka Gulch bridge. This route climbs a creek that drains the large valley above the road.
Approach time: 15 minutes from the car.
Descent: Walk off right.
Season: Late fall/early winter.
Road/Highway the climb is visible from: Colo. 110.
Access issues: None.

315. Yet Another Iced Up Chimney (WI 4+, 120 feet) ★★★
9.95 miles up Colo. 110. (2.05 miles past the Eureka Gulch bridge. Like Tempered By Fire, this chimney sits right above the road on the left, in a left leaning chimney.
Approach time: 5 minutes from the car.
Descent: Scramble off left.
Season: Late fall/early winter.
Road/Highway the climb is visible from: Colo. 110.
Access issues: None.

316. Burns Gulch Falls (WI 4+, 100 feet) ★★★
9.95 miles up Colo. 110. (2.05 miles past the Eureka Gulch bridge. Burns Gulch was once mistakenly called Niagara Gulch on a BLM sign and thus there's some confusion over the name of this route. (The real Niagra Gulch lies further down the valley, and is home to the Whore House Hoses.) Anyway, Burns Gulch is the major drainage coming in on the right side of the valley and boasting a big, prominent waterfall, Burns Gulch Falls. It lies pretty much opposite Yet Another Ice Up Chimney. To reach Burns Gulch Falls, scramble down from the road, cross the river, and hike to the base of the falls.
Approach time: 25 minutes from the car.
Descent: Walk off left or right.
Season: Late fall/early winter.
Road/Highway the climb is visible from: Colo. 110.
Access issues: There's an old mine off to the right, with the only bridge around. Don't use the bridge or go near the mine. The owners are extremely anti-trespassers. You can pretty much cross the Animas River anywhere, when the snow's deep.

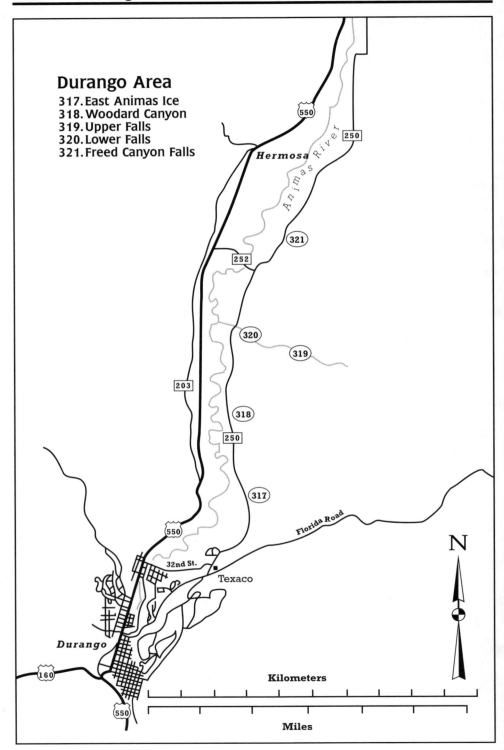

Durango Area
317. East Animas Ice
318. Woodard Canyon
319. Upper Falls
320. Lower Falls
321. Freed Canyon Falls

SOUTHWESTERN MOUNTAINS

Durango
(Routes 317-315)

'What's the sense in all this?"
—Warren J. Harding, "Downward Bound," 1975

Durango is one of the biggest cities in southwestern Colorado, and has one of the biggest climbing populations around. Unfortunately, the amount of ice climbing to be found there is not commensurate with the population, and the climbs that form are generally in condition only during the height of the ice climbing season. Still, the handful of climbs located here can offer a visitor a couple of days' worth of entertainment.

All of the immediate Durango area's ice routes are located on the east side of Animas River Valley, on the western slopes of Baldy Mountain, at the East Animas rock climbing area, and in Woodard Canyon, Haflin Canyon and Freed Canyons.

Access is an issue here as much as anywhere else in the state. Indeed, every route described here — with the sole exception of the Haflin Canyon ice routes — require an approach across private land. For ice climbers, that means the obvious: be cool, low-key and totally respectful. Lotsa noise, nudity, beer drinking in the parking area after climbing, and general debauchery ain't a good idea. The two short ice climbs — Falls Creek and Animas City Mountain — that exist along County Road 203 on the west side of the valley are currently closed to ice climbers.

Getting there: The East Animas rock climbing area, Woodard Canyon, Haflin Canyon and Freed Canyon are accessed by driving north, out of Durango, along the East side of the Animas River Valley on County Road 250 (East Animas Road). There are numerous ways to reach County Road 250.

From downtown Durango, drive north on Main Avenue to 15th St. and turn right. Follow 15th to Florida Road, and turn left. Follow Florida Road north to County Road 250 (East Animas Road). There's a Texaco station at the intersection. Turn left here. This is also a good place to reset your odometer.

The East Animas Rock climbing area is reached by following County Road 250 (East Animas Road) north for exactly 1.8 miles to a small parking pullout on the right hand side of the road, in front of a house, No. 1852. Please do not park in the driveway. The residents don't appreciate it.

Woodard Canyon is the hardest canyon to find in the Durango area, but the ice climbing is worth the effort. From the parking area for East Animas, drive north on County Road 250 (East Animas Road) for 2.05 miles. (From the Florida Road—County Road 250 intersection, it's 3.85 miles to Woodard Canyon.) Pull off on the side of the road. There are few landmarks here to help tell you've reached

Woodard, but look for a fenced yard on the right (east) side of the road, with brown, wooden corner posts. Woodard Canyon should be visible behind this yard, to the east.

Haflin Canyon is easy to find because a Forest Service sign designates the trail-head.

From the parking area for East Animas, drive north on County Road 250 (East Animas Road) for 3.7 miles. (From the Florida Road—County Road 250 intersection, it's 5.5 miles to Haflin Canyon.) Pull off on the side of the road.

Turn right onto a gravel road on the right side of the road, which accesses a Forest Service works facility. Park on the left side of the gravel road.

To reach Freed Canyon, Durango's most reliable ice climb, drive north on County Road 250 (East Animas Road) from the County Road 250-County Road 252 (Trimble Lane) intersection for 1.0 miles.

(From the Florida Road—County Road 250 intersection, it's 7.7 miles to Freed Canyon.) As with Woodard Canyon, there are few landmarks here to help tell you've reached Freed Canyon, but look for a fenced field on the right (east) side of the road. The field is just a few hundred feet south of an old barn (on the left) and a light brownish house (on the right).

Freed Canyon is the heavily wooded canyon directly behind the field, to the east.

317. East Animas Ice
(WI 5, 60 feet) ★

East Animas is the climbing area behind the house, No. 1852. The Watch Crystal is the largest, flat-faced cliff behind the house. To reach it, walk up County Road 250 to the next driveway, the driveway for the next house north, No. 1866. Walk 10 feet up the driveway, then skirt right, along the property boundary, to the base of the cliff.

This area rarely has ice, but it is reportedly good when its in. The gully just left of the Watch Crystal is the place to watch for an impressive icicle to form.

Approach time: 5 minutes

Descent: Rappel off trees at the top of the route.

Season: Only forms during very cold spells in a rare year.

Road/Highway the climb is visible from: County Road 250 (East Animas Road), Highway 550.

Access issues: So far, access has not been a huge problem, but every now and then access becomes an issue. Climbers hanging out after climbing and drinking beer, making noise and generally whooping it up has nearly shut the access down a few times. Be very cool. Pretend you're a model citizen.

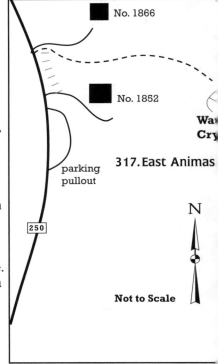

318. Woodard Canyon (WI 4-5, 120 feet) ★★

Skirt the fenced yard to its right (south) and wander up the canyon for 15 minutes to the climb, a nice pillar that starts with easy ground. A gully continues up above the pillar, but most parties only climb the pillar.

Approach time: 15 minutes.
Descent: Rappel off trees at the top of the route.
Season: December-early March.
Road/Highway the climb is visible from: County Road 250, barely. Highway 550, definitely.
Access issues: None at present.

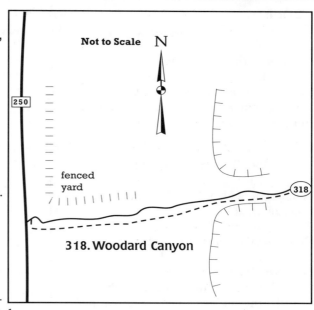

318. Woodard Canyon

Haflin Canyon Ice Climbs

At the parking area, a sign designates the public trail into Haflin Canyon. Follow this trail for ten minutes into the canyon. Near an old, small green, building that's always locked up, the trail branches.

319. Upper Falls (WI 5+, 120 feet) ★★★

The left branch goes to the Upper Falls. The Upper Falls are about a 1.5 hour hike (it's about 2.5 miles). The trail comes out above the falls so it's necessary to rappel in to climb the route. (Rap off trees.) This climb doesn't form much, so it's a good idea to ask locally before making the hike.

Approach time: 1.5 hours
Descent: Rappel off trees to the base of the route, then climb out.
Season: December-early March.
Road/Highway the climb is visible from: None
Access issues: None.

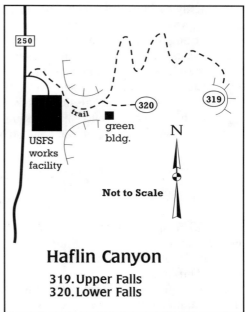

Haflin Canyon

319. Upper Falls
320. Lower Falls

320. Lower Falls (WI 4-5, 60 feet) ★★★
The trail branch that goes straight goes to the Lower Falls. This is about a 15-minute hike.
Approach time: 15 minutes
Descent: Rappel off trees at the top of the route.
Season: December-early March.
Road/Highway the climb is visible from: None
Access issues: None.

321. Freed Canyon Falls (WI 5, 75 feet) ★★★
A nice pillar regularly forms in the canyon behind the field, although it's not visible from the road.
Approach time: 5 minutes
Descent: Rappel off trees at the top of the route.
Season: December-early March.
Road/Highway the climb is visible from: Highway 550, especially in the Hermosa area.
Access issues: This approach requires crossing private farmland. To date, crossing the field has not been a problem, but in 1996, brand new and highly authoritative 'no trespassing' signs went up. What is an issue is parking along the County Road 250. Because there's no shoulder, snowplows have a hard time getting around cars here. Park sensibly and as out of the way as possible. Park down the road if you have to. If ice climbers aren't careful, "No Parking" signs, parking tickets and fist fights with plow drivers (generally big, strong people) could result.

321. Freed Canyon Falls

Highway 550
(Routes 322-327)

Along U.S. 550, between Durango and Silverton, are numerous ice climbs and climbing areas of interest. Although they are spread out and require some driving, these climbs offer a nice alternative to standing in line at any of the canyon areas close to Durango.

Cascade Creek, near Purgatory ski area, is as good as it gets in the San Juans.

The locations of the climbs in this section are listed from south to north, starting from the little town of Hermosa, just a few miles north of Durango. Hermosa is where U.S. 550 and County Road 203 meet.

If you're coming from the north, the first climb will be the Molas Creek Pillar, on Molas Pass. This is about 10 miles south of Silverton, and once at Molas Pass (there are signs everywhere telling you you're at Molas Pass), you can do the math and figure out how far it is to the rest of the routes. Remember, math is your friend.

Getting there: To reach the first climb in this area, Highway Robbery, from the intersection of Highway 550 and County Road 203, drive 5.7 miles north to the large, brown San Juan National Forest sign on the right, and park. Highway Robbery is in a gully on the hillside to the west (left).

4.3 miles north of the big brown San Juan National Forest sign mentioned above, above an Adopt A Highway sign, is the outrageous Seven Year Itch. It'll be as obvious as a mugger breathing down your neck.

The next area of interest along U.S. 550 is the Cascade Creek area. This little canyon is Durango's answer to Ouray's Box Canyon and offers some of the finest ice in the San Juans. Situated below a bend in Highway 550 (but not visible from the road) about a mile north of Purgatory Ski area, the walls of this short canyon boast a thick coating of ice throughout the season.

Parking is available at three separate spots around the bend. To reach the base of the routes, rappel into the canyon from any side. Avalanche danger is low.

Continuing north along U.S. 550, the first high mountain pass reached is Coal Bank Summit. North of Coal Bank Summit 2.6 miles, Deer Creek (though I think its got a sign saying West Lime Creek) trickles down from the west (left, if you're headed north). The limestone cliffs a few hundred yards above the creek offer a myriad of ice routes, most of which are vertical, but short. Avalanche danger can be high.

About a mile north of West Lime Creek, Highway 550 makes a huge sweeping turn as it passes through the Lime Creek Valley. The Lime Creek Curtain is tucked uphill from the curve, on the left, in a narrow gully that drains into Lime Creek. It is visible (just) from the road. Avalanche danger can be high.

Molas Creek is located just north of Molas Pass, which is three and a half miles north of Lime Creek. (For reference, it's about 10 miles south of Silverton.) A huge nearly flat basin atop which Molas Pass sits makes Molas Pass feel less like a pass than a high point in a prairie. Regardless, Molas Creek drains the entire flat basin area. About a half mile downstream the creek goes over a small cliff band, creating the Molas Creek Pillar. The cliff band can be reached by parking at the main Molas Pass parking area, and descending into the creek's drainage to the north, or, by parking at a small pullout on the right, about a mile north of the pass itself. From the pullout, walk or ski back right (southeast) towards the low point in the basin. Follow it until you reach the cliff. Walk down to the right (north) side of the falls.

Highway 550 Area

322. Highway Robbery
323. Seven Year Itch
324. Cascade Creek Area
325. Deer Creek
326. Lime Creek Curtain
327. Molas Creek Pillar

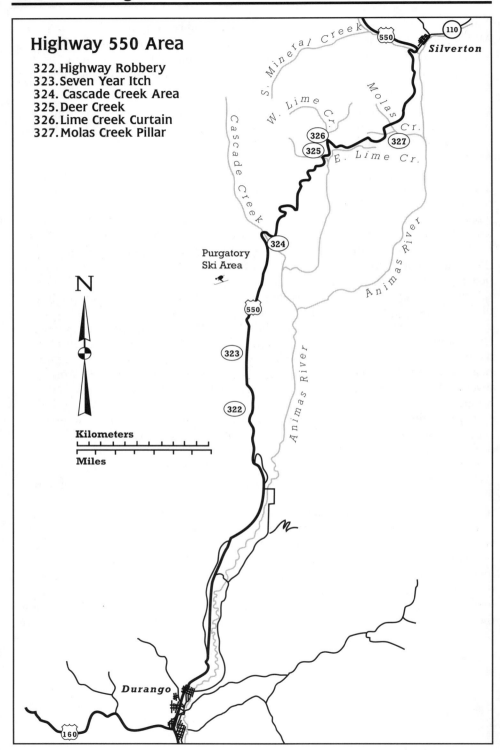

Highway 550 Routes

322. Highway Robbery (WI 3, 100 feet)
Approach time: 20 minutes
Descent: Rappel off trees at the top of the route.
Season: December-April.
Road/Highway the climb is visible from: Highway 550.
Access issues: This approach requires crossing private farmland, but access has
    not yet been a problem.

Seven Year Itch

323. Seven Year Itch (WI 5, 300 feet) ★★★
Several curtains and column spill down the wall creating a desperate classic. Park
on the road and slog through the snow up to the route.
Approach time: 20 minutes
Descent: Rappel off trees.
Season: Early December-early May.
Road/Highway the climb is visible from: Highway 550.
Access issues: This approach requires crossing private farmland, but access has
    not yet been a problem.

324. Cascade Creek Area (WI 2-5, various routes, lengths) ★★★
Like the Uncompahgre Gorge in Ouray. Killer pillars, wild curtains, classic cruis-
es.
Approach time: 3 minutes
Descent: Rappel off trees to reach the base of the route.
Season: November-late May.

Road/Highway the climb is visible from: Sometimes, when snow conditions are right, you can see ice through the trees from U.S. 550 as it circles the canyon.

Access issues: None.

325. Deer Creek (WI 5, 80 feet)

Approach time: 15 minutes
Descent: Rappel off trees.
Season: Late November-May.
Road/Highway the climb is visible from: Highway 550.
Access issues: None.

326. Lime Creek Curtain (WI 5, 300 feet) ★★

Unlike the title suggests, this route is more than just curtains. There are three steep sections.
Approach time: 15 minutes
Descent: Rappel off trees or scramble off.
Season: Late November-May.
Road/Highway the climb is visible from: Highway 550, barely.
Access issues: None.

Nils Gram on Cascade Creek

327. Molas Creek Pillar (WI 3-4, 70 feet) ★★★

Despite the fact that you can't see it until you're on top of it, the Molas Creek Pillar is worth the ski in. Oftentimes, a number of mixed variations form up on the left side.
Approach time: 20 minutes
Descent: Walk off.
Season: Late November-May.
Road/Highway the climb is visible from: None.
Access issues: None.

Lime Creek   Photo: Jeff Singer

Seven Year Itch

Photo: Jeff Singer

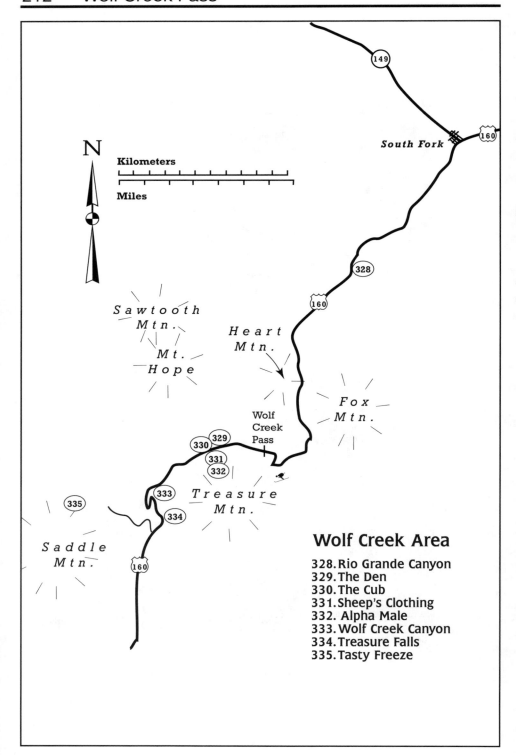

N

Kilometers

Miles

South Fork

149

160

160

328

Sawtooth
Mtn.

Mt.
Hope

Heart
Mtn.

Fox
Mtn.

Wolf
Creek
Pass

330 329
331
332
333
335
334

Saddle
Mtn.

Treasure
Mtn.

160

Wolf Creek Area

328. Rio Grande Canyon
329. The Den
330. The Cub
331. Sheep's Clothing
332. Alpha Male
333. Wolf Creek Canyon
334. Treasure Falls
335. Tasty Freeze

SOUTHWESTERN MOUNTAINS

Wolf Creek Pass
(Routes 328-335)

"It was important to stay cool as security diminished ... "
—Doug Scott, Alpine Journal, 1970

Wolf Creek Pass offers almost as much ice climbing as some of the better known Colorado ice climbing areas, scattered along U.S. Highway 160 as it crests the pass. However, with the exception of the local tourist attraction of Treasure Falls, the majority of the routes here are generally overlooked.

Wolf Creek Pass lies between the towns of Pagosa Springs and South Fork, on U.S. 160. The top of the pass is about 19.4 miles west of South Fork, and about 22.7 miles east of Pagosa Springs (at the intersection of U.S. 160 and U.S. 84 on the east side of town).

For the sake of clarity, these routes will be described from east to west. That is, from the South Fork (east) side of Wolf Creek Pass to the Pagosa Springs (west) side.

Helpful Hint: Don't park where you'll be plowed in. Wolf Creek Pass has one of the highest annual snowfalls of anywhere in the lower 48 and plows do double time on the road.

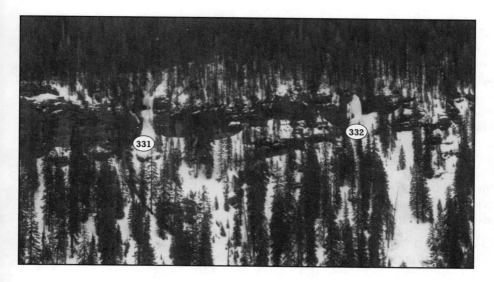

Left to right: Sheep's Clothing, Alpha Male

328. Rio Grande Canyon (WI 2-5, dozens of routes and difficulties) ★★

The first ice climbing area of note along Highway 160 is the Rio Grande Canyon, on the east side of Wolf Creek Pass. This is a narrow limestone walled canyon, about two miles long, through which the South Fork of the Rio Grande flows. Highway 160 parallels the river through this canyon, just north of the river. The canyon is not continuous, but rather, a series of sporadic cliffs on both the north and south sides of the road which produce bountiful quantities of ice in the winter.

The canyon lies about 10 miles west of South Fork (about 32 miles from Pagosa Springs). There are numerous parking areas along the road side. The best ice is found at the east end of the canyon, on the south walls of the canyon. Short steep routes about, from WI 2 to 5. Unfortunately, the approach includes crossing the Rio Grande.

329. The Den (WI 2-5, various) ★

2.9 miles west of the crest of the pass. On the west side of Wolf Creek Pass, a number of small waterfalls abound, some just off the road. At the 2.9 mile mark, a small cirque will become obvious a few hundred feet up the hill to the right (north), behind a sign saying "Vehicles over 30,000 GVW use right lane."

Park on the roadside and follow the small creek that passes next to the sign up the hill. On the left is a WI 4-5 waterfall, 100 feet. To the right are a handful of easier routes.

Descent: Descend by walking off to the right.

330. The Cub (WI 3, 60 feet)

4.5 miles west of the crest of the pass. This small waterfall lies about 4.5 miles west of the crest of the pass, uphill from the bottom end of a runaway truck ramp. It's visible from the road. Don't park on the ramp itself. (Big fines!)

Descent: Pretty much whatever you want to do.

331. Sheep's Clothing (WI 3-4, 70 feet) ★

4.5 miles west of the crest of the pass. Across the valley from the truck ramp are two obvious waterfalls. The left one, Sheep's Clothing, is easier. To access these routes, park a few hundred feet downhill from the truck ramp on the south side of the road. (You can also park here for The Cub.) Between this parking area and the routes is a steep, gnarly, snow-filled valley. The further west it goes, the deeper it gets. So, walk back uphill a few hundred yards until the valley is fairly easy, then cross over to the climbs. Walk along the top of the cliff band housing the routes and rap in. The edge of the cliff band is often blown relatively free of snow while the slope below is usually deep with snow and hard to cross. Snowshoes are recommended.

Sheep's Clothing usually offers low angled climbing to a steep curtain at the top.

Descent: Rap in to base of the climb.

332. Alpha Male (WI 5, 80 feet) ★★

4.5 miles west of the crest of the pass. Right of Sheep's Clothing, Alpha Male generally forms with a short steep step, then low-angled ice to a final 30-foot vertical section.

Descent: Rap in to base of the climb.

Tasty Freeze

333. Wolf Creek Canyon (Various grades, various lengths)

7.12 miles west of the crest of the pass. Wolf Creek Canyon is also of interest to ice climbers, but the long, arduous approach will definitely keep the hoards away. This canyon lies uphill from the massive bend in Highway 160 just east of Treasure Falls. (It's 7.12 miles west of the crest of the pass, and about a mile east of Treasure Falls.) A number of high quality climbs form in this canyon, all of which can be checked out from Highway 160, further up the pass.

334. Treasure Falls (WI 4-5, 130 feet) ★★★

8.2 miles west of the crest of the pass. This spectacular waterfall is a year round tourist attraction and one of southwest Colorado's most classic lines. It lies just off Highway 160 and is almost impossible to miss, as in recent years a small parking area has been built, and signs added along the road pointing out the falls.

Just for reference, Treasure Falls lies 14.5 miles east of Pagosa Springs, and 8.2 miles west of the crest of the pass. A trail leads south from the parking area a short way to the falls.

Descent: Descent is via rappel.

335. Tasty Freeze (WI 4, 500 feet) ★★★

Tasty Freeze is the massive blue strand that forms up on the northeast face of Saddle Mountain, which lies north of Highway 160 in the West Fork of the San Juan River Valley.

To reach this route, follow the West Fork Road, which intersects Highway 160 0.7 miles west of Treasure Falls. (The West Fork Road is 13.8 miles east of Pagosa Springs.) Follow the road north — past a number of commercial outfitter operations and Forest service campgrounds — for just over 3 miles. A gate, private property, and the end of the road, bar further progress. Park here. Then hike along the telephone line towards the mountain. Keep your eye on the face of the mountain, and try to head towards the route. The approach takes 3 hours, and involves some really awful bushwhacking, but the route is one of the finest in the San Juans. Do this one during a dry winter. Avalanche danger is usually extreme.

Descent: The first ascent party left screws, as well as rapped off trees. Bring rock gear, screws, and slings, just in case.

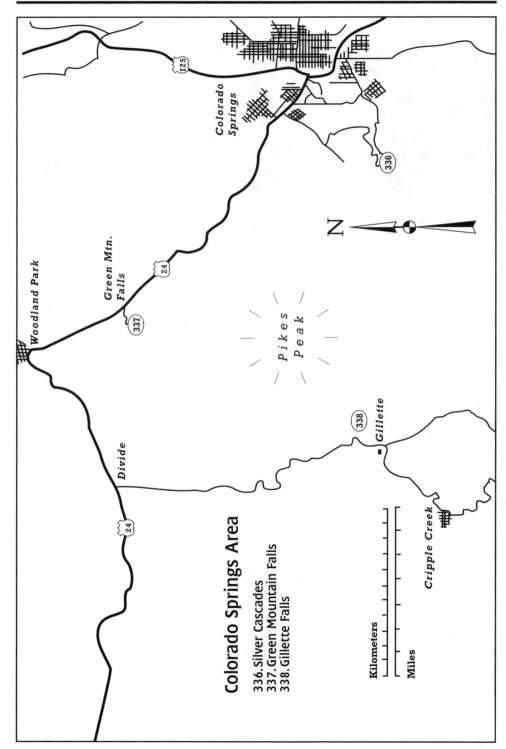

Colorado Springs Area

336. Silver Cascades
337. Green Mountain Falls
338. Gillette Falls

EASTERN COLORADO

Colorado Springs Area
(Routes 336-338)

"The best stuff is on private property,"
—Colorado Springs ice climber ducking under a fence.

The Colorado Springs area offers some excellent ice climbing, the only problem is it lies on privately owned land and is off limits to climbers. Hence, ice climbing in the area is somewhat limited.

The most popular venues in the immediate area for ice climbers is a small, low-angled flow called Silver Cascades in North Cheyenne Canyon.

Gillette Falls, lying an hour's drive from town (followed by a two-three hour hike) offers probably the best ice climbing in the area.

North Cheyenne Canyon

Silver Cascades lies in North Cheyenne Canyon, just downcanyon (east) of Helen Hunt Falls, a popular tourist attraction.

Getting there: To reach Helen Hunt Falls from downtown Colorado Springs, take I-25 south to Exit 140, and follow signs towards Colo. 115 and Colo. 122. At Tejon, turn right, and follow it south. After half a mile, Tejon curves right and becomes Cheyenne Boulevard. Follow Cheyenne Boulevard west (towards the mountains) for about 2.5 miles and turn right, onto North Cheyenne Canyon Road. (If you go straight here, you end up at Seven Falls, a privately owned waterfall and tourist attraction.) Follow N. Cheyenne Canyon Road for 2.65 miles to Helen Hunt Falls area.

There are several parking areas on both sides of the road. A short, well-built trail leads several hundred yards south, up to Helen Hunt Falls.

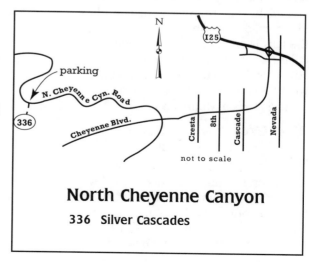

North Cheyenne Canyon

336 Silver Cascades

Helen Hunts Falls is, basically, a wide, 250-foot rock slab down which a small creek trickles into a small valley. The falls don't freeze entirely and are of little interest to ice climbers except during very cold periods.

Before you reach Helen Hunt Falls (at a point about halfway between the parking lot and Helen Hunt Falls) the trail crests a low ridge and makes a sharp right turn. At this point, Helen Hunt Falls will be visible to the right. Silver Cascades will be visible directly ahead, through the trees across the small valley that contains the creek draining Helen Hunt Falls. Duck under the fence and descend straight into the small valley. Go downstream about 250 feet, and Silver Cascades will be up to the right.

336. Silver Cascades (WI 1-2, 150 feet of WI 1 followed by 15 feet (f WI 2) ★

150-200 feet of very easy, soloable ice is followed by a short (15 feet) steep section of WI 2 that offers some good bouldering or easy leading.
Approach time: 15 minutes.
Descent: Descend by downclimbing on the right side of the falls.
Season: Midwinter
Road/Highway the climb is visible from: None.
Access issues: None.

Green Mountain Falls

Green Mountain Falls — the namesake of the town — is not generally known as an ice climb, however, the falls can offer some very easy leads and practice climbs.

Getting there: The town of Green Mountain Falls lies 13.8 miles west of I-25, on U.S. 24. Turn south off U.S. 24 (Exit 141, Cinnamon St.) into the town of Green Mountain Falls and drive 0.5 miles. Tale a right on Belvedere Avenue. and follow this 0.8 miles to its end. Park in the cul-de-sac. An dirt road leading to the falls is on the south (left) side of the cul-de-sac, heading into the mountain. Hike 10 minutes up the road to a bridge, where a large metal tank sits.

This is Green Mountain Falls.

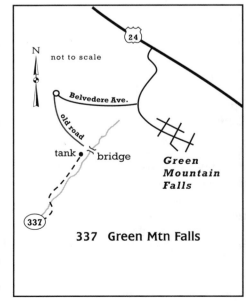

337 Green Mtn Falls

337. Green Mountain Falls (WI 1-2, various lengths) ★

On the creek embankments just below the bridge are a number of short WI 1-2 flows that offer easy leads and top-ropes. To the right (west) of the tank, a small trail continues up the hill. Follow this for about 500 feet to the main falls. They are not very steep but offer a good place to learn.

Approach time: 15 minutes.

Descent: Descend by downclimbing the falls.

Season: Midwinter.

Road/Highway the climb is visible from: Limited views are available from U.S. 24.

Access issues: None.

Gillette Falls

Despite the long drive and three-mile approach hike required to reach Gillette Falls, it offers the best ice climbing in the Colorado Springs region.

Getting there: Gillette Falls is located near the tiny (one house) town of Gillette, which lies halfway between Divide and Cripple Creek.

To reach Gillette Falls from Colorado Springs, take Highway 24 west. After 20 miles, you'll pass through the town of Woodland Park. Continue 6.3 miles west on Highway 24 until the small town of Divide. Turn left onto Colo. 67, which heads towards Cripple Creek. 13.5 miles down this road you'll reach the town of Gillette, which is nothing more than a house and a bend in the road. At the bend, turn left, onto Teller County Road 81, which heads towards Victor.

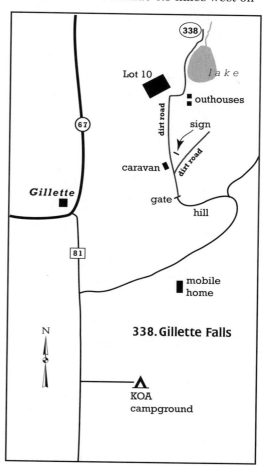

Follow this south for several hundred yards (.25 miles) to the first dirt road on the left. Go through a gate. (If you're turning into the KOA campground, you've gone too far.) Follow the dirt road 1.05 miles as it goes up a gentle slope and curves left, then up a short, steep hill, then drops down to a gate. This gate marks the entrance to the Timberline Fishing Club, which allows ice climbers to pass through the Club's property. The gate is usually locked and you'll have to walk from here.

Follow the dirt road across the creek, past the caravan on the left and up the road for about 1.5 miles to the reservoir. (Stay left at each branch in the road, except for the last branch, which leads to lot No. 10.) Skirt the lake on its left side. Usually there's a trail, then follow the creek that drains the valley to the north. After about a mile and a half, Gillette Falls and the various flows associated with it will become visible up to the left, on the wall of the valley. Bushwhack up to the climbs.

338. Gillette Falls (WI 2-5, various lengths, many variations possible) ★★★

There are several different climbs available, from thick waterfall ice to thin mixed climbs. Some are quite long.

Approach time: Allow 2 hours.

Descent: Rappel from fixed anchors or trees.

Season: Midwinter.

Road/Highway the climb is visible from: None.

Access issues: The Timberline Fishing Club allows ice climbers through the property without any problems. Be cool, though.

Appendix

Suppliers

The following stores stock ice climbing gear and their staffers usually have pretty good knowledge of current ice conditions in their area.

Backcountry Experience
780 Main St.
Durango CO 81301
800-648-8519

Boulder Mountaineer
1335 Broadway
Boulder CO 80302
303-442-8355

Casa de Madera
680 Grande Ave.
Del Norte CO 81132
719-657-2336

Gore Range Mountain Works
201 Gore Creek Dr.
Vail CO 81657
970-476-ROCK

Mountain Chalet
226 N. Tejon
Colorado Springs CO 80903
719-633-0732

Mountain Sports
821 Pearl St.
Boulder CO 80302
303-443-6770

Neptune Mountaineering
633 S. Broadway, Unit A
Boulder CO 80303
303-499-8866

Ouray Mountain Sports
722 Main St.
Ouray CO 81427
970-325-4284

Summit Canyon Mountaineering
732 Grand Ave.
Glenwood Springs CO 81601
970-945-6994

Summit Canyon Mountaineering
549 Main St.
Grand Junction CO
970-243-2847

Telluride Mountaineer
216 E. Colorado Ave.
Telluride CO 81435
970-728-6736

Telluride Sports
150 W. Colorado Ave.
Telluride CO 81435
970-728-4477

The Mountain Shop
632 S. Mason
Fort Collins CO 80524
970-493-5720

The Ute Mountaineer
308 S. Mill St.
Aspen CO 81611
970-925-2849

Wilderness Sports
Summit Place Shopping Center
Dillon CO 80435
970-468-5687

Bob Bohus on Silverpick Falls, Telluride   Photo: Bill Pelander

Index

Access: It's everybody's concern

The Access Fund, a national, non-profit climbers' organization, is working to keep you climbing. The Access Fund helps preserve access and protect the environment by providing funds for land acquisitions and climber support facilities, financing scientific studies, publishing educational materials promoting low-impact climbing, and providing start-up money, legal counsel and other resources to local climbers' coalitions.

Climbers can help preserve access by being responsible users of climbing areas. Here are some practical ways to support climbing:

- **Commit yourself to "leaving no trace."** Pick up litter around campgrounds and the crags. Let your actions inspire others.

- **Dispose of human waste properly.** Use toilets whenever possible. If none are available, choose a spot at least 50 meters from any water source. Dig a hole 6 inches (15 cm) deep, and bury your waste in it. *Always pack out toilet paper* in a "Zip-Lock"-type bag.

- **Utilize existing trails**. Avoid cutting switchbacks and trampling vegetation.

- **Use discretion when placing bolts and other "fixed" protection.** Camouflage all anchors with rock-colored paint. Use chains for rappel stations, or leave rock-colored webbing.

- **Respect restrictions that protect natural resources and cultural artifacts** . Appropriate restrictions can include prohibition of climbing around Indian rock art, pioneer inscriptions, and on certain formations during raptor nesting season. Power drills are illegal in wilderness areas. *Never chisel or sculpt holds in rock on public lands, unless it is expressly allowed* – no other practice so seriously threatens our sport.

- **Park in designated areas,** not in undeveloped, vegetated areas. Carpool to the crags!

- **Maintain a low profile.** Other people have the same right to undisturbed enjoyment of natural areas as do you.

- **Respect private property.** Don't trespass in order to climb.

- **Join or form a group to deal with access issues in your area.** Consider clean-ups, trail building or maintenance, or other "goodwill" projects.

- **Join the Access Fund.** To become a member, *simply make a donation (tax-deductible) of any amount.* Only by working together can we preserve the diverse American climbing experience.

The Access Fund. Preserving America's diverse climbing resources.
The Access Fund • P.O. Box 17010 • Boulder, CO 80308